Kind Regards

Kevin Thomas

March '95.

Managing Your Internal Customers

Managing Your Internal Customers

The Key to Getting Better Results

KEVIN THOMSON with
KATHY WHITWELL

FINANCIAL TIMES
PITMAN PUBLISHING

PITMAN PUBLISHING
128 Long Acre, London WC2E 9AN

A Division of Longman Group UK Limited

First published in Great Britain 1993

British Library Cataloguing in Publication Data
A CIP catalogue record for this book can be obtained from the British Library.

ISBN 0 273 60161 X

Phototypeset in Linotron Times Roman
by Northern Phototypesetting Co. Ltd., Bolton
Printed and bound in Great Britain
by Biddles Ltd, Guildford and King's Lynn

CONTENTS

FOREWORD

In recent years, 'internal marketing' has become a term increasingly used within organisations. However, it is seldom developed in an integrated manner. 'Managing Your Internal Customers' is the second book by Kevin Thomson which addresses the topic of internal marketing linking this to Total Quality and Human Resources. In his earlier book, *The Employee Revolution: The Rise of Corporate Internal Marketing* Pitman, 1990, the author demonstrated the importance of managing internal communication in order to successfully address external markets. This new book offers a practical approach to everybody, to help them address the internal market-place. It highlights the importance of the tactical activities involved in developing an integrated marketing and communication programme across the whole organisation and its customer supplier chain.

Many organisations have failed in the implementation of quality programmes because of neglecting the need to market such initiatives internally. This book illustrates why the discrete elements of internal marketing, such as quality initiatives and customer care, have failed to achieve the results that were anticiptated. Drawing on their in-house and consulting experience, the authors offer illustrations of how to use internal marketing activities to achieve dramatic improvement in performance. In particular, they point out the importance of gaining the total commitment of people throughout the organisation in order for such initiatives to succeed.

Research carried out at the Cranfield School of Management has found that activities which fall under the heading of 'internal marketing' are not well developed in most organisations. Internal marketing activity therefore often lacks integration and focus. In a recent book, *Relationship Marketing* (Martin Christopher, Adrian Payne and David Ballantyne, Butterworth Heinemann, 1991) we argued that internal and external marketing needs to be aligned to achieve a successful relationship with customers. *Managing Your Internal Customers* offers an approach to linking Marketing, Quality and Human Resources which integrates the key elements of the customer supplier chain. It also examines the important task of raising awareness of the need to strategically manage communication across the diverse audiences within the organisation.

This book is of importance to any manager concerned with developing their internal activities in support of improving the organisation's interaction with external customers. It takes a step by step approach to internal marketing, applying many of the concepts from the traditional marketing arena, to this new area. It offers a logical argument as to why Quality, Human Resources and Marketing need to be considered as an integrated whole. Managers responsible for helping co-ordinate internal and external marketing activities will find the book provides valuable insights to improving organisational performance.

Adrian Payne
Professor of Services Marketing
Cranfield School of Management

PREFACE

THE INTEGRATED MARKETING JIGSAW – THE HOLISTIC APPROACH

'Holistic' tends to take on the meaning 'if you don't do the whole (istic!) lot at once then you are sunk'. Fortunately, this is not the case here. The integrated marketing concepts which will be built up during the book do not offer a closed loop that you cannot break into if you don't do it all. The entry points are everywhere.

It will be surprising if, with much of what will be described in this book, you won't be nodding, and saying to yourself 'Yes, we do that'. As they say – you didn't get where you are today without doing something right.

The book will advocate that the things that you are doing right can be done that much better, once viewed through the eyes of a marketeer. To do this however, does require what can be variously described as *the big picture*, *the overview*, *the strategic plan*, or, the latest buzzword, *the holistic view*. The problem with a holistic view is that unless you can see the whole, then the parts may in themselves not appear as clear as you would like.

This book can, therefore, best be described as a jigsaw. You can start anywhere. You can pick it up and go back to it at any time. You will start to see smaller pictures emerging as you build up each section of the jigsaw that you are looking at.

To carry the analogy further, the problem that you may have, is how much, or how little, of the picture on the box lid you can see already. Until the late 1980s the same jigsaw analogy applied to myself and the team, and organisations we worked with; except we had no picture, and often no pieces.

As a team we have been involved in this tremendously exciting area for well over 30 man years. Much of the integrated marketing work I have been involved in, until a few years ago was of a tactical nature. During the 1980s for example, the biggest area of concern for many organisations was in the field of customer service, so this was where the big internal marketing budgets were spent.

The pattern of a total approach has only recently emerged. This has

evolved with the increasingly complex needs of the internal customer becoming more like demands. It has evolved even further with the recognition that a Quality approach demands everyone to look after their own customers in the customer supplier chain.

This book will explore the background, processes and methodologies that can be used to tackle the needs of all customers, whilst not taking a rose tinted view of the internal customer. Unlike external customers, the internal customer does not have a choice when it comes to some of the very tough demands the organisation places on them.

Throughout the book each piece of the jigsaw is built up to give as much of a mini picture as possible. To create obvious points of reference, some of the main sections will sum up with a 'jigsaw piece' summary.

TARGETING

1 The 'strategic' thinker

If you need to see the big picture first and then fill in the details go straight to the chapter entitled 'Using a Model to Manage Change in Your Organisation'.

2 The 'tactical' thinker

If you like to first build up the details about the subject you are interested in then go to 'A New Management Attitude' and 'The Customer Chain Segmented'.

3 The 'implementers' and 'influencers'

For those looking to introduce change through a focus on the internal customer and who believe that integrated marketing might assist in this process, I have spent a long time on the build up to the arguments needed. I am constantly in front of decision makers who need the reassurance that what they can see immediately as the big picture, is backed up by people who know what they are talking about. The first part of the book is devoted to the background on the organisation and its people. It not only provides answers, but also some of the tools to use.

4 The decision maker

Decision makers usually like to know two things: what something will do for their career, and by implication what it will do to improve the organisation. 'The Benefits of People, Marketing and Quality Working Together' is the chapter that pulls together the features and turns them into what can best be described as 'the nice thing for your organisation is . . .'

You will be pleased to note that just like external marketing, the nice thing about integrated marketing is that there are a lot of nice things about it!

5 The marketeer

Firstly a personal note: like the word buccaneer I prefer this way of spelling 'marketeer', rather than 'marketer' which conveys none of the spirit employed by the pirates of old! As someone who will be familiar with much of the marketing jargon in this book, I suggest that you resist the temptation to say 'been there, seen it, done it'. When the concepts, strategies, tactics, tools and techniques of marketing are applied internally to the organisation, it is a much more difficult process than dealing with external customers.

Secondly a note of caution: if only it were as easy as appealing to external customers. They simply buy the products. They don't spend half their life living and breathing in the environment which makes the products and services you have to market.

Thirdly my recommendation: to gain the greatest understanding of how and why the methodologies of Quality and human resources need to be intertwined with marketing, it is worth reading the whole book. The world of the intenal customer could then be your oyster.

6 The training/personnel/HRD specialist

For those of you who are on the look out for ideas for your next course, you will not be disappointed. This book is a 'handbook'. It has been written to provide usable tools and techniques to help organisations facing the critical problems, such as recession, that are facing them in the 1990s and beyond into 2000.

However, having worked long and hard on these concepts, ideas and methodologies, the ones contained within this book are copyright – yes that means you! Having been involved in training, I know the temptations to 'borrow' ideas. You are, however, welcome to adopt the sound marketing principles involved.

7 The quality director/manager

My advice to you would be to read the book from cover to cover! A sure way to achieve success with Quality is to integrate it with marketing, or indeed adopt the principle of marketing to sustain it.

8 Skimming the book/exam notes

As a summary, a reminder, a pre-prepared set of notes, a quick reference and easy to remember quotes, I have included a summary of key points in each section. These are the jigsaw pieces that build up to form the complete picture.

Should my views ever become the basis for a standard text on this emerging discipline, then simply tear these pages out or copy the contents on to your shirt cuff prior to going into exams!

9 The back of the book sums it up

Last but not least, if you are looking for a quick summary, and confirmation of what is being said throughout the book then there are two articles reprinted here.

The first is by Professor Adrian Payne writing in the *European Management Journal*, September 1991, and is entitled 'Internal Marketing: A New Perspective For HRM'. It argues that human resource management needs to take on marketing skills. As he believes – 'Concepts and techniques from marketing can provide means by which HR managers can be more effective'.

The second article is by the author writing for the Chartered Institute of Marketing in The Science of Marketing series in the magazine *Marketing Business*, also in September 1991. This article was targeted at marketing people, encouraging them to get involved in human resource development (HR)! 'Looking at the employee as a valued customer is the focus of the new discipline of internal marketing.'

These are the same messages coming from two different angles. They are targeted at two different internal target markets. This is what marketing is all about.

ACKNOWLEDGEMENTS

This book is dedicated to Julie. She has suffered over a computer that kept crashing, from a nasty virus called 'bookitis'. She gave her all, and weekends too, for little more than a 'thank you', a stick of rock, and a big 'didit' from me.

Thanks also to Kathy Whitwell for her contributions to the concepts and developments in the book. And to the team for all their input, especially to Kathryn Young and Andrew Flint.

Finally a big thank you to all those people in the organisations quoted throughout the book.

INTRODUCTION

At the end of the 1980s many organisations had gone through considerable change. This change had been driven by what were often called 'Cultural Change Programmes'. These usually included Customer Service and Total Quality Management (to keep things simple and in line with current usage I shall be using the terms TQM and Quality rather than Total Quality Management). Subsets of these types of programmes also created changes within organisations. These included: Just In Time, BS5750/ISO9000 and Throughput Accounting.

Most of these programmes, whilst focusing on the ultimate customer, were internally driven. They focused on the new 'internal customer' who was placed very firmly within the newly created concept of the 'customer-supplier chain'. Marketing departments rarely got involved with the internal changes going on in the organisation. Marketing people themselves had to refocus on customers who were becoming ever more sophisticated and requiring more and more closely targeted messages.

The age of relationship marketing was starting. Some marketing commentators attempted to merge the external and internal changes going on, notably John Fraser-Robinson in his book *Total Quality Marketing* and Nigel Piercy in *Market Led Strategic Change* and later in 1991 from Adrian Payne in *Relationship Marketing*. However, the mainstream disciplines of marketing for the external customer, Quality for the internal customer, and human resources for the employee, stayed well apart. While the customer-supplier chain had become a piece of corporate folklore, nobody really got to grips with managing the concept.

It was at this time that my long term involvement with both external and internal marketing led me to develop a strategic approach with our clients which I entitled 'Corporate Internal Marketing'. This strategy for dealing with the internal customer, using classic marketing principles, was laid bare for all to see in *The Employee Revolution*. This book looked at a strategic approach and covered the reasons 'why' organisations should think about merging their internal communications under an overall marketing-based approach.

In the short time since the publication of *The Employee Revolution* a lot has happened. Most people in organisations now know that they need to be focusing on external and internal customers at the same time. They have recognised that Quality programmes and customer service programmes need an ongoing commitment, and large degree of what is now recognised as internal marketing. The net result of this is that people no longer need to know 'why' they should be looking after and communicating with all their customers, internally and externally. What they want to know is 'what' and 'how' they should be doing it. In other words internal marketing know how.

Managing Your Internal Customers is an update of *The Employee Revolution* giving the 'what' to do and 'how' to do it as the key focus. Much of the strategic approach in the first book has been retained as a move from a large picture to individual jigsaw pieces would be too big a jump.

In addition I am delighted to be able to update many of the case studies and introduce new case studies of organisations who have 'boldly gone where no organisations have gone before' and have greatly benefited as a result.

This new book is aimed at key decision makers and influencers in the fields of Quality, Human Resources and, of course, Marketing. The nature of the subject will also be of interest to managing directors who are now beginning to recognise that it is not enough to leave the subject of communicating with customers up to others. A recent survey by the Chartered Institute of Marketing highlighted the fact that in these recessionary times, the chairmen of many organisations were also beginning to focus strongly on all marketing issues. It is my hope that they would look to this integrated approach to communicating with all of their customers, internally and externally.

In addition to those interested in an *overall* approach for their organisation, it has become increasingly clear that individuals in many departments within organisations are also looking for the marketing and communication tools and techniques to enhance their *own* image and get closer to their own customers. 'Downsizing' – the euphemism for getting rid of people and departments and bringing the skills in from outside, means that no one is safe. This book attempts to provide the know-how for everyone to market themselves from within.

We are now a number of years on from the interventions, exhortations and teachings of the gurus like Tom Peters with *Excellence*, and Philip Crosby, Juran, Demming etc. with *Quality*. Everyone now knows that it is not enough to just want cultural change to occur. The only way to make things happen in the internal environment, is to win the hearts and minds of every single employee. *Quality* and *Excellence* tried to do this but are now generally seen as having failed to live up to expectations.

> ***In simple marketing terms Excellence and Quality are both products developed within the internal market, for the benefit of the external market. These products both focus on customers – inside and out. They now need to be better marketed, throughout the customer-supplier chain, in almost all organisations. In addition, all newly created 'suppliers' in the chain now need the marketing skills to market their* own *products and services, to all of their own new found 'customers'.***

They need these skills in order to get their customers to want to buy into, and be satisfied with what they produce as suppliers. It is now recognised that everyone must also be able to get nearer to the marketing objective of being 'closer to the customer'. Once again what is needed is the know how to be able to do this.

This book will address what Peters and Crosby et al. had only been able to uncover in the 1980s as tactical examples of good marketing in quality driven environments. They did not have a strategic approach to communication.

The work done by the author and his team within both major organisations and small companies is based on the fundamental practices of marketing. This is brought together with years of experience in marketing, HR and introducing TQM into organisations.

If organisations are to take their people with them into the next century, then, in today's extremely marketing conscious and sophisticated environment they must practise the disciplines of Quality and marketing at the same time. Both of these focus on the customer, on meeting customer needs, and on an integrated approach. Yet Quality and marketing have not, so far, begun to work together.

Managing Your Internal Customers looks to integrating the disciplines of Quality, human resource development and marketing throughout what is commonly now recognised in organisations as the customer-supplier chain. In this book, I have updated and added to the concept of internal marketing to encompass marketing in the whole of the customer-supplier chain, both inside and outside the organisation. Internal marketing is still applicable when only dealing with the internal customer. When internal marketing and external marketing are combined throughout the customer-supplier chain, I have called this approach integrated marketing. There should be no breaks in any chain.

WHAT IS THE CUSTOMER-SUPPLIER CHAIN?

As the book is all about this concept, it is worth covering this at the start. I have assumed throughout the book that everyone knows all about the basic Quality concepts, but in case any readers are unfamiliar with the concepts, the 'customer-supplier chain' simply means that there is a continuous link between you the customer and your suppliers. This is *anyone* who supplies you with a product (physical output) or service (professional help). This applies whether or not they are paying for what you produce. It applies inside the organisation and outside. Therefore this covers:

external customers
internal employees
external suppliers

In simple terms – everyone is a customer or supplier in a chain of people who all interact to get the final product or service to the end customer.

AN INTEGRATED MARKETING APPROACH – A QUICK SUMMARY

Integrated marketing takes a holistic view of an organisation. It responds to the needs of *every* customer for a quality product or service throughout the customer-supplier chain.

Internal marketing creates an inspiring *internal* climate in which motivation and morale thrives. This occurs by developing a framework of targeted communication aimed at everyone inside the organisation, and integrating with the external communication.

Together with Quality and human resource development, these ensure that both the internal people relationships, and the business' resources, are working in harmony to achieve the organisation's *customer driven*, strategic and tactical goals.

1 CLOSER TO CUSTOMERS – INTERNAL AND EXTERNAL

INTRODUCTION

The first steps on the route that brings you closer to your customers is a policy review for integrating marketing, human resource development and quality.

Are you customer facing?
Are you totally committed to quality?
Have you decided your vision, mission and values? – Have you communicated them? – How well?

DO YOU SEE YOUR EMPLOYEES AS CUSTOMERS?

I could use up a lot of space in this chapter telling you what you should be doing to develop a policy intended to get you closer to your customers. However, with a little help from a classic research tool you can be doing it yourself. This book is all about giving you the tools and techniques to be able to get closer to everyone in your customer-supplier chain and the first tool you need is a method to assess your potential, to help you see where your strengths and weaknesses lie.

HOW ARE YOU DOING SO FAR?

Many organisations will already have begun to look at their quality procedures and how they manage resources. You may have gone through the hoop that most Total Quality programmes contain: producing and communicating your Vision and Mission. In essence these are:

- where your leaders are taking you.
- how you go about meeting your customers needs.

Also, if you have achieved BS5750/ISO9000 you will have looked at another area of your organisation's policies, a Quality policy itself. You need this as the starting point for BS5750/ISO9000.

If you haven't gone through the formal Total Quality, or BS5750/ISO9000 routes then you still may have done these informally.

In addition to these you may also have looked at the human resource (people) aspects of your organisation and attempted to create a set of Values. These will provide the focus for the 'soft' issues like honesty, trust, etc.

Before you decide to change anything you need to review where you are, and how you are doing with them. To assist in this process, and to let you do it yourself, I have included my version of the tried and tested marketing tool, the SWOT analysis. This will help you to get a clearer focus on your overall position with your customers, inside and outside your organisation.

Figure 1.1 is a form entitled SWOT-on Policies. Fill this out for your own organisation, concentrating on the Strengths, Weaknesses, Opportunities and Threats of your policies for getting closer to meeting your customer needs. For ease of reference these are shown under the titles: Vision, Mission, Values and Quality – you may give them different titles or not call them anything at all. Whatever you call them, those policies will be attempting to do one thing: keep your customers coming back for more – be they internal or external.

Here is an example:

Strengths:

Your Comments – Introducing Total Quality Policy has produced good results.
Your Rating – 3
Your Reason – Returns are down to minimal figures; and reducing!

The data you enter will provide you with valuable information on the strengths and weaknesses of the customer orientated policies within your organisation. The SWOT process will be discussed in greater detail later, as it can be used for other areas, as well as policy. Once you have completed this form, the next step is to look at integrating marketing, with Quality, and human resource development. This policy of integration forms the basis of this book.

Why should you complete the analysis? What is a SWOT Analysis? Is it worth it? Do you have the time? Are you the right person to be looking at this?

It is worth listening to what another marketeer says about the importance of the SWOT Analysis. The following is taken from the book *The Marketing Plan* by Malcolm McDonald, Professor of Marketing Planning and Director of Distance Education at Cranfield School of Management.

> 'Now let's look at the Marketing planning process itself . . . Audits are essential, but who in your organisation will carry them out? Unfortunately the ideal people are probably the busiest – the line managers. They know the job: they are involved – and they are much cheaper than outside consultants. The problem is finding the time.
>
> They have to be given a clear idea of what you want them to do, or because they are specialists they will suffer from a kind of tunnel vision.
>
> *Appraisal Procedures Must Be Standardised*
> A standard company-wide critical appraisal is needed – hence the need to institutionalise and systematise the procedures in order to make the appraisal easier.
>
> 1) Corporate objectives
> 2) Marketing audit
> 3) SWOT analysis
>
> Having done the marketing audit, the marketing planner's next move is to find out what the company's objectives and strategies in marketing must be. To do this he must analyse the information gathered by the marketing audit in something called a SWOT analysis.
>
> *Strengths Weakness Opportunities Threats*
> The SWOT analysis should be a brief document focusing on key factors; e.g. key differences in strengths and weaknesses between the company and its competition, and in other opportunities and threats. A summary of reasons for bad or good performances should be included. It should be a concise, interesting analysis which appears in the eventual marketing plan, not the audit.'

The SWOT Analysis in Figure 1.1 has the simple strength of combining the marketing audit, external or internal, and the SWOT analysis itself. It does this on one document that can be completed by anyone. That should save time!

AN INTEGRATED POLICY – MISSION AND VISION

Having completed the SWOT analysis you have probably decided that your customer facing policies could be improved. Quality is all about constant

SWOT - ON POLICIES

Your Overall Comments About Your Policies - Vision/ Mission/ Values/ Quality	Your Rating	Your Reason For This Rating
	Fill in one arrow e.g. 1 2 3 4 ▷ ▷ ▶ ▷	
STRENGTHS When it comes to policy, what are your main strengths?	Strong → Very Strong	**WHY?**
1. ______	▷ ▷ ▷ ▷	1. ______
2. ______	▷ ▷ ▷ ▷	2. ______
3. ______	▷ ▷ ▷ ▷	3. ______
WEAKNESSES What are your main policy weaknesses? i.e. where you fall down.	Weak → Very Weak	**WHY?**
1. ______	▷ ▷ ▷ ▷	1. ______
2. ______	▷ ▷ ▷ ▷	2. ______
3. ______	▷ ▷ ▷ ▷	3. ______
OPPORTUNITIES What new policy ideas do you have that will provide you with any opportunities?	Good Idea → Very Good Idea	**WHY?**
1. ______	▷ ▷ ▷ ▷	1. ______
2. ______	▷ ▷ ▷ ▷	2. ______
3. ______	▷ ▷ ▷ ▷	3. ______
THREATS What/who provides your policies with a threat in any way?	Threat → Very Strong Threat	**WHY?**
1. ______	▷ ▷ ▷ ▷	1. ______
2. ______	▷ ▷ ▷ ▷	2. ______
3. ______	▷ ▷ ▷ ▷	3. ______

Figure 1.1 SWOT analysis

improvement and integrating previously disintegrated functions is one way to achieve it.

We have already established that the fundamental starting point of integrated marketing is the wealth of knowledge and experience of three key disciplines that have affected the dynamic changes in business today. These are marketing, Quality and human resources.

The different languages and concepts of these three disciplines, when added together, provide a very powerful tool to tackle the strategic and tactical ramifications that 'change' has on all organisations. For all organisations where Quality is the key policy, the Mission and Vision are fundamental. Therefore, the starting point for an integrated marketing and Quality approach must also be an organisation's Mission and Vision. What do the words mean?

The Mission

The Mission is starting to reach the very heart and soul of many organisations. Starting at the 'top', it is being discussed in boardrooms throughout the world, and from there generally, but often not successfully, cascades (falls in a downward direction) towards the employee. However, we hit the first snag: these are the same employees who for years have been left very much to the vagaries of their immediate boss. They are now expected to partake of a new direction for the company that has taken the 'bosses' often days of painstaking debate. Even worse, the new direction is communicated under a mystifying title of 'The Mission Statement'. This is either given to the employee verbally, by managers who themselves wonder what it really means, or it goes up on the wall as a paragraph on a piece of paper. Some of them may actually read it. The Mission statement on its own cannot solve an organisation's problems, particularly if it is badly communicated.

A Mission for Integrated Marketing

> ***The Mission of integrated marketing is to put a stop to the type of internal communication, advertising, PR and promotional activity that would put most organisations out of business if practised externally.***

Does this sound a harsh judgement on the way the internal customer is marketed to? Turn then to the external customer and the vast amounts of time and money that are being put into customer care, advertising, promotions, etc. Even after all the spending, there is often a huge gulf between how the external customer should expect to be treated and what actually happens. It is a fair assumption that this is because all too often internal people are not even treated as well as the external customer.

Indeed, the internal customer is usually perceived as someone who is paid to take on anything that is given to them (or thrown at them), and not seen as someone who should be 'sold' to, or even marketed to, professionally.

The Mission statement at the end of this section (Fig. 1.2) is there only to provide an overview of the function of integrated marketing. It will help you realise that concepts like the Mission statement do not stand on their own; they need to be put into context. It is only a 'statement' because you, the reader, cannot be expected to buy into a set of words on a piece of paper. It matters not a jot that these words have been lovingly produced, nor that they *should* mean something to you, even that they *should* increase your desire to act on them. A lot more needs to happen.

Integrated marketing is all about getting into the psyche of the target buyer throughout the customer-supplier chain. It is about creating people who are ready, willing and able to change their attitudes, understanding and their behaviour towards the new and the different. The Mission is simply a way of expressing this.

The Vision

The vision must be held by the leaders of an organisation – be they national or local. It is a picture in their minds of the future. Here is the basis of my vision; given at the end of the section (see also Fig. 1.2).

A Vision of Needs Marketing

> ***The Vision needs marketing in every organisation if it is to succeed. And not just the words need to be marketed, the leaders who hold the vision need to be marketed as personalities in their own right. A classic example of this is in politics. An ongoing marketing campaign at local and national levels is vital to motivate people throughout the organisation, no matter what its size.***

The basis of my vision of integrated marketing is that it will happen in most organisations within the next decade. The understanding provided by Quality and knowledge of the customer-supplier chain, will have produced an environment where the strategies and tactics advocated by an integrated approach to marketing will be the norm in all 'Excellent' and 'Quality' organisations.

THE MISSION OF INTEGRATED MARKETING

To match the customer needs and values, throughout the customer-supplier chain, with the products and services that are created throughout the organisation. This must be done in order to fulfil the mission of the organisation and the vision of the people in it.

In simple terms, to be able to say
'You, the customer, think we are the best'

MY VISION FOR INTEGRATED MARKETING
In the next decade, just as external marketing took a place in business practice, the same will happen with an integrated approach to marketing, throughout the customer-supplier chain.

By the year 2000 everybody will be doing it
(well almost!)

Figure 1.2

AN INTEGRATED POLICY – THE INTERNAL CUSTOMER-SUPPLIER CHAIN

Everyone has customers. Everyone has suppliers. Everyone knows this. It is the recognition that everyone is a customer which should set off the recognition of a need for the marketing process, but this has not yet happened. It *should* happen whenever the issue of conformance to customer requirements is raised, and this should happen whenever the establishing of a customer requirement is raised.

How do you know what the customer requirements are, or might be, if you aren't listening to them?

Quality, marketing, and human resource management can work together to change the way an organisation treats internal customers.

In essence, a Quality programme, by its own definition, must be a marketing programme. It will be seen later that the marketing steps taken to bring a product to the external market place, are just as applicable to any individual or team attempting to have their ideas accepted by the internal market place.

Clearly, a tremendous amount of work has been done at a technical level in terms of systems and measurements in Quality. I am not suggesting that the 'baby gets thrown out with the bath water'. If the basic premise is that Quality is all about customers, this simply means that marketing principles should be added. Indeed, with much of the interaction being on a one to one basis, then the setting of requirements and agreeing the terms is part of the complete marketing and *sales* process.

Organisations spend large sums of money training and re-training sales people, and they spend large sums of money on marketing. The role of sales and marketing is to constantly service the customers' needs and to be constantly monitoring feedback. Marketing people can then respond to customer problems and opportunities with whatever changes and new introductions are needed. This requires a high degree of skill.

The same could also be said of the skills needed by each internal customer in assessing and delivering against their customers' needs. The steps taken by people when getting together in a Quality programme are effectively a marketing process – they must be, if the people are all customers. If everyone were trained in this process it would ensure the following:

1 The tactical execution of any strategy will focus on the gathering of customer data via structured research.
2 The needs of the internal or external customer on a one to one basis will be met by the recognised use of sales and marketing techniques. These ensure customers get the right products and services at the right time in the right way.
3 The distribution of the best of the products and services being provided internally will be done by the use of targeted marketing.
4 The constantly updated needs of the market place will be measured in terms of the ultimate marketing aim of the organisation, e.g. satisfied customers at a profit.
5 The language used to inspire the individuals will be one of marketing and selling. This allows every individual to use tried and tested techniques on their own customers.
6 The focus is on customers' needs and meeting them, in a positive and exciting way.
7 Training people to use a marketing-based approach will provide incentives – new skills and personal development. This will be of major benefit to those people who have been trained in the technical aspects of this type of programme.

Does this sound like a takeover of Quality programmes? It isn't. The point is that any type of programme will require the added awareness and use of marketing and sales tools and techniques. Indeed, as the workforce become more and more sophisticated in their needs and desires, and better trained to handle the people aspects involved in all jobs, there will be a need for even greater use of the sophisticated external marketing techniques.

This is backed up, albeit perhaps unwittingly, by Crosby. In the section below I quote from his book *Quality is Free*, where he talks of the Fourteen Steps of Quality. I have added my comments in *italics*.

Step One: Management Commitment

Action. Discuss the need for quality improvement with management, emphasising the need for defect prevention.
i.e. sell them the idea that providing the right products and services to internal and external customers is a good idea – also target the message on one of the features of the programme.

There are plenty of films, visual aids, and other materials available to support this communication
i.e. there is a target market who are unlikely to be sold the ideas by unskilled people. The hearts and minds of these people will only be won over by sophisticated marketing techniques.

and later . . .

Step Five

Action. It is now time to share with employees the measurements of what non-quality is costing. This is done by training supervisors to orient employees.
i.e. sell them the ideas as well
and by providing visible evidence of the concern for quality improvement
i.e. show them the research
through communication
i.e. marketing
material such as booklets, films and posters.
N.B. although no mention is given of the need to ensure that the 'quality' of this material meets the customer requirements!

Don't confuse this with some get-motivated-quick scheme
i.e. these marketing people are only capable of short-term hype not long-term strategic campaigns!

It is a sharing process, and does not involve manipulating people.
So why the need for all the sexy marketing material, and the selling process at

senior level and 'orienting employees'? Of course it involves manipulating people. People love to be sold to, they love to be persuaded to buy into things they might not have considered before. Marketing and selling are not dishonourable professions, there is nothing wrong with using the skills – but don't over-use them and pressurise people into short term decisions that will later affect their long term buying. Most marketing and sales people want long term customers. It makes a lot of sense, as the most expensive customers to reach are those who have not bought the product before.

This (sharing with employees) is an important step. It may be the most important step of all.

i.e. 'Quality' is just like every other product or service which requires people to buy. As a product and service being provided by the organisation, it needs internal marketing and selling. In addition to this, the product must meet customer requirements – and that to the external world is the function of Marketing.

Service and administrative people should be included, just like everybody else.

i.e. There are other target markets who must be considered – whether or not they should be treated as 'just like everybody else' would be a function of the research into their needs and requirements, and their acceptance of the creative approach used.

and finally . . .

Step Fourteen

Repetition makes the programme perpetual and thus 'part of the woodwork'. If quality isn't ingrained in the organisation, it will never happen.

i.e. This is a people orientated, long term, on-going programme – or in marketing terms – an internal customer, targeted, strategic campaign. It is aimed at turning non-users into users, who, through constant advertising and promotion, are encouraged to perform repeat purchases.

The difference between Quality and marketing isn't just in the words, it is a whole mind set.

Marketing has the ability to provide supporting professional skills. These will ensure that customers' requirements are met. It is through marketing that the tactics needed to listen to, gather, and share the best practices of the organisation are instilled in every individual. The commitment to continue is driven by consistent targeted messages.

Quality programmes are all about generating tactics from below. Constant improvement comes through constant input from everyone. This will only truly come about when the processes and techniques of marketing are used by everyone, i.e. when they are all able to market and sell their ideas.

AN INTEGRATED POLICY – IS IT WORTH IT?

Integrating these disciplines has some other results worth mentioning at this stage. Many organisations want results like these below, but don't know how to go about achieving them. They include:

1 Increased monitoring of customer needs throughout the customer-supplier chain.
2 More involvement in improving quality.
3 More and better suggestions.
4 More innovation.
5 Improved communication.
6 Better targeted training programmes.
7 Better targeted Quality programmes.
8 Greater efficiency and effectiveness.

> ***The payoffs must of course also outweigh the investment. To prove this actually happens, the quality of the measures and the levels of success are vital. Marketing techniques like research can be used to provide these measures.***

So, the concept of shifting the organisation to a total customer focus through an integrated marketing approach looks like a 'good idea'.

MARKETING – A POWERFUL TOOL!

When considering adopting an integrated approach to marketing, remember that in most organisations marketing is already perceived as a very powerful tool. The same power can be shown to apply to marketing in the customer-supplier chain. Marketing is also an exciting area to be involved in, often with large budgets! It is always easier to shift attitudes if managers who are implementing plans know that they have the financial, as well as the emotional, backing.

The sum of the results from an integrated approach with TQM, HR and marketing should be much, much greater than the parts, i.e. of separate investment in traditional internal communication, training and quality.

An integrated approach should mean integrated budgets. This in itself should mean *more chance of success and greater cost savings.*

2 MARKETING – AND THE FEAR OF CHANGE IT BRINGS

If you have decided to change and become customer facing, is anything stopping you?

THE REACTION TO CHANGE FROM INTERNAL CUSTOMERS

There is one major problem that marketing anything new brings into organisations – *fear*. Recognising, and acknowledging, this problem is fundamental to achieving the Mission. It is vital for those organisations that want to rely on their people to help them achieve their goals in a positive and motivated way, in other words, be committed.

In those organisations that have recognised that change needs to take place, recognition of the fear factor by the leaders of the organisation is critical. Good leaders do not ignore problems, they take them into account. Human frailties are not there to be steam-rollered, they are the stuff of marketing; a challenge to be met.

As an example where the external marketeer uses the fear factor in external customers to drive an advertising programme, the pet food industry is classic. People do not know for sure whether their pets are happy with their food or not, so they are persuaded to purchase branded goods which are inevitably premium priced. People are afraid that if they don't buy branded products, they are not being kind to their animals. This fear factor is not ignored, it is traded on. Hence, '9 out of 10 cat owners who expressed a preference said their cats preferred it'.

So, it is worth exploring fear, and the other human reactions that the introduction of any change will produce amongst internal customers. These reactions will need to be taken into account when considering an integrated marketing strategy for a future shift of attitude, practice, or culture.

Does fear sound too strong a word? I don't believe it is. And not just one aspect of fear arises out of the enormous changes that go on within organisations. Unfortunately there are a number.

Fear of change itself

One of the greatest challenges in any programme of change is to tackle the inherent fear that people feel when looking to a different future. It may be that the future is better, but if there is the slightest chance that there is likely to be any uncertainty about it, it can safely be assumed that there are going to be barriers. These barriers are actually intended to destroy, or at least hinder the introduction of, the new order of things.

The future may or may not concern people, but it is the fact that their view of it is unclear which causes the problem. So, fear and the resulting barriers cause one of the greatest challenges to any introduction of change. My grandfather used to say:

You can't change a man against his will he'll hold the same opinion still

The corollary to that statement is that you cannot communicate with people who do not want to listen! It is usually fear which produces a 'knee jerk' response in the individuals in organisations. This response is not unrecognised, but all too often there may be an attempt to calm the fears of individuals, that then goes too far the other way to appease. Appeasing people in itself can produce totally the wrong results, often even greater negative reactions. This occurs when individuals feel they are in a strong position because people are going out of their way to placate them. They know that what is being introduced is fundamentally right, it is just that they may not be happy about it personally.

It is at a very early stage in the process of change, that key individuals who are likely to become major sources of discontent and disruption can be detected. They are simply hitting out as a means of protection. They are afraid of change.

I often get asked by human resource professionals, (especially when introducing an attitudinal campaign, such as customer service), what to do about the desperately negative people who are, or will, undermine their major investment in these new campaigns. Surprisingly, experience suggests that these people are a primary target market. They need to recognise the 'hooks' that will turn them on. They also need to be given the opportunity to see that their world is not going to be turned upside down. They need to have the policies and plans of the organisation clearly laid out. Change is only a problem if it is not goal-directed. Negative people often end up as greater champions of the new ideas than those who already appear to be practising many of them. Why? The reason is simple – when people are coming from a low attitudinal base, the removal of the fear barrier allows them to make enormous changes. The simplest analogy is well documented. Consider the hundreds of thousands of people who have been 'converted', in religious terms, to various 'causes'.

Personal experience of many a training course shows that the last thing that should be done with 'Fred in the corner', who is causing havoc with his negative vibes, his caustic comments, and pointed remarks, is to kick him out. In most cases the 'Freds' of this world are afraid of the changes that are apparently being forced on them. However, once they 'see the light' then woe betide anyone who tries to criticise the trainer or the programme! In essence, they are now in a new comfort zone. This will produce a level of acceptance of anything new that will be absorbed into their *modus operandi*.

Interestingly they will probably then accept almost anything that the instigator of the change wants to throw at them. The fear will be removed through a belief in the person who can 'see' into the future, and will make sure that Fred is OK.

> ***Surprisingly it is the person who seems to be the paragon of virtue who is the person to watch out for, and the one to whom you need to target your messages carefully.***

Why? They fear that they will lose the status they had prior to any change. Not only is everyone else accepting the new ideas that often only they thought they were practising, but also they are no longer the focus of attention. This results in a loss of standing or visibility and so may even affect their chances of promotion.

They feel that the attention is not on them but on a new leader who is driving forward new ideas and concepts. The result for anyone trying to target internal marketing or sales messages, is that these people can become the most difficult to reach. They don't want to listen. As far as they are concerned, they are already doing what is being asked of them. They seem to feel, (judging by the feigned indifference, and sometimes supercilious attitude of people on many a training course or workshop) 'I don't have to bother with this'. In reality it is another type of fear which is another problem the marketeer must be aware of. This is well known to the people we all aspire to emulate, the Japanese.

Fear of loss of face

This is not an Oriental phenomenon; it affects every organisation. It is this fear which creates entrenched positions and negative attitudes in people. Examples of how people try to overcome this serve to illustrate the severity of the problem. The following copy, for example, is typical of that used to try and persuade internal customers to do things that they don't want to:

THIS CUSTOMER SERVICE PROGRAMME WILL HELP YOU BUILD ON YOUR STRENGTHS

Translated into what it really means – but you dare not say it!
WE HAVE HAD TREMENDOUS COMPLAINTS FROM OUR CUSTOMERS ABOUT THE APPALLING ATTITUDE AND PRACTICES OF OUR STAFF AND WE ARE JOLLY WELL GOING TO CHANGE THE WAY YOU DO THINGS!

or . . .

YOU ARE INVITED TO ATTEND A FIVE DAY MANAGEMENT DEVELOPMENT WORKSHOP IN LEADERSHIP SKILLS.

Translated again . . .
THE PEOPLE REPORTING TO YOU ARE HAVING BIG PROBLEMS WITH THE WAY YOU ARE TREATING THEM, SO WE HAVE DECIDED TO PUT YOU ON A COURSE.

Is this overstating the case? Is there more than a grain of truth behind these statements? The real problem is that if anyone says that they have a *better* way of doing things, as opposed to saying, for example, 'here is a *different* way of doing things that you *might* like to consider', people get defensive.

People get defensive because all too often things are presented in a way that makes it appear that the way they were doing it before was wrong. To people who don't like criticism, this means a loss of face.

Hence, the introduction of 'change', which implies things being 'better', also infers that what went before was 'worse'. For those people who are not prepared to admit fallibility, or for those who believe that what they are doing is right, it comes as a shock to be told that things could be better. The 'soft sell' is inevitably necessary.

> ***Yet, compare this to external marketing; when anyone launches a 'NEW' and 'IMPROVED' product, it is usually eagerly awaited!***

The fear of 'loss of face', is just one of the many reasons why marketing to internal customers inside an organisation will always be more difficult than external marketing. Internally in most organisations there will be an aversion to anything new. In contrast, in the external market place people are always demanding almost everything to be new!

The manufacturer is not criticised for making it better. Why? Because the consumer is not personally involved. With no personal involvement in producing the product, it is unlikely that they will say 'I'm not going to buy this because you didn't do it better before'. They are more likely to praise you for improving and developing it.

Fear of losing one's job

Is fear of losing one's job a major consideration when thinking of change or is this another example of overstating the case? First hand experience of a number of projects shows that it is one of the biggest concerns of many employees of both large and small organisations. Think of the introduction of information technology (computers). Lately, the recession has created massive uncertainty.

How can internal people be expected to react to marketing messages bringing in change, when they believe that keeping their head down is the way to keep their job.

If you think about it, almost any change in an organisation could do the same. For example, better management development programmes produce the need for fewer managers. This is generally accepted as a part of the current methodology for bringing about 'flatter structures'. Many managers are very worried about flat structures and the effect, not only on their future prospects, but on the job they are doing now.

Unfortunately, the same can be said about improvements of almost any kind. If the individual perceives them to be a threat to their position or their future, then they will resist them. This makes the role of marketing to the internal customer a lot more difficult than marketing to the external customer.

Fear of failure

Taking on anything new as a task or hobby at home allows for a period of private experiment 'where no-one can see'. It might take hours to put the flat pack kitchen cupboard up, but it is in the privacy of your own home. The same is not true at work. Under the full glare of colleagues and the bosses, the pressures to adopt and adapt to new practices and principles are increasing daily.

These are real pressures to those who feel they cannot cope. The individual who refuses to accept that they are unable to change will once again self-justify their incapability as being someone else's fault, for example, 'they are throwing too much at us again'. However, it may be that they feel that the end result will be that the organisation will sooner or later not require their services. In the meantime any failure, whether it is accepted by others as part of the individual's learning curve or not, is often perceived by the individual themselves as personally unacceptable.

Matters are made worse by the prevalent culture in most organisations that failure is taboo. The result of this is that creativity and innovation are stifled.

If people do not attempt anything new, then they cannot be seen to be failing. Resisting change protects people from the glare of failure.

In one organisation, this fear had created a culture which spawned long memos blaming everyone else for failure, or even potential failure. These memos were universally recognised by the acronym TCIC – Thank Christ I'm Covered.

This may be amusing, but recent analysis of how managers spend their time suggests some frightening statistics. In one management survey the figures looked like this:

Time spent justifying your existence – 1/3
Time spent covering your back (TCIC) – 1/3
Time spent actually being productive – 1/3

If you think of the amount of time spent on writing and reading unnecessary memos and the wasted time spent in meetings because of the fear of exposure and failure, the figures become more familiar. What has this got to do with integrated marketing? It is against this attitudinal background that the new messages need to penetrate.

To give a concrete example, which will be covered in more depth later, in one of the UK's largest clearing banks I encountered an unspoken cultural axiom which virtually all the managers seemed to adhere to. Summed up it can be expressed in a way akin to a government warning about smoking:

SPEAKING UP CAN DAMAGE YOUR FUTURE WEALTH

If it is accepted that communication is a two way process, this kind of barrier creates a major problem when it comes to marketing to the internal customer. And it doesn't just stop at fear . . .

Pride

Pride creates major barriers to marketing anything new into organisations. Pride forces people to appear to have done everything themselves in order to be recognised. This of course leads to promotion, pay rises, etc., or so they believe. In turn this creates the problem often referred to as NIH – Not Invented Here.

'Not Invented Here' arises through an unwillingness of people to admit that they could not or did not think of something. Alternatively, to say that someone else has improved on what they have done, they see as tantamount to failure. As we will be seeing later, one of the most important ways of changing an organisation is that of introducing Best Practice. This helps everyone to overcome NIH. It is interesting to compare the attitude of the same people who practise NIH when they are acting as external customers.

If every new product in the external market place was rejected because the potential customer hadn't thought of the idea, there would be very few products on the shelves!

This barrier to change has been recognised within organisations and considerable time and effort now goes into getting people to be involved with any change going on in the organisation. The key word being used when it comes to gaining acceptance in organisations, is *ownership*. This runs alongside another of the fashionable concepts being discussed about the way to change organisations through people, that of *empowerment*.

Sometimes, however, things can go too far and the organisation loses its own power through the assumption that the individual, or often Quality teams, can take total responsibility for the decision making process. In one organisation, I came across a very competent administration manager who expressed astonishment that a quality circle had spent eight man-days designing a form for a new system that he had produced in eight minutes. His view that it was his job was correct.

Indeed the practice of consulting others to provide ownership is widespread and the costs can be horrendous. Is it necessary? In a thriving organisation it is probably only necessary on critical issues. Individuals who are very busy, but who feel that communications are good and who do not perceive themselves to be under threat, will, I believe, willingly accept someone else's ideas.

It may be worth stating again that whilst these negative attitudes may need to be altered, they also have to be accepted. Until the day when the individual feels safe, secure, motivated, rewarded, etc., in the job that they are doing, the barriers are put up simply as a survival mechanism. If everyone in the organisation is doing the same, then you have a cultural problem.

However, Quality says that everyone has a customer, so it is no longer an organisational issue about how to tackle attitudinal and other barriers to change. It is up to every supplier in the customer-supplier chain to find out what makes their customer tick. One of the first tools to use is coming shortly!

Complacency

There can be much put under this banner. This can include a number of attitudinal barriers. All of these will have to be taken into account when marketing into the customer-supplier chain.

> ***Complacency, lack of commitment, lack of enthusiasm, etc. are perhaps an even greater threat to marketing in organisations than the strong reactions, like fear, already covered.***

This is typified by the reactions of the people in one office in a Welsh Regional Health Authority that I visited – complete apathy. The only colourful thing about the office, its people and its atmosphere, were a host of postcards on the notice board – all of which were of the same fundamentally sad nature:

YOU DON'T HAVE TO BE MAD TO WORK HERE – BUT IT HELPS

It shows a basic flaw in how work is perceived – as a bore. Yet these individuals are the same target markets who will enthusiastically fly half way round the world to do the same thing day after day on the beach. It is not the monotony of jobs which cause the attitudes to be negative, it is how people react to the monotony. These negative attitudes form the fundamental stumbling blocks to any marketing campaign to the internal customer.

THE POINT IS MADE

There are many self-improvement books appearing on station and airport bookstands throughout the world, designed to help individuals combat the kind of attitudinal problems just described, and there are many specialist books on organisational behaviour. This book is not intended to compete against any of these. There is a general recognition by human resource specialists that attitudes are a major cause for concern and an area that needs tackling. This concern, however, is often restricted to affecting mainly training, getting on with the job and, perhaps in a more nebulous way, on the 'culture'.

To the marketeer it is absolutely vital to know all of the barriers to communication and motivation, if any successful marketing activity is going to take place. These problems must, therefore, be understood.

In depth research and analysis will be covered later. In the meantime what follows is a very useful tool that helps identify what your customers are like. The benefit of this method is that it only takes a few seconds to complete and analyse.

A CUSTOMER STYLE INDICATOR

If human reactions like fear, pride and 'not invented here' affect how people react in organisations, then one of the strongest ways to counter this is to use classic marketing techniques like targeting a message to overcome these reactions. It works on people as external customers so why not try it within your organisation on your internal customers?

Why? Because carefully targeting your message within your organisation may be even more critical to success than targeting your external customers. Your internal customers can have much more to lose if they decide whether or not to follow a course of action e.g. their jobs. Whether you are trying to influence them or even just help them, saying the right thing, at the right time in the right way must be the better option – especially if you have to overcome fear and all the other barriers people put up at work.

I promised this book would contain practical tools and techniques for handling communication in the customer-supplier chain. Each of these techniques is rooted firmly in marketing practices. As is the case with so many skills, they are really straightforward, but they are often made more complicated than they need be.

Being responsible for introducing marketing skills, often into large organisations, we have to apply the KISS principle to everything we do. KISS stands for **K**eep **I**t **S**hort and **S**imple or in the USA Keep it Simple Stupid! Following this maxim ensures that in large organisations everyone is able to understand, relate to, use, and want to reuse the skills. I do not apologise for this. Our experience shows it is vital.

The following tool has been used in organisations as diverse as Royal

Mail, Butlins Holiday Worlds, Midland Bank and Thomas Cook. It also now forms part of the core management skills at the British Rail management centre, 'The Grove'. It is used in the Foundation Business Programme and Advanced Business Skills under the title Practical Marketing and Communication for Non-Marketing Managers, as are the other tools and techniques in this book. It has a good pedigree!

Called the Thomson Whitwell Customer Style Indicator, it provides a quick, easy and accurate guide to a customer's style of thinking, acting and reacting. Once you know the type of customers that you are dealing with, then marketing to them is much easier.

> ***External marketing uses many techniques to determine the customer requirements. What is needed internally is a 'user-friendly' way that*** **anybody** ***can use.***

Try it first before going through the explanation. It is so easy that it only needs the little bit of explanation and the example included of how to complete it. If you do not like writing on books please jot your scores on a piece of paper. The rest of this chapter will make much more sense if you can refer to and relate to a real example – yourself.

What does it mean?

The Customer Style Indicator is based on two well known psychological concepts using shapes and shades. The first is called Geometric Psychology which was developed in the United States. The Indicator shows that people who react to certain shapes that please them, will tend to have similar personal characteristics, all akin to that shape. Understanding people's character must be the first stage in understanding them as customers and getting closer to them. British Telecom use this for training receptionists.

The second concept was developed by a German psychologist called Luscher. It is detailed in an interesting and innovative book entitled *The Luscher Colour Test*. Dr Max Luscher, who was professor of psychology at Basle University, tested over 60,000 people by asking them to rank a range of colours in order of preference. According to *The Observer* newspaper:

> 'He based his personality test on the theory that a person's preference for certain colours is directly related to the 'emotional value' of these colours. The colours people prefer, dislike, or are indifferent to, are indicators of basic personality traits.'

As with Geometric Psychology, the rankings provided consistent profiles of

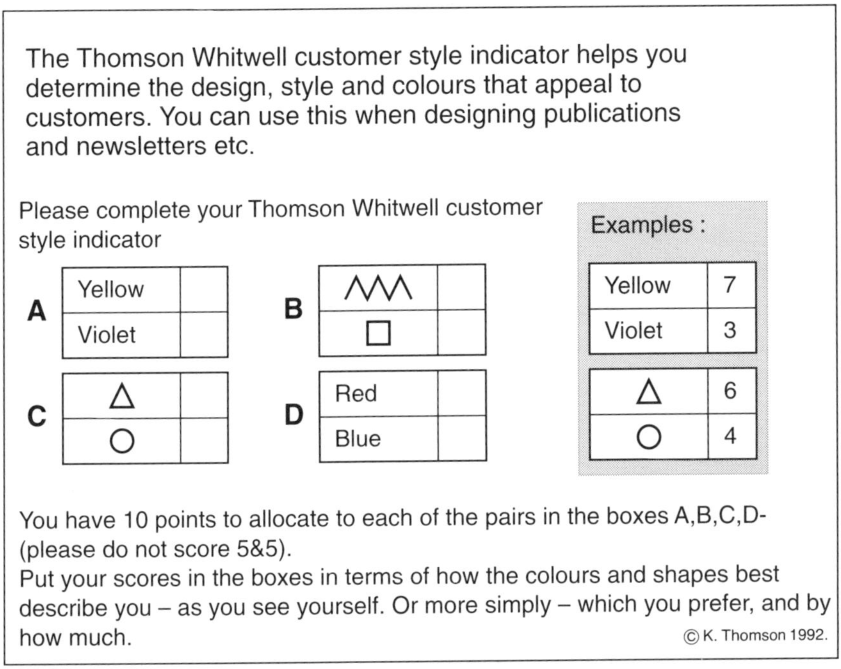
The Thomson Whitwell customer style indicator helps you determine the design, style and colours that appeal to customers. You can use this when designing publications and newsletters etc.
Please complete your Thomson Whitwell customer style indicator
A
Yellow
Violet
B
C
D
Red
Blue
Examples :
Yellow
7
Violet
3
6
4
You have 10 points to allocate to each of the pairs in the boxes A,B,C,D- (please do not score 5&5).
Put your scores in the boxes in terms of how the colours and shapes best describe you – as you see yourself. Or more simply – which you prefer, and by how much.
© K. Thomson 1992.

Figure 2.1 The Thomson Whitwell Customer Style Indicator

people. Creating a consistent customer profile is the first step in being able to target messages precisely to target audiences as well as individuals.

There are major advantages in putting the two together to create a profile that can be used for marketing to customers throughout the customer-supplier chain. The nature of these indicators is such that the data can be used for a variety of purposes, not least of which is creating a language.

> ***Marketing people use the simple language of ABC_1C_2 when targeting messages (see Chapter 7). Now you can use the Thomson Whitwell Customer Style Indicator to do the same targeting job. It uses the powerful language of geometric and colour psychology. It's also a lot more interesting and dare I say fun – this is why people like it!***

How did you score? In our experience the tests done by the psychologists on the colours and shapes provides an exceedingly high hit rate when identifying people's characteristics. Sometimes however, and you may be one of them, people will choose colours or shapes that they subsequently say represent nothing like them, or so they think. We find that colleagues will often tell them otherwise! Even if it is 'wrong' it allows the supplier to, at the very least, discuss what is right.

People always ask for the explanations, so we have put this on a separate page (Figure 2.2) we are happy for this part only to be copied.

Of course everyone has some of each of these characteristics, but core traits will be picked up. The higher the scoring the more likely people are to display the traits. Once you know what your customers are like then you can start to deal with them much more effectively.

How can the Customer Style Indicator be used?

There are a number of powerful benefits in using this process to discover your customers' preferred style. It can be used individually or for large target groups who display similar characteristics. It is a method of defining your customers' preferences when it comes to targeting in any of the following ways:

1 Design style
2 Colour
3 Copy to use for printed material
4 Language to use when talking, presenting, training etc.
5 Non-verbal approach with body language

How does targeting a message work? Think of the last magazine or paper that you read. How many of the adverts appealed to you, did nothing, or turned you off? Why? Because the design, colour, wording of the copy and the overall approach may not be right. This leaves aside the possibility that you do not want the product!

If you get your customers to tell you first what they like in each of these areas then you are far more likely to get the message right when you do try to communicate with them.

From a personal point of view, I wish in my earlier career as a marketeer I had the techniques of pre-testing the style preference of target customers. I believe it would have made an enormous difference to deciding the communication approach, for example on TV, in the press, magazines, etc.

> ***As it was, and still is, the creative approach is often decided by the creative people. They may or may not be in tune with customers. Now you can do it yourself.***

It is not just TV advertising that needs the right approach to customers. Internally within the customer-supplier chain, the Customer Style Indicator

Yellow	Bright, cheerful, positive, extrovert, speaks before thinking
Violet	Reserved, quiet, shy, introvert, thinks before speaking
Squiggle	Ideas orientated, innovative, creative, excitable, enthusiastic, chaotic, energetic (wears you out!), likes to do their own thing
Box	Structured, dependable, cautious, meticulous, detailed, task-orientated, does what is asked
Triangle	Leader, dogmatic, decisive, determined, ambitious, confident, definite, likes to tell others what to do
Circle	Harmonious, likeable, people orientated, reads people well, emotional, good communicator, good listener, adaptable, likes to check with others before acting
Red	Hot, emotional, impetuous, easily provoked, very flexible, moves deadlines to suit themselves, likes to play
Blue	Cool, reserved, organised, can be inflexible, likes to plan

Figure 2.2 The shapes and shades defined

Yellow	Fun Exciting Opportunity Can do 'Let's do it now'
Violet	Maybe If We'll trial this first 'Let's approach this cautiously'
Squiggle	Idea New Innovative Creative Future 'Think what it might do'
Box	Tried Tested Reliable Data Past 'This has proved to work'
Triangle	Profit Goal Success Control Growth 'Look what this will do for your career'
Circle	People Feelings Comfortable Team 'Other people are happy with this'
Red	Do it now Play with this 'It will be all right on the night'
Blue	Planned Organised Factual 'This has to be well thought through'

Figure 2.3 The words to use to target your message

can be used for the simplest of communication vehicles, such as the memo. The way to target messages is to use the words that will appeal to each characteristic the customer displays.

To give a simple example, the office manager may have the strongest characteristics of being 'blue' and being a 'box'. In other words, he is someone who is organised and will concentrate on details, not ideas.

The Marketing Manager who is attempting to communicate with him is a 'yellow squiggle'. In other words someone who is likely to be disorganised, talk a lot and be interested in ideas, not detail. If these two get together there is a definite clash.

If, however, each uses the language of the other, then they will be able to get through. In marketing it is called targeting. Try it, it works.

Figure 2.3 shows the words that will appeal. When it comes to design and colour, these should also reflect the customer preferences as well. As you can imagine, if you like a box shape then a boxy design, e.g. grids, charts, bar charts, will be appealing. If you like yellow and red then McDonalds type corporate colours may appeal to you. If you think of blue, an IBM or ICI corporate colour says a lot about the type of organisation.

External customers are persuaded to buy products from advertising. This uses colour, music, cartoons, drama, stories, design, jingles and anything else that makes people sit up and take note. Why should it be any different when they walk through the office or factory door? No wonder they are bored with internal communication!

If the only way to get people to change is to get into their psyche and to target messages to them, what is stopping it happening? Must marketing to the internal customer be dull and boring? If it means the difference between a motivated and unmotivated workforce isn't it worth a try?

Targeting large or small target groups

The Customer Style Indicator doesn't just have to be used on individual customers. It can be used to ascertain the characteristics of small or large target groups, even extending to whole organisations. To give an example: within the Thomas Cook organisation, as might be expected, the travel consultants, who are the people who help you choose your holiday, are likely to be 'yellow squiggles'. They may have to be outgoing and be ready to take risks in sending people to places that they may have never been to.

The foreign exchange cashiers are more likely to be 'violet', as their role keeps them behind the safety screens away from direct contact with customers. However, they are still likely to be 'squiggles' as they are sending customers into the unknown. This is unlike a cashier in a bank who is more likely to be a 'box' dealing with situations, facts and figures which are based solidly in the here and now. This was borne out by research with cashiers within the Midland Bank.

With the Thomson Whitwell Customer Style Indicator you can target any group with similar characteristics. This can be done with design, style, language and copy.

When you, as a marketeer, have this type of data, either for individuals or whole organisations, you are able to ensure that the messages that you want to get through are not only received and understood but also 'bought into'. With the vast majority of internal communication not even being received, never mind understood and bought into, this is a major step forward for communicating within the customer-supplier chain.

Does this all sound like marketing 'hype'? It is wise to remember that it is the 'hype' that helps sell every product from a BMW to a Mars bar. And no one said that managing people by marketing to them had to be boring. It is often because the training of management skills is boring that it fails. Having said that, there is a far more serious side to marketing to customers.

Try the Customer Style Indicator on your friends, if you are concerned about trying it on customers. As the *Evening News* said of the Luscher Test, 'Will serve not only as a serious psychological tool but also the party game of the year'.

SUMMARY

- **Fear of change itself is one of the fundamental problems to be faced by the marketeer looking to influence customers in their customer- supplier chain.**

- **People feel that they are admitting they did something wrong by accepting a 'new' way of doing things. This creates a fear of loss of face. It creates a resistance to new methods and practices.**

- **The role of integrated marketing is made much more difficult through the well founded fear of job loss from recession, competition, mergers, flatter structures and new technologies.**

- **Any new introduction will be resisted if it is felt it will adversely affect people. Marketing in the customer supplier chain is basically concerned with new introductions!**

- **The solution to the problem of understanding how people will react is to find out what they are like first. The Customer Style Indicator may help.**

3 THE BENEFITS OF PEOPLE, MARKETING AND QUALITY WORKING TOGETHER

WHAT'S IN IT FOR ME AND FOR THE ORGANISATION TO ADOPT THIS APPROACH?

In short, people, marketing and Quality working together must be the biggest single benefit – to the individual and the organisation. Together they can produce better results.

Hard and soft benefits

In my previous book, *The Employee Revolution*, I outlined many of the benefits of an integrated approach. These benefits were often considered to be 'soft' as they impacted mainly on the people issues. These included:

Empowerment at all levels.
Opening up of communication channels.
Reduced need for union need influence.
Increased motivation.
Improved innovation.
A recognition of creativity.
. . . and many more.

Most organisations have started to recognise and, perhaps more importantly, measure, some 'hard' benefits of introducing Total Quality. Imagine these benefits magnified when they start to work together with the ones outlined above:

Increased revenue.
Profits up.
Reduced costs – from increased staff efficiency and reduced initiative failures, to name but two.
Improved margins.

Committed customers with lifetime relationships.
. . . and many others.

Here are two brief examples.

Quadrant (Royal Mail Catering), recently had the daunting task of taking approximately 30 per cent out of the pay packets of its catering grades, to bring the organisation in line with others in the commercial world. With a foresighted Personal Director, Dermot Courtier, who combined marketing, human resource and communication tools and techniques, they achieved a massive 3:1 Union vote in favour of the cuts. The processes they adopted were measured for their effectiveness and possible use again. All of the measures proved successful. One question asked of all staff was 'Should we use this process and format again?' Bearing in mind the message communicated, only 22 people out of 1,500 said no – an amazing result.

By using this potential problem as an opportunity, Quadrant not only remained in business, something a no vote would have put in jeopardy, but it also improved its image and credibility with its people.

Jennifer Shipside, Group Brand Communications Manager of Thomas Cook, is currently piloting a programme in two of its UK regions, looking for between 5 and 10 per cent increase in revenue by 'sharing the wisdom of people' via Best Practice and Team Listenings. So far, the results look very positive, with both hard and soft benefits showing.

These are the sorts of benefits recognisable in a committed organisation, one that focuses both at micro and macro levels on all its customers in the customer-supplier chain.

Everyone knows the 'hard' benefits of introducing Quality. What about the overall benefits of integrating Quality with marketing?

Empowerment at all levels

One of the biggest problems that managers used to face in an organisation was the feeling of being unable to act and make decisions. This may have been as a result of a fear of the consequences of 'sticking their neck out'. It may be the constraints placed upon them by their superiors. This is exemplified by some very low levels of expenditure authority vested in some very highly paid people.

Much of this has changed. There is also a new desire for it to be changed, but the vestiges of the past are steeped in many cultures. The speed of decision making that is required today is unlike anything that people have encountered before. Levels of bureaucracy have been removed in incredibly short time scales and this has forced a greater need for decisions on fewer and fewer individuals. Yet the self same individuals have not been given the support and skills that they feel they need to be able to respond to the new challenges facing them. The benefit of empowerment can lead to increased pressure.

Dealing with these needs of the internal customer naturally involves the use of management skills and techniques. These are, for example, problem solving, decision making, planning, leadership skills and team skills. They are also the technical skills needed to deal with a changing environment that boasts whole new methodologies in the workplace. In addition to these skills there is a whole new organisational environment and culture in which people have to operate. A large part of this environment is generated by the one certainty that does exist in business today, summed up by saying 'nothing is as certain as tremendous change'. In the UK, the Management Charter Initiative, for all the criticism it is facing, is attempting to provide standards for managers in the 1990s to be able to deal with all the things that are thrown at them.

On top of these changes, the other certainty is that, as the structures get 'flatter', the pressures get greater.

What are these pressures?

Greater demands from customers
Greater demands on workloads
Greater demands on time
Greater demands on effectiveness
Greater demands from people around them
Greater demands from home
Greater personal demands on improved quality of life
Greater demands from 'above'
Greater demands to produce and increase profitability

And so the list goes on, and it adds to the list of pressures that create intrinsic fear in individuals; for their position, their status, their security and their jobs.

The net result is an enormous strain, especially at middle management level. The easiest way out of this, for those who are in the unfortunate position where the organisation does not invest in the training, development and the communication processes, is to retreat to a 'safe position', where they believe they cannot be harmed. It is one where they put a squeeze on just about everything, to prevent or delay decisions being made. This is classically referred to as applying 'control'.

This is best exemplified by what I describe as the 'egg timer effect' (see Figure 3.1). It may not have any basis in qualitatively researched data, but the power of its message has been attested to in the many organisations that have had this theory presented to them.

In essence, the result of this middle management 'squeeze' is to produce an amazingly powerful counter to the attempts at opening up the communication channels. This prevents 'empowerment' even getting off the ground. The squeeze prevents the internal marketing of ideas, products and services. This can be to, or from, those individuals who are on either side of the internal chain of command.

In turn, it prevents not only the individual concerned from making decisions, but also restricts and prevents those above or below from making decisions, because the information that allows this to happen is not flowing. Marketing is all about opening distribution channels. Imagine the power of opening up the middle management 'squeeze'.

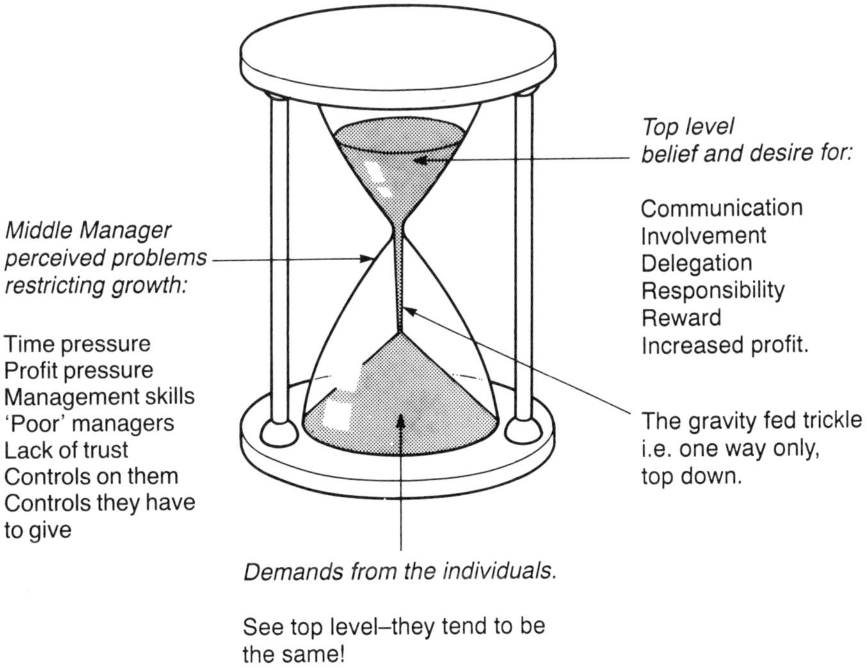

Figure 3.1 The bottleneck to growth

The employee revolution has then begun

In my last book, *The Employee Revolution*, written at the end of the 1980s, I used the analogy that 'employees' were no longer prepared to lie down and accept the type of 'top down', autocratic and bureaucratic styles of management. (Just like the peasants revolted against the aristocracy in the French Revolution 200 years ago.) In the depths of a world recession as I write in late 1992 it is easy to say that any employee revolution, where they are demanding more power, will soon be quashed – if it ever really gets going. With profitability being driven down, with margins slashed, with workforces reduced to the bone and with everyone being afraid for their jobs, surely the employees can go back to being 'told' what to do? Some managers think so.

The opposite is the case! With people having so much to do, most organisations now recognise that they have to be left to get on with it. People must be empowered to get on with it themselves or the organisation will be unable to get the goods out of the door. Leaders are looking for empowerment to happen as much as the 'employee' is having to take on the responsibility of being responsible for themselves. Empowerment is now recognised as the key to survival, if not success.

So, the people want empowerment as well as the leaders want it to happen. The question is how can it happen? This question is critical to understanding the new style of organisation in the 1990s – customer facing, responsive at local level, fast, adaptable, quality driven and one that is no longer searching for, but has found, 'excellence'.

The way to empowerment of people throughout the customer-supplier chain is to meet their needs. This can be done by providing them with the internal products and services, like training and information technology that they need to get on with the job. But, you may be saying, we already do that.

Do you truly meet your internal customer needs or do you decide what you think that they want?

Of course you may train them, but is it the training they feel is necessary? Have you researched their needs? Of course they are given the tools to do the job, but do they really meet their needs? Because they are more responsible and closer to the needs of their customer and to what needs to be done, they are demanding more responsibility for their own fate. They want to be allowed to meet the needs of their customers, who they in turn should be researching.

The interesting thing about the 'egg timer effect', is that it shows that the hopes and desire of those above and those below the individual who is controlling the squeeze, arc almost always the same. It is not until the squeeze is opened out that the start of empowering all the individuals in the organisation will happen. The second characteristic of the 'egg timer' itself, which makes this model so pertinent, is that the flow, (in this case of information), is always downwards.

Opening up communication channels

In one organisation the downward 'cascade' of information was described in one qualitative research group as being 'from that shower at head office'! Too often people believe that information is something to be handed down from decision-makers to the people at the lower levels. This need not happen, but let's look at the problem first.

Team briefing adds to the problem

This type of 'cascade' is embodied in the methodology of the 'Team Briefing'; almost a military style 'tell' session, with a concession to the people after they have been 'briefed' to say what they think. Having been presented with a *fait accompli*, it is not often wise to say what you think! In addition to this, the flow of locally targeted information often dries up. This is because it comes from managers who are controlling and squeezing information. They do this in a bid to retain their authority. It often leads to only two or three briefing groups being held because they soon dry up, and lose their credibility. The attempt at communication is seen to have failed. This, of course, puts the squeezing manager back in a strong position and they are then the sole source of information transfer. They no longer have to expose themselves to groups.

The process moves back to a one to one basis and so they return to the old practice of 'divide and rule'. However, this need not be the case. It will be shown later how targeted messages do not need to be delivered by managers who are not capable of delivering them, or at least are reluctant to do so.

Yet the pressure is on. Not for less responsibility but more. People want to use their brains. The ESSO research by MORI highlighted that people want involvement. Once they get involved, they will be able to take responsibility.

It is through the targeting of key information to all levels that the individuals will start to demand greater and greater autonomy. Why? Because information is power!

This does not mean that a reduction in 'leadership' is required. People need and want strong leaders. What is needed is a lessening of the levels of control-orientated management.

The key issue for individuals in the organisation becomes the responsiveness of those around them to the decisions that they are making. These people either above, below, or colleagues, become the customers who benefit or otherwise from the decisions. The opening up of communication will ensure that the speed of response allows the decision maker to know very quickly if they have made the right decision or not. By opening up the communication, the people feel that the information being targeted at them meets their needs and they will increasingly demand that these need to be taken into account.

Reduced need for union influence

If it is accepted that the key need of employees is to be left to get on with it; and the leaders of the organisation are doing all in their power to ensure this happens, then the great 'us and them' divide will disappear. So, what about the Unions?

Everyone knows that unions are no longer the force that they used to be. Is it any wonder that their power is diminished when everyone wants the same thing in an organisation? The cry for greater involvement, greater training, better conditions and generally better wages has been met in most cases, with some notable exceptions in lower paid unskilled jobs like catering. Is it any wonder that their power is lessened when Governments are committed to keeping inflation low and everyone knows that spiralling wage costs are a thing of the past? Is it any wonder, when the last thing that anyone wants in a world recession is to go on strike? And what will happen if they do? Foreign competition is soon able to step into any gap.

It is also true to say that very few good organisations want to get the most for the least amount of money. Additionally, very few good organisations are insensitive to the needs of their people, especially when they are contributing so much. They may no longer be able to afford to provide them as much, be it pay, benefits, etc. but that is down to external pressures rather than a philosophy of screwing every last thing out of them.

Leaders in organisations want, and desperately need, motivated, adequately paid people who are ready, willing and able to give their all. So, the need for unions to try to force this to happen has more or less gone.

It is my belief that whilst in power in the UK, the Conservative Government would like to claim all the credit for it. It has done a lot, but it is probable that Quality has (silently) done more to destroy Union power than any other single change in the last decade.

However, there have been many other influences. Greater competition, flatter structures, greater levels of communication, attitude surveys, better training, and better meeting of customer needs throughout the customer-supplier chain, all help towards empowering the individuals, and reducing the power of the unions.

The need disappears to leave 'employee' power in the hands of the Unions, who may be perceived to be using it in a way not acceptable to the individual, e.g. politically.

Empowering people also does not mean a full scale socialist revolution in the work place! It means everyone accepting greater levels of responsibility to assist the organisation. These changes are not only desirable, they are vital if the organisation is to survive.

Increased motivation

There is a new wave of morality that is sweeping through organisations as they move down the paths of 'Excellence' and 'Quality'. Very few people have recognised it yet but the more popular term for it would be 'religion'.

The work being done by consultants, human resource specialists and the like, is almost akin to that of missionaries. They go into the organisation and 'spread the word'. They provide the basis for their 'high priests' to be trained, often called 'champions'. They leave their 'bibles', often called manuals, with the converts. They tell their parables of other 'good Samaritans' doing excellent things all over the world. They can now also create the impression of immortality by appearing on the everlasting medium of a training video. They are called gurus by their disciples.

Finally, people are prepared to travel great distances to hear their words of wisdom, or in the case of Tom Peters to be harangued about their corporate sins (like not putting the janitor's name on his picture in the Annual Report and Accounts, when the CEO, of course, is named).

Is this analogy with religion going too far? With the demise of the Church, especially in the UK, it is perhaps a good thing that someone is taking up the role of provider of spiritual guidance.

Read this set of values from one organisation. To produce these words, a tremendous amount of soul searching went on; and a great deal of debate took place, all of which ended up with what appeared at the time to be perhaps the fastest change in some people's outlooks that they had ever experienced. Not everyone was hit by the fervour created, but there was a fundamental recognition that the ways of the past would not be tolerated.

WE VALUE – RECOGNITION OF INDIVIDUAL CONTRIBUTION, TEAMWORK, HONESTY AND INTEGRITY, SOCIAL RESPONSIBILITY, MUTUAL RESPECT AND INTEGRITY.

Interestingly this organisation was recently acquired by another with a totally different set of values. The whole process must start again. Is this like being reborn?

These attitudinal shifts occur as a direct result of people interacting with others in a structured way. The debates and discussions are even provided in 'company time', so that unlike church, the individual does not have to invest their own time. Attitudes towards the organisation, customers and colleagues are discussed effectively in the context of more 'honourable' methods of making a profit, e.g. through improving internal and external relationships. The individual must, therefore, consider both their personal and work ethics. To give two simple examples:

— Customers should never be looked down on in any way, such as calling them 'punters'.
— Colleagues' needs should be respected, e.g. no smoking at work, even in the unlikely event of smokers being in the majority.

What has religion got to do with marketing? A lot. Without being in any way sacrilegious, religion provides an interesting parallel. For centuries it has been one of the best sold and marketed 'products and services' the world has ever seen.

Now the same type of messages are suddenly becoming important in the work place. In fact, the fervour created by strong belief, is exactly that desired by most organisations. Look at what is happening in Japan. It is not the methods and practices (like Just in Time etc.) which ensure that the levels of quality and cost are almost unbeatable. It is the people's total commitment to these technological and production 'gods' that guarantees their total domination in so many markets.

Much of the work by the western 'experts' in these areas is little more than an attempt to verbalise the actions required, rather than translating those messages into a language that the target market wants to buy into. Very few advertising agencies would now suggest that global advertising campaigns really work (that is not to say a global marketing strategy can't work), so why should people think that global Quality programmes should work? The marketing message today is 'Think global, act local'. Quality needs to take the same approach.

> ***I have seen more people 'switched off', than 'switched on', by campaigns themes like 'zero defects' and 'right first time'. If you are a long way off getting it right first time, unlike the Japanese, then frustration will soon set in and the whole programme may be doomed to fail, or to not even get off the ground.***

Unfortunately, this perception of a manic approach to Quality is worsened by business programmes on TV featuring Japanese style quality in action. Examples of this ability to create in-built trust, loyalty, commitment, enthusiasm etc, usually involve British workers in Japanese owned factories in some far flung new town in the UK. They are either doing physical jerks at some ungodly hour in the morning, sitting in groups in the single level canteen having a pep talk, or sitting in Quality Circles. This does little to create a desire for change in others.

I am not decrying the validity of what is happening in these organisations. The point is that the message being given to these employees is coming from a different source than before. They are more likely to be disposed to buy into this message because they are effectively in a 'foreign' environment. The old adage applies, otherwise they would not have gone for the job in the first place – 'When in Japan do as the Japanese do'!

This same employee commitment is desired by Western organisations. However, they cannot change the culture without changing the deep rooted beliefs of everybody. In a telephone poll survey of British companies who had tried to introduce JIT, 90 per cent failed in the first three months. Why? The answer lies, firstly in the quality of the marketing in the launch, and secondly in the trust placed by the individuals being asked to change their ways. If the target market lacks the basic trust in the organisation and its motives, then nothing will move them to buy the new products and services being offered.

The needs of the individual at a basic, emotional level are for those often reiterated virtues that are heard in church; trust, integrity, respect etc.

Consider then the possible objectives of a customer service campaign. These are not definitive, but serve to show the close proximity of religious teachings:

1 To provide your customer with a level of service that you would expect when you are buying products and services.
i.e. Do unto others as you would have done to you.

2 To ensure that the customer is treated with the utmost respect even when it appears that they are being 'awkward'.
i.e. Turn the other cheek.

3 Deal with complaints in a tolerant, friendly way.
i.e. Let he who is without sin cast the first stone.

4 Welcome the customer in a polite, friendly way.
i.e. Be a good Samaritan to these total strangers that you are being asked to deal with.

5 Ensure our 'Children's Policy' is adhered to as they are important customers today and in the future.
i.e. Suffer the little children to come unto me.

It is the targeting of these messages into the hearts and souls of the individual that forms part of the brief in this and many other internal marketing campaigns. Trust can be produced when long term customer satisfaction is aimed at. This occurs when marketing to the customer produces a customer-facing culture. The organisation itself must change to prove to the individual that it means what it says.

The individual will not, for example, practise any new technique or skill for long if the manager does not practise it. The individual will not give of their best if all they are doing is being taken advantage of. The individual will not respond to greater amounts of responsibility being thrust on them if the respect for their contribution is not forthcoming. So, what can be expected with greater levels of effective marketing throughout the customer-supplier chain?

1 Greater levels of research, and simple 'listening', backed up by response, leads to greater levels of trust.
NB This is not to be taken lightly. The trust placed in the brand and its values by the external customer is dearly bought.

2 Better targeted messages homing in on specific needs. This leads to greater commitment to the organisation.
NB This is the same as external marketing finding the hooks that make the customer eager to buy.

3 More improved information means the individual will be more loyal. The mushroom theory of 'keeping everyone in the dark and feeding them fertiliser' is nonsense.
NB The external marketeer who fails to keep their products and services in

front of the consumer will (owing to their short term and fickle nature) soon end up with a dead product.

4 Pride develops when an individual knows that they are trusted and that this recognition is demonstrated to others.
NB The new car in the driveway is a powerful testimony to pride and how people will go out of their way to seek and to demonstrate it.

5 Finally, the biggest buzzword in both Quality and in human resource development circles today is 'ownership'. This is created through the very processes of marketing, which shows the individual that they are just that – individuals.

Effective marketing throughout the customer-supplier chain demonstrates that people's needs are being met. Researching and delivering to customers' present and future requirements, is practising what Quality preaches.

IMPROVED INNOVATION

The one demand that is placed on the external marketing department, above all else, is providing the customer with something NEW, NEW, NEW.

This may be in the products and services themselves, in the advertising, the promotion, or, for the sales force, it may be in the form of new markets, conference themes, incentive schemes, or in the packaging, branding or Corporate identity. There are always demands for things that are new.

The pace of change itself has created an almost insatiable beast demanding the new. If it isn't new and improved, then there must be something wrong with it!'

There are one or two products and services which don't appear to change, but on closer inspection they are moving as rapidly as the latest piece of information technology – well almost. For example, Fairy Liquid appear to have used the same adverts for 25 years, and indeed the basic story of parent, child and bubbles at the sink has not changed (with the odd foray into other creative ideas on the way), but the advertising production techniques are as up to date as you would expect and we now even see a *man* at the sink!

The external customer is literally assailed by everything new, every day. The same is now happening in the work place. The latest advance in information technology is new one day and out of date the next.

People management techniques and practices change every time someone brings out the latest management best seller. The individual at the sharp end experiences a constant stream of new messages.

Recognition of creativity

On top of all this, everyone in the organisation is now being viewed as a vital cog in the wheel of improving quality. They are also expected to contribute to the creative input. Compare this with the classic case of Post-it Notes. The inventor who worked in 3M had to secretly market the product before the company saw the possibilities. People are also expected to be immediately capable of handling the process of innovation to bring these ideas to the market place. Finally, they are now recognised as a crucial part in meeting increasingly tough profit targets.

Without wishing to beat the marketing drum too hard, it is the techniques of those two key skills of creativity and innovation that rest with the marketing function.

> ***Marketing people spend their entire existence in managing creativity and innovation. They do this in order to satisfy the external customer. These skills and processes can, and should, be transferred to everyone.***

Just as importantly, it must be recognised by everyone in the organisation that both quality and innovation are only meaningful if they are placed in the context of customers and their needs. Hence, the other marketing skills such as research, design and testing also come into play. There are still further skills which are vital in this process of improving quality and managing information. These have been touched on elsewhere under the general headings of problem solving (sometimes referred to as problem prevention), planning and decision making. This is where combining marketing and human resource skills will prove invaluable.

Consider these definitions:

Oxford English Dictionary:

Create: Bring into existence, give rise to, originate.

Perhaps it is also worth mentioning the part of the definition which is sometimes used by other non-creative people in the organisation. This happens when their cosy world is shattered by the goings on of the creative individuals who are forever challenging the order of things. Creative people are always looking to replace, renew, restructure and reject things with their new ideas, viz. – **Create:** make a fuss.

To quote Tom Peters from *In Search Of Excellence*, who quotes Quinn:

> 'Most corporations fail to tolerate the creative fanatic who has been the driving force behind most major innovations. Innovations, being far removed from the mainstream of the business, show little promise in the early stages of development. Moreover, the champion is obnoxious, impatient, egotistic, and perhaps

a bit irrational in organisational terms. As a consequence, he is not hired. If he is hired, he is not promoted or rewarded. He is regarded as 'not a serious person', 'embarrassing', or 'disruptive'.'

Oxford English Dictionary:
Innovate: Bring in novelties; make new.

The difference is that creativity brings ideas into existence. Innovation turns them into products and services. Marketing puts the two into context by establishing a number of things within an organisation.

1 If customers want NEW, NEW, NEW, then the organisation must ensure it gives it to them.
2 If it takes an 'upsetting of the (internal) apple cart' to get new ideas into the system to replace the things that customers no longer want, so be it.

   It is not the creators and innovators that we ought to be coaching and counselling about their pushing and shoving of others (and generally in the process, dulling their desires to be at the leading edge) it is the ones who are getting upset. These people are not the holders of 'all that is right', they are the ones who will let the competitor overtake you.
3 Failure is success. If you have failed then you have tried. Something like 95 per cent of all new products fail in the first two years. It is a good job that the innovators of these did not give up and go home because, if they had, we would not have the other 5 per cent!
4 Most creativity and innovation relies on everybody in the organisation to contribute. Therefore, everybody should receive the training to assist the organisation to meet its overwhelming need to improve quality and innovate.
5 Most creativity and innovation is stopped through the attitude of the creators, e.g. worry or fear that it won't succeed. The attitude of the other people involved also stops creative potential, e.g. worry or fear that someone else's ideas will succeed and highlight their inadequacy. The introduction of a process which ensures that does not happen will help alleviate the biggest stumbling block to both processes.

The only problem here is that, whilst everyone has got hung up, quite rightly, on Jan Carlzon and the 1,000 × 1 per cent improvements, i.e. think small not big, there appears to be very little evidence of the skills training to enable the process to occur. Where it does occur, the tendency is for there to be a concentration on improvements in quality of existing products, services and internal procedures and practices, rather than creativity and innovation.

One excellent example of a focus on the existing products and services in a quality improvement programme that also ran with a strong slant on innovation, is in the Royal Bank of Scotland. The entire programme they ran, called 'Where People Matter', began as an internal campaign to focus on customer needs. As a consequence of its success, the programme's theme was carried into the external marketing, with the theme 'Where People Matter' being applied to their TV and press campaign.

> ***The power achieved from both an internal and external marketing campaign can ultimately be aimed for in most organisations. This is a truly integrated marketing approach.***

In the Royal Bank of Scotland, the individual branches and departments have two elements operating under the title of 'Service Circles'. The first of these, entitled 'Doing It Right' is the activity which . . . 'looks at the services we provide for both internal and external customers. It looks at what we do and how we do it. This activity will establish the standards of performance that our services need to meet. It will also identify the problems that prevent us from meeting the required standards and develop ideas to overcome'.

To do this there are 10 steps in the Royal Bank of Scotland process. Of these, the three key steps that are effectively marketing orientated are:

1 Identify customers (the target market)
2 Establish the requirements of the customer (research customer needs)
3 Communicate the actions (advertise the improved products and services)

The second activity in the programme allows the individuals at branch and department level to concentrate on the major area of innovation under their control, i.e. the service they give. Ideas for new products and services for the whole Bank are gathered and put into practice. The framework of existing products at any given time in most organisations leaves little room at local level for major innovation, specifically on product. This is not to say that a great deal can, and should be done at local level to meet and surpass the needs of customers. It is in this 'surpassing' of the needs of customers that the process of innovation takes place. It assumes that the innovation brings with it a level of service that is not either expected or even requested. Hence the title the Bank has given this process 'Surprising The Customer'.

To quote the 'Where People Matter' programme again . . . 'This activity . . . is to examine our *means* of communication with our customers, internal or external, to ensure that we are using them most effectively. If we are to gain a reputation for being more effective and more personal in the services we provide, our means of communication must be looked at closely'.

Once again there are three key marketing orientated steps which are exactly the same as those previously stated. Whether looking at 'new' or just 'improved', the customer requirements are paramount. These three activities form the core of an internal marketing process which will be detailed later under the titles 'Listening, Gathering, and Sharing'.

So, back to the central premise that if customers are involved, then so should the role of marketing. Where it is involved, it will keep that focus paramount simply by its language, and its processes and innovation will be fundamental to what everyone recognises of the soap powder syndrome: 'New and Improved'; in other words keeping up with, and ahead of, the customer.

> ***Innovation throughout the customer-supplier chain can become one of the greatest benefits of a marketing based approach to Quality.***

Together with empowerment at all levels and 'trust', this achieves the key needs of the organisation and the individual. This is the desire to get on with the job in an environment that lets them do it. It does this by giving people the attitude, awareness and ability along with the opportunity to continually improve.

SUMMARY

- Empowerment at all levels is the result of the information explosion. Once people are targeted with the right information, they will demand to be allowed to act. Sales and customer service will increase.
- Increased revenue by gathering and sharing the wisdom of the people.
- Improved communication by opening up the communication channels.
- Reduced Union influence.
- Reduced costs as fewer initiatives fail.
- Increased motivation as people learn to trust the organisation to 'do as they would be done to' and then they will give their all.
- An organisation focused on goal – the customer.
- Improved creativity starting with the removal of fear and acceptance of failure.
- Innovation is the key to future customer satisfaction.
- If customers are involved in the equation, then marketing won't be far behind in pushing forward the skills to meet their needs.

4 SOME KEY TERMS USED IN HUMAN RESOURCES DEVELOPMENT AND TOTAL QUALITY MANAGEMENT

The main purpose of including some of the definitions of concepts and terms is to set the scene for future terminology. It begins to allow a merging of the three disciplines of Quality, marketing and human resource development (as practised by personnel and training specialists). This whole process of merging will in itself produce the key strategy of 'total customer focus'.

So it is worth outlining the human resource development issues that will crop up when practising this new discipline. This section describes some HRD techniques and issues, and relates them to the techniques of internal marketing. (Also see *Internal Marketing: A New Perspective for HRD* page 250, Adrian Payne.)

Training – tell or sell

The *Oxford English Dictionary* defines training as follows:

> **Train:** Bring (person, child, animal) to desired state or standard of efficiency etc. by instruction and practice.

What I find interesting about this definition is that it makes no mention of whether or not the person (child, animal) actually *wants* to be trained. It then goes on to say that the methodology is by instruction and practice. This would imply a situation where people are told what to do, must go about doing it, once they have had the chance to try it out through practice. There is no mention of encouraging *motivation*. It reflects the still prevalent view of many unenlightened trainers (the type of people who wouldn't read this book so they won't be upset by my calling them that) who have a 'must do' mentality. (I first discovered this in the catering industry.) This happens because trainers, managers and supervisors feel that they have the power of the organisation behind them to instruct employees to act in such a way as to achieve set standards.

Today, the final desired outcome may be exactly the same, to achieve set standards, but using an autocratic 'tell' method will be less successful.

Training has come a long way and, as a subject, is well covered by others. Almost by default, training professionals are beginning to adopt many internal marketing techniques to add to their existing tools and techniques.

Coaching, counselling, appraisal, influencing

These are called inter-personal skills in human resource development terms. What have they to do with internal marketing?

> ***They could be dramatically enhanced by sales and marketing skills, if in the appropriate circumstances, people are viewed as customers who need to be marketed and sold to.***

At this point, to prevent people switching off if they view marketing and selling as something a little bit sordid, it is worth telling the story of one executive who felt the same. He came to a course he had been asked to attend on selling to internal customers entitled 'Selling Yourself'. His boss phoned me up some two months after to say how, during his salary review, the executive had used all the principles he had been taught. As a result, the boss had given him more than double the increase he had intended!

If this is not enough to convince you, then simply reflect that the internal manager has only the same basic tools as the sales person on the road. To get the most out of the people they deal with, sales people have only their brain and their mouth. They are perceived to need training to deal with external customers. Their level of revenue is dependent not just on the product they sell, but largely on the skills they bring to bear when influencing the potential buyer. Is it not true then, that within organisations massive amounts of revenue are lost through an inability to communicate and persuade people? If the internal customer needs to buy into the products and services then the internal sales person has to sell, and the internal marketeer to market.

Workshop – training by another name?

This is the term often used to describe a training session. Workshops are more popular and therefore more fully subscribed than when the same subject is promoted as a training session.

Assuming that people need to be 'sold' via an interactive process that creates debate and persuasion, the term workshop should mean just what it implies. It should be an opportunity to work through ideas and concepts which need time to be accepted.

The fact that workshops should be interesting and fun, is not an added bonus, it is part of the process necessary to create the maximum absorption.

It is sad and indicative, however, that some senior people only feel comfortable attending 'workshops', or the even more euphemistically named short training course, an 'appreciation'; but they expect employees to go on training courses – assuming that there is a budget for such unproductive activity!

Conferences

Having chaired a recent conference on Internal Marketing, I can give you the type of feedback that I am increasingly becoming exposed to. It is indicative of the way things are moving in terms of how people want to learn.

People feel that the conference process itself inhibits learning. It is a one way flow of information which does little to create that key stimulus to learning – that of interaction.

This is not to say that conferences do not have a place in the field of human resource development, they very much do. The huge, and perhaps main, benefit of holding them is that they can create a great deal of *impact*. This may be vital when the perceived need of the people is to see commitment being demonstrated to the subject in question. If, however, they themselves are already committed and feel that the organisation is committed, then a conference may be one of the most expensive ways of getting the fewest number of messages through. This of course excludes the memo!

Another benefit of the conference, if it is held in an exciting place, is for pure reward, e.g. sales conferences. Again this may be valid and once started is difficult to stop, but as a vehicle for increasing understanding, it is very limited.

In one organisation in which I worked, the annual conference for approximately 300 people cost £¼ million, and that was in the early 1980s! It was held abroad. The total time away was two days, but the total conference time was just two hours. If impact or reward are the only objectives then the conference may well be the answer, but some serious questions must be asked if the main requirement is absorption, especially if people see a conference as the chance to 'have a good time'.

In addition, the conference becomes a problem because of the very nature of such exciting and prestigious events: how to make them ever more exciting and prestigious year after year. This leads to an escalation of cost, an escalation of expectation and a diminution of the main aim of the conference: *impact*, as delegates watch 'yet another hyped up event'.

In short, in terms of the new approach to marketing to internal customers, events and conferences alike are very limited vehicles. They may be extremely valid in external marketing when impact is necessary to launch that new car or plane in a blaze of publicity, but to the internal customer they can go so far as to have a negative impact.

There is one such case extremely well known in the brewery industry. The marketing people decided that the best way of telling over 1,000 pub managers of the 'way forward', was to fill the Albert Hall and inform them that they were not just part of one concept, i.e. pubs, but of 16 newly created brands. This was done at the time of a dramatic reduction in the number of pubs due to increased competition and falling volumes. So, all this money was being spent on the event and people were being made redundant! To add insult, the managers were being 'told' that the product they knew and loved would be shoved into a concept that they could not relate to. The result effect on the business can be imagined!

So marketeers beware! The same thing happens internally as happens externally! If people are upset they can be put off the products and services forever. The ex-MD of this brewery company will testify to that!

This leads us on to the next type of event which is gaining more and more critics.

The one day road show – is it worth the money?

Similar to a conference, the aim of the one day road show is to create impact, on a large, but more limited number of people, e.g. 30–100. However, only skilled presenters working from pre-arranged scripts can control this sort of number. Again, the level of *impact* may be high but the *absorption* is likely to be correspondingly low.

These events can have their place in a well orchestrated campaign. By themselves they are of limited value.

SOME KEY TERMS USED IN QUALITY

It really depends on who you are reading when it comes to definitions about Quality. For the purpose of this book, as the focus on customers is one of constant change in the market place, I have quoted extensively from the definitions used in the book by Imai entitled *Kaizen – The Key to Japan's Competitive Success*. I have added comments *in italics*, where appropriate and I have added a few extra definitions of my own. It will be obvious that there are, and should be, very strong links between Quality and marketing.

The basis of marketing is constant measurement. The same is true of Quality. The two are so close that putting them together should not be difficult.

Definitions of quality

(from *Kaizen – the Key to Japan's Competitive Success*. Imai. My comments in italics)

Analytical approach (to management improvement): an approach based on learning from the evaluation of past experience. *The marketing approach to this is called research.*

Check Points and Control Points (Jidohka): a word coined to describe a feature of Toyota production system whereby a machine is designed to stop automatically whenever a defective part is produced. *This is the type of constant feedback that a powerful customer complaints system provides.*

Cross-Functional Management: the interdepartmental co-ordination required to realise the policy goals of a KAIZEN and a Total Quality Control (TQC) programme. After corporate strategy and planning are determined, top management sets objectives for cross-functional efforts that cut laterally through the organisation. *This can only happen with an efficient, targeted communication system.*

Cross functional management is the major organisation tool for realising TQC improvement goals. (While cross-functional management may resemble certain Western managerial techniques, it is distinguished from them by an intensive focus on the follow-through to achieve the success of goals and measures.) *The essence of any marketing campaign is that it is a campaign with an intensive follow through to ensure the customer buys into the messages. Current internal communication tends to be tactical and very short lived.*

Deming Cycle: The concept of a continuously rotating wheel used by W. E. Deming to emphasise the necessity of constant interaction among research, design, production and sales, so as to arrive at an improved quality that satisfies customers (see PDCA Cycle).

Thomson Cycle: *The concept of a continuously rotating wheel used by K.M. Thomson to emphasise the necessity of constant interaction using research with customers to ensure satisfied customers (see PDCA Cycle).*

Improvement: improvement as a part of a successful KAIZEN strategy goes beyond the dictionary definition of the word. Improvement is a mind set inextricably linked to maintaining and improving standards.

In a still broader sense, improvement can be defined as KAIZEN and innovation, where a KAIZEN strategy maintains and improves the working standard through small, gradual improvements and innovation calls forth radical improvements as a result of large investments in technology and/or equipment.

Customers continually demand improvement. Every marketing strategy and tactical execution must accept customers' demands will be constantly changing.

A successful KAIZEN strategy clearly delineates responsibility for maintaining standards to the worker, with management's role being the improvement of standards. The Japanese perception of management boils down to one precept: maintain and improve standards. *A successful marketing strategy recognises that it is the responsibility of the supplier to be constantly checking the standards demanded by the customer.*

Just in Time: a production and inventory control technique that is part of the Toyota production system. It was designed and perfected at Toyota by Taiichi Ohno specifically to cut waste in production. *The customer expectation is not 'just in time'; every marketeer now recognises that the customer wants things 'yesterday'!*

KAIZEN: KAIZEN means improvement. Moreover it means continuing improvement in personal life, home life, social life, and working life. When applied to the workplace KAIZEN means continuing improvement involving everyone – managers and workers alike. *Marketing through the customer supplier chain is based on exactly the same premise.*

Kamban: a communication tool in the 'just in time' production and inventory control system developed by Taiichi Ohno at Toyota. A Kamban, or signboard, is attached to specific parts in the production line signifying the delivery of a given quantity. When the parts have all been used, the same sign is returned to its origin where it becomes an order for more. *Any visual signboard or poster is a classic marketing technique for making customers sit up and take note.*

PDCA Cycle: The PDCA Cycle – Plan, Do, Check, Action – is an adaption of the Deming Wheel. Where the Deming Wheel stresses the need for constant interaction among research, design, production and sales, the PDCA Cycle asserts that every managerial action can be improved by careful application of the sequence, plan, do, check, action (see also Deming Wheel).

The Ten Point Wheel: *The integrated marketing sequence in the Thomson Cycle follows the same process as PDCA – going into greater depth, i.e. create, develop, design, test, launch, measure, systemise, sustain, promote and improve. There is one enormous difference with the Thomson Cycle. Unlike the Deming Wheel it has a hub: research. Research at every stage allows the Wheel to move along.*

Policy: (in Japanese management): in Japan the term is used to describe long- and medium-range management orientations as well as annual goals or targets. Another aspect of policy is that it is composed of both goals and measures, that is, both ends and means. Goals are usually quantitative figures established by top management, such as sales, profit, and market share targets. Measures, on the other hand, are the specific action programmes to achieve these goals. A goal that is not expressed in terms of such specific measures is merely a slogan. It is imperative that top management determine both the goals and the measures and then 'deploy' them down through the organisation.

The integrated marketing model puts the leaders who create policy firmly at the bottom, supporting the rest of the organisation. The goal is stated in the marketing plan. The measure is research, throughout the customer-supplier chain.

Policy Deployment: the process of implementing the policies of a KAIZEN programme directly through line managers and indirectly through cross-functional organisation. *This is the same process in internal marketing.*

Policy Prioritisation: a technique to ensure maximum utilisation of resources at all levels of management in the process of policy deployment. Top management's policy statement must be restated at all management levels in increasingly specific and action-oriented goals, eventually becoming precise quantitative values. *This is backed-up by the policy of precisely measuring customer requirements at all levels.*

Process-Oriented Management: a style of management that is also people oriented in contrast to one that is oriented solely toward results. In process-oriented management a manager must support and stimulate efforts to improve the way employees do their jobs.

Such a style of management calls for long-term outlook and usually requires behavioural change. *In order to support, stimulate, and create behavioural change, the manager must be able to meet the employee's needs – their customer. The way they can do this is detailed throughout this book.*

QC (Quality Control): according to the Japanese Industrial Standards (Z8101–1981) definition, quality control is a 'system of means to economically produce goods or services that satisfy customer requirement.'

Marketing: *is defined in simple terms as a means to ensure the right goods and services are produced to satisfy customer requirements (at a profit).*

When QC was first introduced to Japan by W.E. Deming in 1950, the main emphasis was on improving product quality by applying statistical tools in the production process. *When marketing was first truly introduced in the 1950s the main aim was selling products by applying broad brush advertising techniques.*

In 1954, J.M. Juran brought the concept of QC as a vital management tool for improving managerial performance. Today QC is used as a tool to build a system of continuing interaction among all elements responsible for the conduct of a company's business so as to achieve the improved quality that satisfies the customer's demand. *Today marketing is a tool to build a system of continuing interaction throughout the customer-supplier chain.*

Thus, the term QC as used in Japan is almost synonymous with KAIZEN, and although the use of statistics still remain the main stay of QC, it has come to add many other tools, such as the New Seven tools for improvement.

The time will perhaps come when the terms marketing and Quality are also almost synonymous.

QC (Quality Control) Circles: a small group that voluntarily performs quality control activities within the workplace, carrying out its work continuously as part of a company-wide programme of quality control, self-development, mutual education, flow control, and improvement within the workplace.

Focus groups: *small groups that discuss the requirements of the participants in their role as customers in great depth. See later – Listening/Issues Groups.*

Quality: there is very little agreement on what constitutes quality. In its broadest sense, quality is anything that can be improved. When speaking of 'quality' one tends to think first in terms of product quality. When discussed in the context of KAIZEN strategy nothing could be further off the mark. The foremost concern here is with the 'quality of people'. *The foremost concern with marketing is with customers. The foremost concern with an integrated approach to marketing is customers throughout the customer-supplier chain.*

The three building blocks of a business are hardware, software and 'humanware'. Only after humanware is squarely in place should the hardware and software aspects of a business be considered. Building quality into people means helping them become KAIZEN conscious. *The three building blocks of marketing to improve an organisation are* ***Listening*** *to customers,* ***Gathering*** *the 'best practices' necessary to meet their needs and* ***Sharing*** *information with everyone else in the organisation.*

Quality Assurance (at Toyota): quality assurance means assuring that the quality of the product is satisfactory, reliable, and yet economical for the customer.

Research: *research means assuring the quality of the product is satisfactory, reliable, and yet economical for the customer.*

Quality Development: a technique to deploy customer requirements (known as 'true quality characteristics') into designing characteristics (known as 'counterpart characteristics') and deploy them into such subsystems as components, parts, and production processes. Quality development is regarded as the most significant development to come out of TQC in the last 30 years in Japan.

Integrated Marketing: *a technique to deploy customer requirements into the whole of the customer-supplier chain. Integrated marketing will one day be regarded as the most significant development to be applied to TQC in the last 30 years – worldwide! (This is known in Quality as a 'Bold Goal!')*

Q Seven and the New Seven: the seven statistical tools (commonly referred to as the Q Seven) and seven additional tools (the New Seven) that have made an indispensable contribution to the constant evolution and improvement of the Total Quality Control movement.

The Seven Statistical Tools are:

Pareto diagrams
Cause-and-effect diagrams
Histograms
Control charts

Scatter diagrams
Graphs and Checksheets

The New Seven are:
Relations diagram
Affinity diagram
Tree diagram
Matrix diagram
Matrix data-analysis diagram
PDPC (Process Decision Programme Chart)
Arrow diagram

The 4 Ps and the New 4 Ps: *the four areas for concentrating on the external customer for the marketeer (commonly referred to as the 4 Ps) and four new areas for concentrating on the internal customer for the internal marketeer (launched in this book).*

The 4 Ps are:

Product
Price
Place
Promotion

The New 4 Ps are:

Policy
Procedures
Plans
Practices

Standards: a set of policies, rules, directives and procedures established by management for all major operations, which serves as guidelines that enable all employees to perform their jobs successfully.

Best Practice: *a methodology for ensuring standards are marketed into the organisation. They serve as guidelines which will enable all internal suppliers to want to perform their jobs successfully.*

Suggestion System: in Japan the suggestion system is a highly integrated part of individual-oriented KAIZEN. Its design is as carefully plotted, implemented, and communicated as a company's strategic plan. Scrupulous attention is paid to top management responsiveness, and developing a system of feedback and rewards.

Listening, Gathering and Sharing: *applied to Best Practice is a highly integrated part of individual-orientated MARKETING in the customer supplier chain. Its design should be as carefully plotted, implemented and communicated as a company's strategic plan. Scrupulous attention should be paid to the top management's responsiveness to the feedback. Involvement in rewards should occur from management at all levels.*

Japanese-style suggestion systems emphasise morale-boosting benefits and positive employee participation over the economic and financial incentives that are stressed in the American-style systems. (An example of the dimension of Japanese suggestions submitted annually is shown by Matsushita. In 1985 Matsushita employees submitted the highest number of suggestions exceeding six million.) *Internal marketing-style suggestion systems emphasise morale boosting benefits and positive employee participation over the economic and financial incentives that are stressed in the American-style systems (The Midland Bank programme 'Building on Success' changed from an £8 million American-style programme to a £2 million manager-driven programme of local Best Practice).*

TPM (Total Productive Maintenance): total productive maintenance aims at maximising equipment effectiveness throughout the entire life of the equipment. TPM involved everyone in all departments and at all levels; it motivates people for plant maintenance through small group and voluntary activities and involves such basic elements as developing a maintenance system, education in basic housekeeping, problem-solving skills, and activities to achieve zero breakdowns.

Top management must design a system that recognises and rewards everyone's ability and responsibility for TPM.

Internal Marketing: *aims at maximising people's effectiveness throughout the entire length of their employment. It involves everyone in all departments and at all levels; it motivates people towards Best Practice through small group and voluntary activities, and involves such basic elements as listening to customers and communicating to others in the customer-supplier chain.*

TQC (Total Quality Control): organised KAIZEN activities involving everyone in a company, managers and workers, in a totally integrated effort towards improving performance at every level. This improved performance is directed towards satisfying such cross-functional goals as quality, cost, scheduling, manpower development and new product development.

It is assumed that these activities ultimately lead to increased customer satisfaction. (Also referred to as CWQC – Company-Wide Quality Control.)

Total Quality Marketing: *organised MARKETING activities involving everyone in a company, managers and workers, in a totally integrated effort towards improving performance at every level (also referred to 1. as integrated marketing as advocated in this book and by John Fraser-Robinson in his book entitled* Total Quality Marketing, *2. as relationship marketing as advocated by Adrian Payne in his book* Relationship Marketing.

Visible Management: the technique of providing information and instruction about the elements of a job in a clearly visible manner so that the worker can maximise his productivity. (The Kamban, or card system, is an example of this technique.)

Visible Marketing – Advertising!: *the technique of ensuring information gets through to the customer in a clearly visible manner so that the customer is motivated to buy. (Television advertising externally, or corporate videos internally, are examples of this technique.)*

If Quality and marketing aren't saying the same thing as I have tried to demonstrate, then something else needs to be done to ensure customers get what they demand!

SUMMARY

- Training, conferences, one day road shows and other HRD techniques have their place, but evaluate them, and use them with care.

- Many of the approaches used by Quality, are marketing concepts under a different name. A Quality approach to customers *must* therefore be a marketing approach as well.

5 SOME KEY TARGETS AND TECHNIQUES USED IN EXTERNAL MARKETING

Should there be any marketing orientated people reading this they may feel impatient at the thought of reading a chapter on targets. 'Who is he to be teaching me to suck eggs?' Let me explain. The whole point of this section is to place these external marketing terms in the context of the internal market. For example, at present, internal people are called 'employees'; imagine what would happen if they were perceived as 'internal customers'. In groups they would become 'target markets'.

The internal person not used to marketing terminology, or techniques, needs to understand how these terms are used. Then and only then can they be applied. For the marketing person, getting back to basics may serve to reflect on the last time they saw internal people as target customers operating in target markets. (See the article 'Internally Yours' on page 266.) It is targeted at marketing people and was written for the Chartered Institute of Marketing magazine *Marketing Business*.)

> ***This is the greatest challenge to marketing people in the world today. The world's largest untapped target market is the internal customer. Millions of often untouched customers! They are a part of every organisation. They are just waiting for your skills to work on them and for them.***

This is without a doubt the single biggest marketing opportunity of all time. It is the chance to reach people with new products and services – all of which need totally new methods of design and distribution that 'reach the parts that ordinary above and below the line methods cannot reach' to rephrase the Heineken advert. (Can I coin the phrase 'inside the line'?)

The term 'target' is a graphic one. It describes exactly what the marketeer is doing to the customer – aiming! The term is never far from the lips of the marketing professional. It provides a constant and continual reminder of their raison d'être. It highlights just what they would like to do with the marketing message to be portrayed – strike right into the heart of the customer they are aiming at.

It may seem obvious, but the marketeer never attempts just to 'tell' people about the products and services that are being marketed. This would soon create a major problem in the number of sales!

The targeting of messages ensures that a number of things happen:

1. The right *message* is produced – this may range from creating awareness, through to encouraging extra purchase via a promotional campaign.
2. The right *medium* is used – this may mean any form of the printed page through to audio and visual, including TV, press, and radio.
3. The right *markets* are targeted – this may mean a specific segment of a market, or the whole of that market.

It is worth saying that today there are very few marketing people who would suggest that whole markets, or mass markets exist. That is because the level of sophistication of the customer has created a whole series of niche markets.

NICHE MARKETS

It was Tom Peters who said 'There are only niche markets'. He meant that all marketing is about reaching smaller groups of people with far more tightly aimed messages about more highly specific products and services. The same is true throughout the customer-supplier chain.

As the 1990s progress it is clear to everyone that the customers' demands on the organisation and its people are ever increasing. This is often driven by the incredible level of competition which produces ever increasing levels of customer expectation.

In this age of change and huge individual, as well as cultural, differences, it is no longer valid, or profitable, to target customers on a wide basis. Their needs are not only ever increasing, they are increasingly more specific. Individual relationship marketing is now becoming the norm in dealing with external customers.

This same thing that is happening externally, is happening internally. Organisations are becoming a series of niche markets.

As internal people are given more and more responsibility at local level they become more and more demanding of the organisation and their own suppliers, both inside the organisation and out. If they are being measured and forced to deliver a quality product then they will be looking for the same in return. This means that their demands become more specific.

A MARKETING OPPORTUNITY!

Every marketing person should want to break into this new market and apply their skills to making their own organisation really sing. But this just has not happened. Two things emerge from this:

1 To the external marketeer: it is worth questioning the insular stance that might have been taken in the past. They usually acted as though the changes that they tried to bring about with new products and services needed only to be communicated to the external market.
2 To the person responsible for human resource development or Quality: watch out! The past is over and times change. It won't take long for marketing people to take up the challenge of seeing internal people as their next target market.

If the marketeer finally recognises that their market share is declining through internal problems, they may begin to step into other people's perceived territory.

Integration in the past has failed because people could protect their turf with no real pressure on them to change. The world is not like that any more, and if the marketing person does not pick up the gauntlet then the local manager will pick it up whatever happens at Head Office. They are now accountable, so they are forced to take the measures necessary to deliver the goods.

In addition to local ownership of external customer issues, this new level of responsibility also places the onus on the manager to be totally responsible for the people they manage and also those that they bring into the organisation. This also ensures that the ongoing responsibility of internal marketing issues like induction, career paths, company policy etc. is also placed on the line manager. The same is true of Quality issues. As will be seen, these are the very issues which become the products and services that need to be conveyed by an integrated marketing approach.

So, there are implications to human resource development people, Quality people, marketing people, as well as the line manager in this whole area. We have looked at the fundamentals of the HRD and Quality disciplines. Now we can complete the picture by looking at the terminology and techniques used in external marketing, and examining how they might apply to the internal market. For example, if internal customers are now to be grouped together to form target markets, how do you go about defining them? Is it by traditional marketing techniques such as the following?

ABC ANALYSIS

ABC analysis is a somewhat simple way of classifying people in the UK. It sprang out of a realisation that it was too crude to call people 'upper, middle and lower class'. In simple terms, however, it stuck to these same very broad definitions. Having money became as important as having status – a real revolution at the time; and it was only in the 1960s when it really took hold as a common marketing tool. The term is somewhat out of date now but is still used widely in marketing. It serves to illustrate how simple it would be to start off marketing to the internal customer with this type of classification, before moving on to more sophisticated models.

It may be worth pointing out at this stage that the imposition of corporate culture and other factors within the workplace do not readily allow the external marketing classification techniques to apply. However, the concept of segmenting customers, whoever they are, is still totally valid!

Socio-economic groups 1 – the 'As'

Before starting with what the 'A' stands for it is probably best to define 'socio-economic'. This really is jargon. Simply, the 'socio' stands for 'class' and the 'economic' is 'money', thus socio-economic! The 'As' are those with both!

You could therefore be an 'A' if you were a Lord and also a barrow boy, as long as you had lots of money. In the liberal 1960s it was perceived that combining 'socio' and 'economic' would lead to groups with common needs as target markets. So a Rolls Royce was targeted at the 'As' – simple!

Amongst this group would probably be the 'leaders' of companies, such as the Chairman, MD, Board members.

Socio-economic groups 2 – the 'Bs'

These are the next best thing to the 'As'. These are the upper income bracket managerial types. They are recognised today as being amongst the ones with the least disposable income, i.e. the ones with very little to spend, having used it all up at the end of the month on very large mortgages.

Among this group would probably be the senior managers, such as the divisional heads, and those with the title of Director.

Socio-economic groups 3 – the 'C1s and C2s'

This is where things get really interesting, because the two groups are classed under the same general heading of 'C'. This is because it is safe to assume that they have roughly the same amount of disposable income, once they have paid all the basics. The sub-classification then splits out roughly in terms of 'C1' as white collar and 'C2' as blue collar. In today's internal market terms this would probably boil down to 'administrative staff' and 'the workers'. This distinction of course is tremendously blurred because current technology allows 'workers' to work by pressing the same sort of keyboard buttons that the typist does.

Socio-economic groups 4 – the 'Ds and Es'

The 'Ds' are those in society who have little money, e.g. unskilled. The 'Es' are those with little money, e.g. state pensioners. Both of these terms are nice ways of classifying people for whom the marketeer very rarely has affordable products and services. Even if they could afford them, they usually are not in a big enough group to target. There are of course exceptions like retirement homes and pensioners' holidays.

In internal marketing terms these people exist outside the workplace anyway so they would not been seen as particularly relevant, although there are exceptions. In De La Rue, the bank note people, there is a pensioners' 'wall of honour' at head office, proudly proclaiming length of service as a core value.

The point of introducing these concepts in *external* terms is that at least they provide a simple classification for many marketing people to hang their hats on. From here, more sophisticated techniques can be developed. This is not to suggest that the 'ABC' definition should be used internally. It is interesting to note, however, that in broad terms the classifications do correspond to the perceptions of levels, or target segments: of internal people. This could be said to range from the shop floor worker or administrative staff as the 'C1, C2s', the manager 'B', and the ultimate bosses as the 'As'.

So, with a little alteration, the basic classification of ABC could provide a classification of customer segments when marketing to the *internal* customer. At least it might prove just as good a start as it did for external marketing.

Later I will propose that it is only from a common base such as individual, manager, and leader, that greater degrees of sophistication can be added. The greater degrees of sophistication in external marketing classifications are described below.

'ACORN' ANALYSIS

This is an acronym for 'A Classification Of Residential Neighbourhoods'. This technique is often used in direct mail to target people to buy products and services through those delightful letters saying, 'Dear Mr Thomson, We are delighted to tell you, that you have won the opportunity to enter a competition that could bring you, Mr Thomson, the amazing sum of £1,000,000.'

The targeting is done (only hitting certain market segments, in certain geographical areas) through a system which has used the base data of the UK 1981 census (updated in the 1991 census). The targeting is based on research that showed there were almost identical buying patterns by people who live in similar household types, e.g. farmhouses in the country. The question is, could this be applied to the internal customer?

It may be that in the future, people looking for jobs could be targeted in this way, or that they could be screened by their address when they apply. It could also be that an ACORN analysis on the people in an organisation produces a marked propensity to certain ACORN types. This information could be used as the basis for an internal marketing campaign. As part of the battery of tests now becoming available this could prove extremely valuable. Once employed, the targeting of messages to the various ACORN types could also be that much easier. It could also be used to highlight different ACORN types in different geographic sectors of the business, e.g. the South East/London, and the North West could well attract different people to a particular industry.

Just as the external marketing person would build different messages and graphics for a piece of communication material to say, an 18 year old from urban council estates, and to a 50 year old from a rural village, so the same should happen in the internal market place.

LIFESTYLE CLASSIFICATIONS

There are a number of organisations, including research companies and advertising agencies, who have produced new models based on the way a person lives, rather than their income, social background or their abode. The most famous of the terms, although not necessarily an accepted target group (but it serves to give an understanding of the meaning of lifestyle) is the YUPPIE, mnemonic (aren't they all!) for Young Upwardly Mobile Income Earner. Other terms have crept into this lifestyle folklore such as DINKY – Dual Income No Kids Yet.

The essential point about lifestyle classifications is that they pinpoint certain key attitudes in individuals' perceptions of the world and how they fit into it.

Current work in research seems to be reinventing the wheel of Maslow and giving it 'sexy' new marketing titles like 'lifestyle'. In essence, Maslow developed the theory of the 'Hierarchy of needs' that forms the basis of what drives individuals.

For now it suffices to suggest that the more sophisticated forms of targeting like 'lifestyles' will be just as valid in the internal market as in the external market.

'OTS'

OTS is yet another piece of jargon created to pinpoint one of the measures of success of an advertising campaign, usually run on television. As such it provides a pointer to what may well become one of the measurements for the internal marketeer. The term simply means 'Opportunities To See', yet behind it lies a tremendous debate about the validity of the measurement.

Just like a memo which may have been circulated to say 20 people, a TV advertising campaign may also be transmitted with a view to reaching its target audience. But how many people does it need to reach and how often do they need to see it for it to make the type of impact that is deemed necessary? These are the two key measurements. Things start to get complicated at this stage because, just like the unread memo, the TV commercial may not be seen.

How does the advertising agency know that someone has seen their client's commercial? The best measurement that is currently available is taken from a sample panel of people who have their viewing measured.

INTERNAL OTS

The memo which goes out, targeted at 20 people presents the same problem as the TV advert: how do you know that all 20 people actually read it? Of course, you know even less about what impact it has and any changes in behaviour it caused, unless you further research the sales, or the behaviour and attitude, of the target audience. The highly unsophisticated tool of OTS, still used today, caused one advertising agency to be fired by its client, a TV station, when they publicly declared their concern at its validity.

What chance then has the internal person sending out a piece of communication and trying to assess its impact? Sending out 20 memos or 4,000 corporate newsheets may well produce a warm glow of satisfaction as the 'opportunities to see' can be clearly defined. However, these are not like newspapers which people *buy* to read, they are more like the TV advert which is transmitted without their consent. The 'opportunity' may be there, but that doesn't mean they will take it up and 'see' what is in it.

How does this relate to marketing to the internal customer? Take a real example which is typical of today's corporate life, that of the document going out to announce a new policy or practice. I came across a manager who had one such document sent to him to describe the massive changes that were about to hit him and his staff with the large scale installation of information technology equipment. The manager was one of 12 we researched on the implications of this upheaval and fundamental change in method and focus of working practice.

He said of the document, which he had received some two months previously, 'I hope you aren't going to ask me too many questions about this, I only read the document last night, knowing that I was coming here today'. He was, in fact, the only one to have read it all!

In summary, the OTS of a memo, document, etc. is very similar to that of a TV advert; it can be measured by its circulation, just like counting the number of times an advert is on in people's homes. Whether or not it is seen is difficult to measure and albeit crude, the OTS is the only tool that can be used. The message is clear, even though you may be fired for saying it – the 'opportunity' to do something is not the same thing as actually doing it.

This leads on to two other external marketing definitions. These focus on the gathering of information needed to justify the marketing activity, and to prepare for the future – qualitative and quantitative research.

QUALITATIVE RESEARCH

Qualitative research is the gathering of information which provides an in-depth or 'quality' piece of data. It is acquired through discussion in small groups, rather than through a questionnaire to large numbers. This type of research is ideal for certain types of needs. Usually an in-depth analysis of the issues is necessary to get 'under the skin' of the problem or opportunity. Qualitative research is therefore ideal when testing out new products and services. The group will interact to debate their perceptions of what is under discussion.

This type of research is also ideal when the marketeer knows that something is not right about the existing products and services out in the market place. It can also be used where a steer is needed on which way the quantitative data should be positioned and which questions are pertinent to ask.

> ***What is fascinating about the process of qualitative research* inside *the organisation, is that it has an inherent characteristic of involving people in the process. This is of little use to the external marketeer but can be of tremendous use to the whole process of marketing to the customer-supplier chain. This involvement can herald change through advance 'PR'. It can also help convert sceptics, as well as providing examples of real people who have helped in the development of the change.***

The people undertaking the qualitative research process use two key techniques: 'open questioning' and 'facilitation' of the discussion. These are used to encourage the in-depth analysis necessary to get to the real issues. When they are used in the external marketing situation the customer leaves the research group and that is the end of their involvement. In the internal marketing process however, a fundamental change will often have taken place. Through the professional questioning and facilitation, the group member will have had the opportunity to debate and consider the issues in question. This will often lead to them reappraising the issues. In short, they may change their minds about something which they may not have considered before. This is a powerful tool in the hands of the person who knows how to use it.

QUANTITATIVE RESEARCH

This type of research provides a 'quantity' of information, usually sufficient to form a representative sample to ensure that it is a valid basis on which to work. It is interesting that the word most typically used to describe research in human resource development terms is 'survey', not research. This implies something that provides interesting information on events that have occurred, or are likely to occur, e.g. a survey on voting. It does not imply a pro-active measurement process used to provide data on which to make decisions.

External marketing uses the much more specific terminology, quantitative research. This is just one part of a total external marketing methodology. The time will come when this term will be used in internal marketing. This needs to happen if the results are to be viewed by the decision makers in a positive and professional light.

The decision makers are in fact those most likely to want this type of information about the internal marketing process. They will use quantitative data to examine the effectiveness of the investment made in human resource development and in Quality. They will want qualitative research to back up their own value judgements about past issues and future events.

Until quite recently qualitative and quantitative research have been neglected for human resource development and Quality issues. Now is the time to change.

TQM programmes may use many measurement tools (called statistical process control or SPC for short). However, these have rarely been used to measure customer needs and perceptions. The recognition exists that measurement is vital, yet few organisations regard having a policy of research throughout the customer-supplier chain as fundamental to their success, as yet.

The policy of using research to understand the needs of customers throughout the customer-supplier chain needs to be adopted. Also, the research must be carried out by people who are given the responsibility for it.

If everyone now has customers, how can it make sense to bring third party research organisations into organisations to research every single customer in the chain? Yet, all of this requires investment, whoever does the research.

The only way to persuade decision makers of the long term validity of any investment decision, is to keep providing the data which shows that it is working.

Marketeers have learned this lesson very well and will go into board meetings with some very impressive figures that somehow always seem to back up their case – even if the figures are questionable, such as OTS! It is up to those who are going to drive forward the concepts of human resource development, Quality, and integrated marketing to make sure the figures are there for all to see. Otherwise, the training and internal marketing budgets will be the first to be cut, as is classically the case for the budgets for external marketing!

There is no arguing with the type of statement made by Bass, one of the UK's major brewers that 'the figures in the test sites, for the northern division, as researched by Sheffield Business School, following a customer service campaign, showed an 81 per cent increase in beer volume against a declining market'. It is clear that top line and bottom line information like that, together with the 'softer' data on attitudes and 'harder' data on staff turnover, recruitment costs, etc. will have to go a lot further than the all too often heard comment about internal campaigns, 'it was extremely well received'.

SUMMARY

- **External marketing definitions are a good starting point when thinking about your internal markets.**

- **Opportunities to see – your memo or document is not necessarily read, even if it reaches its target market. Even then it is usually only read *once*.**

- **Research inside the organisation is an important source of information. It is the basis of reaching into the mind of your internal customers.**

6 THE IMPORTANCE OF ATTITUDE AND LANGUAGE TO CREATE A CUSTOMER-BASED CULTURE

HOW CAN YOU RECOGNISE AN ORGANISATION PRACTISING AN INTEGRATED APPROACH?

Marketing is based on a very simple concept:

> ***In order to entice customers to do anything new, the right form of persuasion is required.***

So, what is it that creates or reinforces the 'need' for customers to want to act in a positive, motivated way? This 'need' is itself a concept that anyone looking to use marketing techniques in the customer-supplier chain must be able to accept and buy into. To help this happen, the organisations I have worked with found that it is more emotive, and therefore more powerful, to call these needs the 'hooks'. However, the hooks for your customers will not be the same as for the organisation itself.

To continue to use the terminology and concepts of sales and marketing, we have defined the hooks to the organisation and the individuals as the 'benefits'. The changes that are necessary to produce the hooks for the customer in this new approach are called the 'features'.

CONSTANT CUSTOMER FOCUS THROUGH THE LANGUAGE OF MARKETING

It is not enough just to keep repeating how important the customer is. There must be a strategic methodology for ensuring that *every* decision has the customer as its focus. And now for the good news. There is no need to go out and reinvent the wheel to make sure this happens! There are thousands of man-years of experience behind the practices and disciplines of external marketing. With the careful addition of the practices and disciplines of human resource development and Quality, the methods of achieving a constant customer focus are waiting to be applied.

> ***Only by putting external marketing, Quality and human resource development skills together, can an integrated approach to marketing take place throughout the customer-supplier chain.***

From this strategic base, any change to a constant customer focus requires an often enormous attitudinal shift as well as an organisational shift. These shifts must be away from the classic heavy industries' stance of asset facing and from the classic employee stance of inward facing. They must also be away from the supplier stance of stock facing. Finally, they must be away from the all too common stance of a simple revenue focus (dare I say a 'screw the customer' philosophy). The supposed stalwarts of customer focus, the sales force, often have to adopt this focus (be it retail, finance, or any sales force) when the pressure is on to generate the revenue.

In recessionary times, even with the recognition of the vital importance of customer satisfaction, this pressure is increased, not reduced. A recent survey of customer perceptions throughout Europe showed that there is a belief that the UK's greatest problem in dealing with its European partners is UK companies' lack of ability to deliver what their salesmen say they will. In other words, they believe that UK salesmen try to get the order with whatever promises they need to use, regardless of the reality.

The reason why the focus within organisations is on things other than customers, may be a simple one – it is the criteria that are used to *measure* people. These measurements don't force them to see customers as their key criteria. In many organisations the moves to start any constant customer focus are in fact totally thwarted by the often useless traditional management measures used to drive the business. These include sales volume, stock levels, profit, share value etc.

Quality programmes themselves often have measurements for just about every form of quality improvement. But who is asking the customer what they think? Suffice it to say that all too often these measurements are cost driven, or simply revenue driven, when the need is for market-driven measurements based on customer requirements. In order to create the changes that are necessary for a constant customer focus, throughout an organisation, there must be a shift from existing practice.

The attitudinal shift to a total customer focus

The basis of attitudes is in repeated behaviour. If this repeated behaviour is given a new input that forces it to adopt new concepts through a constant use of a new 'language', the shift in attitudes can start to occur.

Table 6.1 shows just some of the customer-focused words that are the very fabric of marketing. Using them throughout the customer-supplier chain is a powerful tool for changing a culture.

Table 6.1 The Attitudinal Shift by the Language of Internal Marketing

Existing word(s)	*Existing focus*	*New word(s)*	*New focus*
Communication	Verbal/written e.g. Memo, Team Briefing	Intergrated marketing	Targeted methods of reaching the customer
Employee	Inward Top Down with a degree of lack of respect	Internal target market Bottom Up	Internal customers with a marketeers respect for their nature and variety
Attitude survey	Inward Highlights communication problems	Customer chain research	Internal customers Highlights marketing opportunities
Manuals/memos	Instructional Downwards	Support Material	Targeted
Conference	Tell Talk at	Launch Event	Involve
Training	Tell Instruct	Workshop	Sell
Inform	Tell Direct	Ownership	Empower
Team briefing	Tell Cascade	Team Listening	Facilitate

And so the list goes on, allowing organisations to pick up the language of their marketing departments – of which sales and its language should be a part.

The organisational shift to a total customer focus

If marketing and its language has power on the attitudinal aspects of the people, the same holds true for the organisational side. Before looking at this however, it is necessary to establish the link between the two. That link is very simply created by perceiving everyone in the organisation as a **customer**.

Quality has produced this recognition through the concept of the customer-supplier chain. However, the time has now come for what Tom Peters calls 'a blinding flash of the obvious'. If it is accepted that all employees are internal customers (and this concept is crucial to all Quality Programmes along the Crosby style) then two key concepts must follow:

1 ***The internal customer's needs must be researched and addressed by marketing.***

This comes down to people being able to say, 'If I am your customer, then many of the internal transactions you have with me as my 'supplier', involve you 'marketing' to me.

2 ***The internal customer also needs products and services from the organisation.***

'If I am an internal customer, then anything that the organisation wants me to buy into must be a product or service. These need marketing, for me to want to buy into them.'

Thus, by introducing the concept of Quality and the customer-supplier chain, it follows that it is fundamental to adopt and adapt the concepts of external marketing to make it work. However, it is not sufficient for one person or department to take this role, for example the communications manager. If *everyone* has customers, *everyone* needs the marketing know-how to deal with them.

The nice thing is that this concept is so easy to grasp, that everyone in the organisation can start to perceive the need for a new marketing-based approach. As an added bonus, for those organisations that have already started to use Quality programmes which use the concept of the customer-supplier chain, the methodology of matching the needs of the internal customers through marketing *must* be the next logical step to take.

It cannot be enough to accept that internal customers exist without giving the people the marketing skills, or the right marketing techniques, to be able to deal with these new found customers.

If the organisation is then viewed as a supplier of the internal goods and services, then the people who are responsible for these goods and services also need to have the skills necessary to be able to get these to the internal market place. These may range from producing a memo, to a dissemination of the five year plan.

The organisational shift in attitude to a total customer focus can start to take place, once the pragmatic skills processes, and techniques of marketing are being used to define, design and refine those internal products and services. From there the move for the people in the organisation to one that is focused on the external customer, is but a step away. This is part of what the concept of Business Process Re-engineering is all about.

If a manager knows that in order to get something accepted internally he, or she, has to go through a *process*, and that the process will create a greater chance of success, then they will buy into it. If, in addition to providing a process, the chances of success are *considerably* enhanced, then the system will be used even more. Furthermore, if the system actually allows the user to be more creative, more efficient, more effective, and most of all more successful, then they are highly likely to want to adopt it to meet their needs.

There are numerous other features that entice managers to adopt integrated marketing. However, it is only when sufficient numbers develop a total customer focus that the organisation will begin to shift. This will be covered in greater detail in later chapters.

Language for an organisational shift

Fortunately, the same language of marketing that is used to create the 'attitudinal' shift is also used in the methodologies and practices that are required for an 'organisational' shift. Table 6.2 shows some examples.

A WORD ABOUT MARKETING JARGON

Having stated that introducing the language of marketing is a fundamental part of the process of moving attitudes and organisations towards the total customer focus, it is worth backing this up. It could be said that Table 6.2 merely shows the same meanings put into marketing jargon.

In all organisations the language used is not a trivial part of the culture that builds up. For example, the word 'punter' is often used in those organisations which have a basic contempt for their customers – no matter how much it is protested that it is an 'affectionate term'. A high level of swearing is also indicative of a culture that breeds bravado and often fear.

Table 6.2 The Organisation Shift provided by the Language of Internal Marketing

Existing word(s)	*Existing focus*	*New word(s)*	*New focus*
Standards	Production 'Must do'	'Best practice'	Internal customers
Directives	Top down 'Must know'	Targeted messages	Customer supplier chain
Suppliers	Cost and price	Supplier Chain Management	Competitiveness and long term relationships
Product marketing	Selling the product	Relationship Marketing	Life time/long term customers

The use of terms like 'screw the business' (or the customers) are part of the language of an organisation which is likely to have future problems. This must be replaced with a language which has customers' needs and long term profitability, at its base.

There are many organisations which have not established *any* common language that their people can understand when it comes to information about their practices or successes. If no one talks about revenue, profit, marketing, strategies, tactics, mission, vision, values etc., then the people are hardly likely to be *able* to get involved in the discussions.

A common language

It must be said that language is only jargon if only a select few are privy to its meaning and its daily usage. Jargon is therefore taboo! The *constant* use of the language of marketing is vital. It is a major feature of organisations that we have worked with, that they start to use this new language as if it were their mother tongue. It provides a focus on the customer that is so strong, it is almost impossible not to get hooked into it.

Imagine *all* of the leaders, managers and staff in an organisation using marketing words and concepts to describe their interactions and relationships – as customers and suppliers. This language of marketing would, in itself, produce a bond between individuals. It would create a marketing orientated culture, or at the very least, start the shift towards a customer focus. The next section looks at this language of marketing together with the language of Quality and human resource development, with a view to merging the three.

SUMMARY

- **Add the practices and disciplines of HRD and Quality to those of external marketing to produce the methods for achieving a constant customer focus.**

- **Use customer-focused language to bring about a change in attitude.**

- **Perceiving everyone in the organisation as a customer is the key to the organisational shift to a total customer focus.**

7 A NEW MANAGEMENT ATTITUDE – SEEING EMPLOYEES AS CUSTOMERS

THE SCENE IS SET

Whether you are a marketeer, Quality, or human resource development professional you may have cause for concern at this point. You may feel a lot of your tried and tested techniques are coming under fire. Excellent! The whole point of gaining ownership is to create debate and challenge existing thinking. It sounds extremely American to say it, but the best word to describe this process is to 'internalise'. In external marketing, the level of internalising of the messages about a new packet of soap powder, for instance, may be very limited. In terms of marketing to the internal customer, many of the issues faced by the target markets will require a great deal of internalising. Issues such as culture, vision of the leaders, information technology, selling skills, etc., are all extremely complex, especially when viewed holistically.

To make things worse, because the speed of change is so rapid, by the time something has been internalised, it is likely to have changed! An example of this would be 'knowledge workers'. These are people who are extremely well paid, who do very specialised jobs which may suddenly become defunct through something like a change in technology. The absorption levels required to become a knowledge worker are considerable. The same is true when someone is required to change jobs. This puts a great deal of onus not just on the individual, but on the quality of the internal marketing message to create the right environment in which new learning is maximised. Additionally, in a recessionary environment, the added pressure on people who fear for their jobs makes communicating to them a very complex and delicate process.

This somewhat sideways look taken at just a few of the definitions of Quality, external marketing and human resource development is part of the build up of the language that becomes the bedrock of the corporate culture. It is this language that creates the first major strategic change, that of *constant customer focus*.

Using terms such as 'target', questioning the impact, and quality of existing communication and of Quality itself, and introducing measures into the organisation which are driven by internal marketing will all result in a new focus. It is also no longer sufficient to call people 'employees'; to just train them, or to assume that by sending out information, it will be read. It is also naïve to assume that just because people are paid they will do what is demanded of them. But surely everyone simply needs to be focussed first on external customers and reminded that they pay the wages? No.

THE EXTERNAL FOCUS BEGINS FROM WITHIN

Is it necessary to focus *first* on the needs of the internal customers? Yes. Only then can people begin to want to understand marketing.

The mechanisms for succeeding with externally focused campaigns like customer service and TQM, will be more readily accepted, once the internal market perceives that it can benefit from them.

The philosophy of embracing the external customers' needs will also be accepted if the individual can see that the organisation embraces his or her needs. Tools such as marketing and selling, which are used to reach the external customer, will be valued if the individual perceives a benefit to themselves by developing these skills.

In short, if the move to a customer facing focus is to happen externally, it must happen internally.

A good example of this is to look to the early attempts at customer service campaigns. They all had one very simple thread, 'Be nice to the customer'. It did not take very long for the resounding answer to come back, 'Why should I be nice to the customer when my manager is not very nice to me!' Today's organisations are faced, not only with their competitors attempting to differentiate themselves by giving 'excellent service', but also with the need to bring in sales.

Now, for example, all of the big banks and building societies, have recognised the need to introduce selling skills throughout their organisation. They often have introduced trained sales staff who sit at desks in the banking hall and respond to customer needs by using their sales skills. The managers have also been trained to apply and manage the process.

Imagine however, organisations only training front line staff in professional selling skills. There are some very sophisticated techniques used to enable them to 'open the sale', to get to the root of the customers' needs through 'open questions', and to 'close the sale' by gaining commitment with 'little yes' questions. It wouldn't take the staff very long to realise that these same techniques internally were not being applied to them. They would soon react by saying 'Why should I bother?'

In addition to this, if all other internal customers are not practising the same techniques, the lack of re-reinforcement will soon result in the investment in the training and development being totally wasted. In other words, it is not just the way that they are expected to behave that is important. They also need to see champions of the behaviour, who they can emulate as well as constant reinforcement from colleagues.

Once the benefits of sales and marketing are realised, this becomes an interactive process that will make people want to buy into it.

WHAT'S IN IT FOR ME?

The beauty of marketing throughout the customer-supplier chain is that it forces people down the route of looking for the benefits, or 'hooks', because they are a fundamental part of its methodology.

Once people realise that it is OK to say 'What's in it for me?', then they will soon be coming out with it in the open, rather than, at present, muttering it under their breath. The external customer has no problem *demanding* to know 'what's in it for me?'

If organisations don't respond to the needs of the internal customer they will soon end up having difficulty attracting and keeping them. Even in recession this is rife within organisations. They may not leave but they sure can 'quit and stay'. In other words quit mentally but stay physically. It is also a fact of life that even if all of this were hogwash your competitor is in the process of becoming more responsive to their internal customer, so you are going to have to respond whether you like it or not!

Examples of organisations in the UK going down the integrated marketing route may as yet be few and far between. This will change when marketing departments start to recognise that a small shift in budgets from totally external to internal campaigns, will produce significant results. Having said that, the programmes introduced by often newly appointed communications, Quality, training or customer service managers in the late

1980s were often good examples of marketing, such as those run by British Airways for the last 10 years on Customer Service.

The concept of the internal customer and the strategy of good internal customer relations is at the heart of all of these programmes. From there, just as with British Airways, the internal campaign can became an external campaign, e.g. 'The world's favourite airline'. This slogan is backed up in the advertising and, in reality, by smiling faces of staff who are seen to be dedicated to customer needs. This is when a truly integrated marketing approach is happening.

Another such programme is the one being run by Butlins Holiday Worlds, part of The Rank Organisation, entitled 'The People Development Programme'. Its aim is to meet the needs of every individual coming into the company, thousands of whom will only work for a very short time scale, often a matter of weeks. Yet the recognition is, that if they do not meet the needs of the internal customer then they will look elsewhere. The net result will be that the external customer focus will not succeed.

All of these, and the many other examples, have at their base the principles and practices of internal marketing. The people putting into practice these exciting changes in culture and working practice may not recognise that they have been doing this under the holistic model developed in this book but they will certainly recognise the elements in their programmes that make them succeed, and sometimes fail.

Marketing's strength is that at least there is a plan and a methodology against which the results can be measured. The first of these, discussed in this section, being constant customer focus.

A WORD ABOUT EXTERNAL AND INTERNAL CUSTOMERS

Marketing as a discipline includes strategic and tactical plans to meet customers' needs. It also encompasses the practices required for selling and distribution.

The whole emphasis is therefore on the customer. In the past, however, this has meant that the focus for the marketing departments has been almost totally external, unless, of course, one or other of the internal departments was seen to be preventing the marketing plan from being realised. This then created the basis for mutually enjoyable meetings of minds, often discussing 'who is to blame this time'.

Once this conflict was resolved, the marketing people could climb back into their shell and mutter strange noises like 'OTS', 'TVRs' and other equally bizarre sayings, and continue on with their weird and wonderful ways. At least that is the view of internal people.

Today's external marketing will only succeed if the whole of marketing throughout the customer-supplier chain is also focused on the final customer. This focus is of a very special nature. The customer needs to become the single driving force of the marketing based organisation. It gives the external marketeer a very simple aim, that of meeting the customers' needs. The word 'meeting' the needs is important because it shows that the customer has a choice. Indeed they can very easily change allegiance to products and services, often on the most irrational basis. They are in a buyers' market and are under no obligation to do anything they do not want. They have an amazing amount of choice, not only of all products in direct competition, but also of other products in indirect competition. It is therefore up to Marketing and Advertising departments to do everything in their power to build the allegiance of the customer. Unless their loyalty is strong enough they can 'vote with their feet'.

Building customer allegiance is the biggest challenge to the marketing orientated company. It is a challenge that is made doubly difficult by the onslaught of the competition. A phrase which drives the marketeer (but unfortunately does nothing for many shop floor assistants who do not perceive customers as a challenge, but a pain) is 'the customer is king'.

Is the internal customer king?

Now imagine the statement 'every customer throughout the customer-supplier chain is king'! It may smack of unions, worker power, loss of control of the organisation by its management and its leaders etc. Why? Because in the past, employees have not had the power to do all the things which they can do when they are outside the workplace, to be as demanding and as fickle as they like. There is no retribution on them as external customers if they suddenly stop buying products or services that they may have been buying for some length of time before.

Now, however, in all but the most autocratic organisations 'empowerment' is seen as vital. So, we are beginning to move towards the employee as well as the customer being king and organisations now want it to happen.

Must organisations lie on their backs and roll over to this new breed of internal customers? The answer is NO. Even if times get really tough, the organisation must meet its own needs.

Sometimes these organisational needs will not meet the needs of the individual, or indeed may be in conflict with them. This is one of the most fundamental differences between internal and external marketing. The difference actually lies in the simplest of words, which impacts on the way the internal person is marketed to. The word replaces the term 'meeting' as in 'meeting the needs of customers' in the short definition of external marketing. It is the word *matching*, and is used in the context of 'matching the needs' of the internal customer. I am not playing with semantics. It is a way of demonstrating that the internal customer should only be treated equally, as much a 'king', as the organisation itself. The organisation cannot become subservient to the needs and wants of the individuals. Therefore both needs must be 'matched' wherever possible. This is where external and internal marketing really differ.

The external marketeer must react totally to the customers' needs. Gone are the days when products could be made in isolation of customers' needs. If a product sells without going through the formal marketing mix then it is either good intuitive thinking, or just good luck. Either way, the producer is at the mercy of the consumer, or at the mercy of the ability of the advertising, promotion and PR departments to affect customers' thinking.

The internal customer on the other hand cannot dictate his terms to the supplier of goods and services – not if the organisation is to remain profitable! For example, they cannot simply opt for more money, fewer hours, etc. when they choose. The internal customer has no choice in complying with certain requirements; therefore the organisation does not exist solely to 'meet' their needs:

However, in these days of fickle people, some internal customers may believe that they do not have to meet the needs of the organisation; that they can make demands.

And so to the crunch. Do the organisation and the individual have to live as two opposing factions? No, it is simply a question of attempting to 'match' the needs of the individuals to those of the organisation. The word 'match' is hereafter used to demonstrate that both have a right to have wants and needs, but they must be compatible.

In the world of external marketing, the producer has no such power over the customer. The marketing function does not have the dual role of marketing the product *and* ensuring any other compliance of the purchaser, like their involvement in a quality programme. They only have to ensure they want to part with their cash and stay committed to do it again and again!

STRATEGY FROM BELOW

'Do as I say, not as I do', was once the war cry of 'The Boss'. It represented his ability to be able to do a number of things (and I use the word 'his' advisedly, as previously there were even fewer women bosses about!):

1 Tell people what to do.
2 Not allow people to answer back (unless, of course, it was with the backing of the unions).
3 Not bother with what people think.
4 Not be concerned about being a role model for the behaviour that was being demanded.
5 Not be too concerned about people as individuals.

It also made the inherent assumption that 'The Boss' knew it all, and could literally command 'his' people in a way that was akin to military rule. In accountancy it is recognised that people are not an asset as they cannot be 'owned' by the organisation. This does not translate into reality, judging by the behaviour of some managers. Unfortunately this is *still* the case with many managers and often includes whole organisations.

All too often managers will perceive that the people working 'for them' are *my* people, that they work 'under them', and are their 'subordinates'. This type of thinking labels people as lesser beings in comparison to the person they work for e.g.:

Less important
Less capable
Less valued
Less intelligent
Less experienced
Less likely to be able to contribute
Less motivated
Less enthusiastic

It also makes an assumption that they are 'more' likely to be a number of undesirable things e.g.:

More in need of being closely watched
More likely to 'cock it up'
More in need of 'rollicking' when they get it wrong
More trouble than they are sometimes worth

The net result of the traditional employee/boss relationship is a lack of respect. Respect is what the external customer is beginning to command. Without it, it is not felt necessary to listen to them. The same respect must now be given internally. There is no way of uncovering internal customer needs if the organisation does not listen. If it does not listen those needs definitely can't be met.

The staggering number of Quality ideas that internal people can come up with (6,000,000 in Matsushita in one year!) and feedback on ways to improve, will not be heard, if the organisation does not listen.

It is through the teaching, and indeed preaching, of marketing concepts, tools and techniques that the needs, wants, desires and ideas of the individuals in the organisation will be respected. Too much is happening now for the average manager to 'do it themselves'. They haven't got the time, so the people 'get on with it'. But, to allow this to happen effectively, people must be given more information – information that lets them do the job effectively. This is the crux of the second strategic change.

A SIMPLE RULE – INFORMATION IS POWER

This rule has been instinctively recognised for generations by people who have worked their way up the organisation. They ensure that they are indispensable (or so they think) by simply keeping things to themselves.

Everyone knows the people in their organisation who withhold things from their subordinates (as they see them), who tell the boss only the 'good news', who block information that would harm their position, who filter information that enhances their cause and who feed information into the grapevine that damages other people. This type of information control leads to massive time wasting, upset and damage to the organisation.

How can internal marketing prevent information control? Because marketing is all about the control of information, its gathering and dissemination in all directions.

To cite just one example. In days gone by, the manager who had unhappy staff could keep that information from those who mattered. It may not have even been considered important that staff turnover was high. Morale was probably not a major issue, motivation would probably be considered to be immeasurable, and there may have been organisational 'Brownie Points' for being seen as a 'bastard'. This state of affairs was prevalent in a number of organisations. Hire and fire managers were feared in case they made it to the top and did unto others what they wouldn't want done to themselves.

Suddenly, however, the transfer of power has resulted in the employees being important. It became fashionable in the 1980s to hold attitude surveys. They often produced damning statistics, and managers who had unhappy staff were being examined under the microscope. In short, the surveys were pieces of information gathered by research and disseminated by internal marketing. The information, once held by the individual, became the weapon to be used to make demands that were listened to.

Look at the concern an employee might feel about the quality of 'communication' they receive. This in itself is a classic sign of the level of dissatisfaction with an organisation. There are a number of other issues, e.g. management attitude. This will affect the morale, motivation and ultimately the effectiveness of that employee. The organisation will then be affected. If the numbers in the research are statistically significant, then positive action should be taken.

There is only one conclusion: the gathering of all data from individuals, en masse, will create a picture which will provide the data for future strategy, both internally and externally. The people in the organisation who are most able to do this are those who are closest to the external customer and can provide the fastest response times in information feedback. These are the people 'at the bottom'. They are the ones who can spot the needs, spot the trends and spot the gaps. They may not be able to verbalise them as well as marketing specialists, but they are exposed to what is happening.

And so to MBWA

There are two main reasons for CEOs wearing out their shoe leather when practising what Tom Peters observed, and then called the technique of MBWA – Management By Wandering About. It is my belief that one of these is a selling function. It is all about the leader having one to one discussions with the internal customer, i.e. a sales call! This allows the people to buy into the enthusiasm, vision and mission of that leader, whoever, and wherever the leader may be in the organisation. Increasingly, this is being recognised as just as vital at local level as at national level.

The other function of MBWA is a marketing one and is one of pure research. Collecting both qualitative research data, and enough quantitative research data on the internal and external issues affecting the organisation, can provide the leader with the basis for future strategy. This information can come from anyone in the organisation, but it comes primarily from the people who have the closest contact with the customer.

However, there is more than a slight niggle with the title MBWA. Whilst stirring the might of corporate management, it vastly undervalues the vital importance of the results it produces, by focusing on and almost trivialising the process in describing it as wandering.

No one entitles research 'Information By Wandering About'. No one entitles professional selling 'Securing Orders By Wandering About'.

Yet now we have a generation of managers who have been led to believe that the way to the hearts and minds of people is through wandering about.

Of course if you are a successful CEO you are likely to have acquired the skills of selling and the skills of getting people to open up. You will be sufficiently aware of what marketing is, to recognise the strategic importance of what you are hearing. You will be able to add up all the anecdotal evidence that accumulates and make some assumptions about what you should be doing. The successful organisations that Tom Peters identified had CEOs who were doing all of this instinctively. He has extolled the virtues of MBWA, yet fundamentally the success has nothing at all to do with wandering.

If you are lousy at selling, researching, and making decisions on that research, then the safest place for you is in the office.

Peters is really extolling the virtues of marketing. He is advocating that time must be spent carrying out the fundamental front end research on the products and services you need to have. Time must also be spent on the selling of your own organisation and its future, to the people who need to be sold to, i.e. the internal customer. If this is not done, the organisation will stagnate and die.

The time has come to turn the concept of MBWA on its head to meet the needs of the enlightened manager in the 1990s. No more 'Wandering About'. The 'W' turns into an 'M' standing for Marketing. The 'A' turns into Ability', and MBWA becomes MBMA:

MANAGEMENT BY MARKETING ABILITY

To give a concrete example, the Chief Executive of Eagle Star shows his commitment to marketing to the people in the organisation, firstly in a published internal article in a highly targeted quarterly news bulletin, and by actually practising what he preaches. It is worth quoting large chunks of the article as this gives the flavour and shows, whether he realised it or not, the methodology of MBMA. Once again the *italics* are mine.

(Taken from *Lifelink* Summer 1989 – Eagle Star, Life Division: The Steve Melcher Interview)

Q: How do you plan to get to know people in the Life Division?
Note the use of interview style rather than an article

A: Well if you looked at my diary, you'll see that I am spending more than half of my time on the road talking to people and meeting them, so that's a big commitment in time.
Commitment to research

Q: Will this travelling around include Cheltenham?
Targeted research

A: Yes, of course, I am concentrating on the branches, and the plan is to get to each branch by the end of October. That should help me to get a good feel for the distribution of the business, which is the critical area at this time.
Strategy from below

Q: Coming on to the challenges facing the Life Division, do you think we have the products to cope?
Providing Marketing Data to the people in the organisation

A: Yes, we certainly have the products to cope, but our success does not depend upon our products as much as on our ability to sell them, i.e. their distribution. In fact we probably have too many products.

What we have to do is cut back on the number of products, concentrate on the ones we are good at and on those which are profitable, and then build a market share in those products.
Not holding back on the 'bad news' validates the sincerity of the sales message

Q: We all face a great deal of change in the months ahead. What are your comments on change?
And now for some classic sales techniques, which are embodied in all 'excellent' leaders – note the 'hooks', note the use of analogies, people see things much better in pictures, and note the assumptive close by saying the word 'we', and note the actual close which leaves no room for doubt that everyone is contributing to the strengths, and helping provide strategy from below.

A: Change is difficult and is all relative to what people are used to. I believe that in order to even keep up with what's going on in the market place, we must not only change but we must also be constantly changing; we must all get used to change as a 'status quo'. We must take on the attitude that there is always a better way to build a mouse trap and once we have built it, we have to rebuild it, keep rebuilding it, and through the rebuilding process, we end up doing things better. Change need not be threatening, but can actually be a motivating force, getting people to want to perform better. We have a lot to do and we are not going to do it all in one month, or even in one year.

I advocate change not for change's sake, but to enable our Division to be more responsive to the changing environment in which we compete. To bring about and lead this change is like rolling a large object, once you get it rolling you have got to keep pushing or you will lose the momentum. I plan to have the corporate reorganisation really on the road by year end. But changing people's minds, habits and attitudes acquired over many years is not going to happen overnight.

We must be careful not to change the wrong aspects of our Division, like the loyalty and dedication to hard work of our staff. I am very optimistic about the future of Eagle Star Life. We have great strengths, a clear idea of the way forward and a workforce which is eager to participate in the process. *Terrific copy!*

So, the 'information' from the Chief Executive is clear, and provides the targeted reader with the power to act on it. It states that there is a 'top down' demand for change, but also a 'bottom up' demand to participate in the change. Additionally it shows both individual employee and manager that the time to listen and talk, i.e. research and sell, is vital. It therefore encourages the people to provide 'strategy from below'. The people are given the information on which they can act. Information is power and the nice thing is that this works to everyone's benefit.

MBMA for everyone

So, Chief Executives as managers should task themselves to Manage By Marketing Ability. This requires listening, and talking to customers and to staff. But what about everyone else? Don't they have customers too? And instead of this research being totally ad hoc, what if it were to be a structured, regular, process and procedure?

> ***What if structured MBMA produced measurable, actionable and usable data for* everyone *to act on? The nice thing about external marketing is that the tools and techniques all exist for managing data about customers.***

These tools and techniques need to be made available to every supplier in the customer-supplier chain. This is what this book is all about. A marketing-based approach using concepts like SWOT will guarantee that everyone gets closer to the customer than ever before.

HOW MUCH CAN AN INTEGRATED APPROACH TO MARKETING BRING ABOUT 'STRATEGY FROM BELOW'?

The answer to this will only become clear once organisations start to practise marketing techniques. Techniques like researching all of the customers' needs. For example, one piece of research conducted by MORI shows the extent of the existing poor communication in organisations. It highlights the attitude problems that are getting in the way. It shows how people are being stopped, when they could help to provide strategic direction.

> ***Even though the people at the 'sharp end', closest to the customer, have a wealth of data and ideas, little of this comes up the communication chain.***

It would be unfair to name the organisation being used here as an example. The temptation of the reader might well be to say to themselves 'Well of course we could not be like that'. My experience of this organisation is that it is extremely well regarded by the staff and is extremely well regarded by the customers – it is among the UK's largest companies. To add credibility to the research I can say that it was commissioned by the organisation in order to publish the data internally. To give it credence, the research company chosen was MORI.

The findings are, I believe, not too dissimilar from what might be discovered in many organisations today. The message that the following statistics contain is that things can really only get better by improving 'communication'; this can only get infinitely better if it is done professionally by internal marketing techniques such as research.

1 Communication: a massive 68 per cent of people feel there is not enough opportunity to tell the organisation about the things that affect their work.
2 Freedom to speak: a frightening 59 per cent of people feel that speaking up can damage your career prospects.
3 Appreciation: over half, 56 per cent feel the organisation is below average in showing appreciation for the things you do.
4 Training: 58 per cent feel that training is ineffective on new services.
5 Communication via the grapevine: almost 50 per cent feel that communication is via the grapevine; 95 per cent of people do not want to receive information this way.
6 Communication from meetings: only 30 per cent of information is felt to come from communication meetings; over 50 per cent would prefer meetings as a part of the communication process.

This is not an untypical set of results from organisations, many of whom are trying extremely hard to 'communicate', but are finding it difficult. The message that the data is giving is that people not only want to be informed, but they want to be able to communicate themselves. Unless this two way process does start, then according to the Henley Centre research produced for Luncheon Vouchers, they will end up citing 'communications' as one of the main reasons for leaving.

So, in terms of the wealth of information that is obtainable, it is definitely worth gathering 'strategy from below'. It is also vital to the individuals. The organisation must increase their involvement and thereby increase their motivation, and their propensity to contribute. This will also reduce their propensity to leave.

This feature of marketing throughout an organisation is achieved by targeting messages and information to everyone in the organisation. However, the way this is done now, through news sheets, circulars, videos, training, conferences etc., is often deliberately targeted straight at the individual. It skirts around the manager. Why? Because there is a recognition that managers often 'filter' information to suit their needs.

This leads on to the next feature of the internal marketing process. It is one that obviates this problem of filtering as far as is possible. There does come a time when the 'soft' approach is not working with certain individuals and they need to go. It is a managerial decision as to how much they are positively contributing to the organisation, its strategies, its goals and its team-work. Most people have had experiences where through no fault of their own, they have not 'fitted'. People who may not work well in one environment may thrive in another. However, if the problem of management filtering information is a general one then the issue must be addressed as an organisational matter.

The words being increasingly used today when referring to improving the effectiveness of managers, in their dealings with others are *Added Value.*

Added value (The internal kind)

To look at a specific example of the power of added value, the experience of ESSO is one that many organisations might like to emulate. The sting in the tail is that, like ESSO UK with its dealers and franchisees, they would have to release control of the ability to manage their managers. This makes them answerable mainly to themselves. How many organisations would be prepared to do that? Then again, with the massive demographic changes, and almost flat organisational structures, the days are not far off when this example may be more the norm.

ESSO Retail UK supply approximately 2,500 sites up and down the highways and byways. These range from the large urban, extremely busy forecourts, to much smaller rural sites. These sites, even those owned by ESSO, are run and managed by franchisees or independent retailers who are not employed by ESSO. The relationship, therefore, is totally different to an ordinary employee-employer one. Like the future patterns, there are no 'direct reporting' lines of authority.

As a result of this relationship, the owner/manager of a site is his own boss. Yet, because there are so many of them it is possible to approach them as a large enough target market to provide credible and meaningful data. These managers are constantly being researched, as would be expected of an organisation that needs to market its products and services to individuals who can make their own decisions about using them or not.

One extremely interesting fact came out of one of the qualitative pieces of research that was carried out on the subject of staff development. The research by MORI showed that the individual staff member felt very strongly about the 'level of involvement and interest' in their job. **This was three times higher than the average Mori found.** I can only speculate on the reasons for this, but I would suggest the following:

1 Flat structures – i.e. the Boss and the Staff! A simple two tier structure. The net result would be excellent communication and little feeling of lack of communication on bigger issues (even though in many organisations these would have no relevance to the average person).
2 Devolved responsibility – the nature of a service station means jobs involve a great deal of responsibility in a number of seriously important areas (health and safety, theft, cash control, etc). Often these jobs are delegated to the one person left on the site to run it. The manager cannot be there on every shift.
3 Fast feedback – as a result of 1 and 2 the feedback would be much quicker than in an organisation where the decision makers are remote.

The net result of these is that the added value from the people in the organisations could be tremendous. When looked at in terms of the amount of input that an employee gives, because they feel 'interested and involved' they provide just the sort of extra input that all organisations are now desperately seeking. This is not just at employee level, it is also at manager level. Their job is to run the site. They can do it putting much less time and effort into the day to day running and let the people get on with this. They can then devote more time to, for example, motivating, communicating, planning, training, building the business, and most important of all, researching customer needs. This is the added value that is generated. The difference in volumes and profitability between average sites and the 'best' sites can be staggering! The question is, do managers understand what it is that people require, in order to be able to target their messages.

The three As

There are in essence three internal customer requirements that can be pointed out to managers. These will provide them with a simple guide for the targeting of messages and information. They are fundamental to understanding what it is that people need when it comes to providing the output that is expected of them. They form the basis for all marketing to the internal customer. Once again I believe that it is important that the language used to describe these is kept simple, memorable, and above all, usable.

I call these requirements or needs, *The Three As*:

1 *Attitude*: How do people feel about what they are doing?
2 *Awareness*: Why are they doing what they are supposed to be doing?
3 *Ability*: How are they supposed to do it?

The order of tackling these is vital. It depends on the situation (for those who are interested, see Blanchard's *Theory of Situational Leadership*), but in most cases the order is as above.

Attitude, awareness, then comes ability

To put this into everyday terms:

1 *Attitude*: People need to feel 'good' about what they are doing if they are to put in the enthusiasm and effort.
2 *Awareness*: People need to know 'why the hell am I doing this?' or even 'why the hell are we all doing this?'.
3 *Ability*: Once they feel good, and know why they are there, they can be shown what to get on with

All too often Ability is *all* that is tackled. It is often felt that it is all that 'employees' need. In other words 'I'll show you what to do then you can damn well get on and do it!'.

The time has arrived where it no longer matters if individual managers do not believe that they also need to cater for the Attitudes and Awareness of the employee. Employees will, and are, demanding to enjoy what they do.

They want to understand why they are doing it. And then they want to be left alone whilst they are doing it. These needs must therefore be met if the organisation is to ensure that it is reaching the people. These Three As are worth exploring further.

Attitude

I first came across the concept that 'attitude training precedes knowledge and skills' when working for Trusthouse Forte. The theory was put to us by Chris Downs, the founder of Customer Service Training Ltd. The basis behind this concept was first developed by an American called Maxwell Maltz. Simply put, it runs along similar lines to the teachings of Dale Carnegie et al and states, 'You are what you think you are, and you can if you think you can'.

In the many years that I have known Chris Downs, he had been one of the UK's leading exponents of the now universally accepted notion that excellent customer service leads to excellent reputations, sales and repeat business. The list of organisations that have run Customer Service Training programmes reads like a Who's Who of Britain's top companies. All of these organisations have doubly benefited from this approach because the added value is not just gained at staff level.

> ***Unlike many other directly targeted 'one day events', attitude training must be given first and foremost to the manager. They then* personally *target the messages, and deliver the 'well done' and 'thank you' to the staff.***

Marketing of Attitude should not just happen in training; it should apply to any form of communication. People can be targeted with 'feel good' messages, from anything like the Mission Statement to the jobs they are doing – as long as the messages are real, and are not propaganda!

Awareness

Philosophers are ultimately concerned with the simplest of questions, 'Why?'. The same is true of almost every individual you meet. The question 'Why?' however, was often left unanswered in the work place. For many years everyone was expected to 'get on with it'.

The question is now a major preoccupation with Chief Executives, Boards, and senior management of organisations throughout the world. This has become the search for the corporate Holy Grail. It is this search for the direction and meaning of life of the organisation that has prompted the days and weekends away, to come up with 'The Vision and Mission Statement'!

Once a Vision and Mission Statement is produced the added value that comes from the senior people can almost be felt palpitating through the corridors. There is the renewed zest for all things corporate. Enthusiasm and team spirit are rekindled in often previously warring factions. The desire to rush out and publish the words of wisdom grips the creators of these new born babes with fervour. Why? Because they have found out 'Why?'. They have come to a personal and common consensus as to the reason for being. Life is no longer just about shuffling paper or juggling budgets, it has meaning and purpose. It is the same need that everyone has at every level in the organisation.

It has taken years to recognise the necessity for viewing 'Awareness' as a prime area for communication. Organisations have been too pre-occupied at all levels with the skills of individuals, i.e. their 'Ability'. This must be changed.

As discussed earlier, the methodology for creating Awareness is not simply running promotional or advertising campaigns. Just as it takes time for the senior people to think things through and absorb the implications, time will also be required by everyone else. Once the internal marketeer has established the best ways for individuals to absorb the required awareness, then added value will also be forthcoming.

The need to create Awareness may not be the same in the different target markets in the organisation. The youth of the past few decades have been brought up in a changed educational system to that of the post- and pre-war era. They have been taught to question. They are expected to think things through. They discuss politics, economics and philosophy and are able to rationalise, as well as produce the creative thinking that leads to cognitive leaps. The UK's exams that pupils sit at 15 and 16 years of age have been described as much tougher than degrees of only a few decades before.

Television, computers, social changes and parental attitudes to the rights of children ensure that they will not sit meekly by and say nothing to the 'boss'. Yet, compare this to the generations before. Their sense of loyalty means an acceptance of an authority which is no longer valid in the context of teams. This, of course, does not deny the responsibility of management and leadership. It simply means that managers cannot expect people to do as they are told, just because they say so. The organisation works because everyone in it makes it work. The power to make it work is no longer vested in the managers. They certainly have very strong responsibilities, but telling people what to do is rapidly going out of fashion!

A fundamental tenet of marketing internally, is that Awareness is vital to the acceptance of a piece of communication, be it verbal or written. This also holds true of external marketing. The consumer, be they internal or external, has a right to know about the products and services that they are buying.

The last few years have seen an explosion in the information about products and services. This includes for example the food revolution, with its focus on colourings and additives. Even the medical profession is being hit by patients not prepared to lie back and take whatever is thrown at them, just because the person pronouncing them is called Doctor. The United States has paved the way for this to go into major litigation if the wrong thing is done to the customer/patient.

The same is now true internally, although some older industries with older work forces may have a few years of grace before they may actually have to explain to their people why they are doing things!

Ability

The skills needed to do a job are becoming more and more complex. This applies to almost every job you can think of. Rapid change means that the simplest of tasks in many organisations may be undertaken manually one day, and the next day the self-same employee could be working a part of an integrated advanced manufacturing system with a computer in front of them. Previously simple tasks, like pressing till buttons, are being supplemented with often demanding selling and inter-personal skills. No-one is safe!

At the other end of the scale, the worlds of finance and technology are spawning a new breed called 'knowledge workers'. These 'knowledge workers' are filling ever increasingly sophisticated niches with their services that are very much in demand one day, and may be totally useless the next.

The massive changes brought about in other sectors produce similar situations. For example, does a manager in a public company or government body, with no experience of say the cut throat world of competition and tendering, have the skills (i.e. ability), to be able to deal with the requirements and pressures put on them?

ITSABILITY

One Government organisation that is rapidly developing the skill and ability to compete in the world outside the public services is the new agency set up to deal with the massive information technology needs within the Department of Social Security. This and similar new agencies have been set up to be more commercially aware. Certain services are also subject to what is called 'market testing'. They are forced to put some or all of the services they offer out to competitive review or tender against the private sector. So how do they set themselves up so they can compete? They do it in the same way as the private sector. They focus on customers, they have mission statements, they have corporate logos, and they adopt Quality and BS5750. They have outside help from the private sector to guide them. But if the private sector counterparts don't have the communication strategies themselves, who will they learn from?

One department of the Information Technology Services Agency (ITSA) we are working with does have a communication strategy; one that is helping it to establish its place as a key supplier of a service that can help the taxpayer save millions of pounds. They are the Procurement Services Section of ITSA, responsible for purchasing. Their ability to communicate is critical. This case study will be covered in more depth later. Suffice to say that having set up a completely new department within a new agency, the communication requirement with all their customers, internal and external, is vital. It has been necessary not only to create an Awareness of their policies, procedures and people, but also essential to create a recognition of their Ability, i.e. in the skills they offer, the service they provide, and the savings they are able to make. In this way their customers are more inclined to use their services. The more they are used, the more they will save.

What of globalisation?

In Europe, no matter what happens post Maastricht, the issues brought about by 1992 have also raised the question of Ability. This Ability is not just learning new languages (and for Britain this is a major problem), but also in learning to deal with different cultures, with the different markets, with the different manufacturing and distribution systems and methods. All of these become crucial to the success of organisations.

Add to this the globalisation of markets, the new philosophies of such systems as Just In Time, Quality, Throughput Accounting; and add to this the massive advances in Information Technology. The net result is a work force that is sorely in need of increased Ability, yet painfully lacking in the awareness of what is about to hit. Consequently they are harbouring low levels of positive attitudes.

The only way to improve the competitiveness of any organisation is to improve the three As – Attitude, Awareness, Ability.

The technique of marketing that helps to identify these is research. It can be done by using whatever method is appropriate. Hold on, I hear the trainers say, training does that with a 'training needs analysis'. Yes, of course it does, but only the issues which require training. Training cannot, for example, tackle the introduction of mission statements, or the attitudes to information technology, or the marketing of strategic and tactical plans. Training cannot tackle the creation of integrated approaches to communicating pay and reward structures. Training cannot tackle the associated actions and plans needed to be produced by the individuals to meet their targets. Training cannot tackle the strategic changes necessary to ensure that communication takes place in rapidly altering global markets; communication to often greatly overburdened people, who have little enough time to 'do their own job never mind spend time talking to others'. (A cry I hear time and time again.)

Training is, however, tackling many of the very important issues that are also covered by the people in communication or internal marketing roles. Customer service is a prime example. The two disciplines of training and marketing to the customer-supplier chain are inextricably linked. Training is one of the key weapons needed in the tough fight to get any new ideas into the internal market place.

To sum up, through improved Attitude, Awareness and Ability brought about by improved communication and training, every individual is capable of giving greatly increased Added Value. This can be measured. More organisations are calculating Added Value and marketing the results to shareholders etc., by producing statistics like profit per employee and added value per employee. The vital internal issues to measure are the Attitude, Awareness and Ability of the people in the organisation.

SUMMARY

- **Focus on the needs of internal customers, and even greater attention to the needs of external customers will follow.**

- **Information is power. Use the information your staff have on every subject from morale, to the requirements of your internal customers. Encourage your people to contribute ideas, and 'listen' to them.**

- **MBMA, Management By Marketing Ability, replaces MBWA, Management By Wandering About.**

- **Added value from the improved contribution of every individual happens by providing internal products and services, such as training. These products and services have to affect the three As: Attitude, Awareness, Ability.**

8 USING A MODEL TO MANAGE CHANGE IN YOUR ORGANISATION

THE ADVANTAGES OF USING A MODEL

Having previously discussed both the features and benefits of an integrated approach, the next step is to illustrate how to apply it in a user-friendly way – by using a very simple model everyone can relate to.

Too often models are complicated. They should be simple and understandable, so that people can actually use them. The other benefits of working from a model are worth stating here, as using the model is the crux of understanding the integrated marketing process.

1 *The Top Of The Jigsaw Box*: The top of the jigsaw box gives the overview, without which, very few people have the skill, patience or tenacity to want to try and put the pieces together. This is what this model provides.

2 *Understanding Grows Through Debate*: The absorption of the facts will be best achieved as each individual element is debated. This model is put forward as a basis for debate, rather than as a fait accompli. The person trying to 'internalise' this new method of seeing things will not be threatened by the new order. They are being asked to consider it, they are not forced to accept it.

3 *Acceptance Comes At Varying Speeds*: The build up of the picture, the facts and reasoning behind it, has taken the author and his team many years of working in this field. For the person coming to this fresh, new ideas take a long while to assimilate, especially if they are not your own! Acceptance of the reasoning behind this model must be at a speed determined by the individual.

4 *Not Everyone Wants To Buy The Concept*: We have tested this model on numerous occasions on individuals in many large and small organisations. It has been further simplified from the model in *The Employee Revolution*, in order to take into account the dynamic, rather than static, nature of organisations.

Using an even simpler marketing model to illustrate the way to integrate the customer-supplier chain, allows the arguments to build up rationally, logically and even more memorably. However there is one big catch!

The concept of marketing into the whole of the chain may not be 'bought' by everyone. The rejection of this idea is likely to come with the realisation that the big picture requires considerable changes on the part of the individual and the organisation.

The arguments that then follow are usually emotional and illogical, but when this happens during discussion, others can criticise this kind of comment. This strengthens their own acceptance of new ideas. Using a model works.

AN INTEGRATED MARKETING STRATEGY

What will bring about a structured approach to marketing the business throughout the customer-supplier chain? Top down commitment?

Yes, once the Chief Executive and Board accept the concept of having an integrated marketing policy, then a number of things start to happen. First and foremost, if the CEO is using a model, then by definition they are approaching the business in a totally structured way. Perhaps for the first time the complexities of the business can be expressed in a way that allows *everyone* in the business to understand what the CEO, and indeed everyone else, is attempting to do, and the methods of trying to do it.

The customer-supplier chain concept is an easy one – even for CEOs!

Previously, the best models of organisational structure were those of the departmental splits of the functions. Everyone realised that, in order to succeed, it was necessary to have a Board, a marketing function, a personnel function, an accounting function etc. These functions then each did their own specialised thing and the business progressed, or otherwise.

The problem is that the approach is not holistic. It simply demonstrates that there are a number of things that are necessary to allow the business to function. Worse, it is divisive in many organisations, where an 'us and them' attitude builds up, as well as localised, parochial perceptions of what the organisation is trying to achieve.

Secondly, the vertical structuring of an organisation no longer works. Not surprisingly this is sometimes called the 'Temple Structure' as each function is in totally separate columns. This is all held down by the weight of the top!

It is also called the 'Silo Structure' as there is no contact between functions, except to lob grenades from one Silo to another!

To overcome this functional split of a business, it is continually necessary to attempt to provide an 'overview' of the business, e.g. its direction, results etc. This often happens by using inadequate and inappropriate vehicles of communication such as the company newspaper, or briefing groups.

Traditional forms of communication tend to further intensify the functional split of a business through their focus on departmental, divisional or even separate company activities.

The 'one piece of paper' approach – integrating the business

The model we use puts down, *on one piece of paper*, the interfaces of all the elements in the organisation, thus integrating the business. It does so in such a way as to stress the importance of both the customers *and* the individuals in the organisation, i.e. the internal customers. It does this at every level, from the front line to the Chief Executive. It also shows the inputs and outputs of the organisation. This is done without specifying the functions or departments.

The 'one piece of paper' approach enables everyone to relate to what is going on in the organisation in a simple way. It does this through showing its activities, rather than its specialised areas of operation. The result is that a previously very confusing array of interrelationships become very clear.

The model places *all* the elements of the business into a marketing framework. This helps generate an understanding of what needs to happen to make the business operate using the customer-supplier chain. In short, the model paints a marketing based picture of business that encompasses the elements of that business. These elements in the model clearly show the areas in which the individuals can expect to be informed, consulted, instructed, etc. In other words, the model shows how communication will take place within the organisation. Before that, more definitions!

Communication defined (communication not communications)

'Communication' in its narrowest sense of allowing individuals at the very least to understand and be able to repeat what they have heard, can only truly occur if the subject matter is placed in context. Where customers are concerned, this means marketing must be involved.

Communication, even in its broadest sense in many organisations, (even today) is not seen as a marketing function. Therefore, it has not been deemed necessary to employ marketing processes, apart from perhaps the powerful use of PR, for the company magazine, Annual Report and Accounts etc.

All too often, however the array of communication that occurs, is thrown into the organisation without any form of context. Individuals are totally confused as to what is happening, why it is happening, and who thinks what is important.

Communications (with an 's') defined

Having defined communication it is worth looking at 'communications'. Today this means the methodology of getting the information from one place to another. This may mean through phones, fax, or through computer networks. This may seem obvious but many people interchange the two words.

All too often organisations will have a 'communications' strategy, without having a communication strategy. That is like building roads and motorways, without having any strategy for what can travel on them, and when. It is like allowing horse drawn carts on the autoroutes in the rush hour!

Common understanding

The model, in essence, paints a marketing picture. Therefore, if everyone can see what the picture looks like, then there will be common understanding. Most people in organisations today only have a very hazy view of their own role in that organisation, never mind anyone else's role. In addition, there is often very little understanding of the overall mission, strategy, structures etc. This often happens it seems, even after they have been explained.

There is a morass of issues in every organisation which have no apparent formal place in the structure of the organisation. The methods and variety of putting things across, and the apparent complexity of the messages that are sent and received, create further confusion.

The model should be simple

The purpose of having a model which is simple is that everyone can understand it. Once the common understanding is achieved, then the individuals can get on with running the business, rather than getting totally bogged down in the process of communication and sorting out the mess resulting from a lack of communication.

Lynette Royle, head of Public Relations at Guinness (post Ernest Saunders) says simply of communication:

> ***In the end, every problem in business can be traced back to one of communication.***

If the organisation does not produce this common understanding today, then there is likely to be a great deal more time spent sorting out the resulting problems. These are usually brought on by a simple lack of clarity and understanding about what is being communicated and why.

Quality assurance as part of the model

Communication with customers isn't just a 'nice to have' it is a 'must have'. However, what communication must you have? BS5750/ISO9000 was created in order to meet customers' need for an organisation which provides an assurance that its systems are documented, defined and followed. To do this it has one simple rule when communicating: **write it down.**

> ***What needs to be written down for BS5750/ISO9000 should be part and parcel of an integrated marketing strategy. That is one that is customer focused.***

This model has therefore been created with BS5750/ISO9000 in mind. So too have the many communication issues which follow from it at a tactical level. These are also covered by BS5750/ISO9000 and include such areas as product design, distribution, organisational structure, and training.

How does BS5750/ISO9000 link into the customer-supplier chain?

Getting feedback from customers throughout the customer-supplier chain isn't also just another 'nice to have'. If an organisation is to have BS5750/ISO9000 then it must have the policies, procedures, plans and practices in place and written down. It needs this to happen for its own internal purposes. It also needs to check that it is able to meet its customer requirements.

CREATING A NEW STRUCTURE FOR YOUR ORGANISATION

One of the key concepts of Total Quality Management is to turn organisational hierarchies upside down. It symbolises a cultural change from 'directive' management to 'supportive' management. Unfortunately it is not very easy for organisations to turn their culture upside down, especially if they are very 'top down' driven, i.e. the bosses like telling people what to do! In addition, for a long time now organisational structures have been displayed in a pyramidal diagram, with the CEO at the top. This reinforces the top down nature of the organisation. In other words, the upside down triangle shape advocated in Total Quality Management is unlikely to take hold. In marketing terms, it is exceedingly difficult to replace a strongly marketed concept, however bad it is!

The upside down triangle as a shape is the wrong way up for the target market, managers and leaders, for them to want to buy it. Also for people in organisations, it is very static. In non-marketing terms (or perhaps it is) it has no pzazzz! Finally, the shape seems to bear no relation to the concept of a chain with each of the links binding customers and their suppliers.

Efforts to overcome the problems of the organisational structure today have ended up with all sorts of organisational models from matrix management to spiders' webs.

So we have a problem; how to portray an organisational model for dealing with customers that shows the following:

1 An organisational chart where customers are at the top
2 A supportive management culture
3 A customer-supplier chain
4 A dynamic, rather than static, situation

We have attempted to do all of these at the same time by moving from a 'top down' model, to one of a 'spinning top' model. This produces a dynamic model with a number of characteristics which will unfold in this chapter. Figure 8.1 shows the spinning top model.

The three requirements for a model organisation

Quality for total customer commitment: enough has been written about the need for an organisation to provide Quality for its customers. This model places this need at the top, where it should be, but is Quality alone enough?

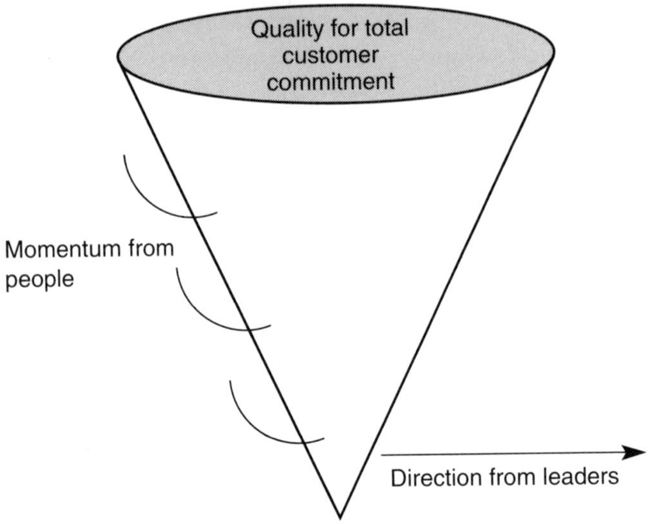

Figure 8.1 The three requirements for a model organisation

Momentum from people: more is being written all the time about subjects like 'Empowerment', 'Ownership', 'Involvement', 'Integration' etc. This highlights the recognition that people are critical to an organisation's success. The model places the people next on an organisation's agenda by looking at their needs as internal customers.
Direction from leaders: a number of organisations have recognised that they have gone too far with subjects like 'Empowerment', 'Ownership', etc. The requirement for strong direction from the leaders of an organisation is now recognised as being the deciding factor in its success.

None of these can operate in isolation. The model puts them all together in the shape of a spinning top providing quality, momentum, and direction. The next chapter takes the model a stage further.

SUMMARY

- Using a model helps you achieve your organisational goals.
- A model helps you see how communications will work within your organisation – and how it links to your external marketing.
- The model should be simple, and provide a common understanding for all your internal customers.
- Quality can only happen through communication, and so forms an important part of the model.
- The model puts leaders at the bottom and customers at the top. Management is supportive and at the same time provides strong direction.

9 MAKING THE MODEL CUSTOMER FACING

QUALITY FOR CUSTOMERS – BUT IT IS ENOUGH?

If there is one single thread running throughout almost every one of the plethora of management books on improving one's business, it must be, it has to be, it should be, it can only be **customers**. The three key words that have been put before organisations to indicate this customer focus have got to be 'Excellence', 'Quality' and 'Marketing'. These may not help clarify what is required and can often obscure the simplicity of the situation. They are all saying the same thing:

> ***People in any type of organisation simply need to understand that they are there to meet customers' needs. This is the*** **only** ***thing that will ultimately ensure that the organisation's own goals and aspirations will be met.***

Marketing to customers has this one basic tenet, and it is worth repeating again and again.

Having already looked at the various definitions, it is worth exploring the similarities between Excellence, Quality and Marketing.

Excellence

The word itself does inspire. It has done a tremendous amount to goad people into action. They still want to reach the giddy heights achieved by the almost innumerable case studies and examples cited in the various 'Excellence' books, even though some of these stars of the 1980s are now faded, or even out.

> ***However, the four secrets of 'Excellence' are, in the end, only ways of satisfying internal and external customers:***

1 Superior service
2 Constant innovation

3 Full use of internal people
4 Leadership through MBWA

Perhaps the link with marketing might have been made earlier, if the titles of the books produced by Peters et al might have been as follows!

In Search Of Customers
A Passion For Customers
Thriving On Customers

Quality

The introduction into the language of 'Quality' of the concept of the customer-supplier chain, has done wonders to make people realise that internal people are not just corporate assets, but are vital links in a chain which can so easily be broken.

I wonder though, if the focus of 'Quality' as a word, has led to yet another search for an intangible Holy Grail. The definition of 'Quality' itself places it in a context most people can relate to i.e. Quality is meeting *customer* requirements, now and in the future.

Is the focus of excellence and quality in the right place?

These two highly emotive words have become part of the language and folklore of organisations. The focus of both Excellence and Quality is in the right place, on customers, but what is the process? If there were a process for everyone to be focusing on customers, wherever they may be, then surely it would entail the involvement of marketing. This is currently not the case.

If the point has not hit home yet (am I repeating myself!) then you will soon see why this must be so. Once everyone is able to concentrate on the customer by using marketing skills then, and only then, will real and lasting change occur.

THE CHANGING NEEDS OF CUSTOMERS

Customers are the focus but what do they want from your organisation? To answer this it is worth looking to see how times have changed. Marketing history is all about customers, products and services. The marketing story since the war is succinctly described in the book *Le Marketing Interne*. (Roughly translated from French this is Internal Marketing!)

I include this reference to show that the subject is well under discussion in the European Community. I had the pleasure, if not the surprise, to be the only British speaker in two days of speeches, at an international conference in Madrid as long ago as 1987. Virtually every country in the community was represented by a speaker talking on one of a large number of issues centred on internal marketing. This was at a time when there were very few in the UK even aware of the subject.

The following summarises the history of marketing, taken from *Le Marketing Interne*. It serves to show the changing focus from inside the organisation to the outside.

The post war history of enterprise

(adapted, updated and added to from *Le Marketing Interne*, by Michael Levionnois, Les Editions d'Organisation, 1987)

1950–1960 The production economy

A period where demand exceeded supply and all the producers had to do was to concern themselves with the process of production and the process of sales.

1960–1970 The distribution economy

A period where supply and demand were roughly equal. In order to survive, the key became the success gained in establishing graphic markets and servicing the needs of those markets. In other words, the battle between manufacturers was supply based.

1970–1980 The marketing economy

The consumer (but not yet individual customer) becomes king. In a European and global economy the reversal of the situation of supply and demand occurs to oust the factory, sales, and distribution led organisations. Supply now exceeds demand and the consumer is faced with an increasingly sophisticated and diverse choice of products and services all vying for their money. The door is open for the marketing professional to meet and create the needs for their particular products and services.

Competition becomes fierce and new skills are needed to meet the rapidly changing needs of the external customer. However, without organisations realising it, this self same external consumer has also become the sophisticated internal employee who, for the moment, mainly requires being better managed and better paid.

1980–1990 The environmental economy

Better described as the Economy of Change. Nothing is now certain. From petrol crisis in the early 1980s to environmental crisis in the late 1980s. From increasing co-operation in the European Economy as 1992 approached and beyond, to the unbelievable events in the USSR under Gorbachev. From massive mainframe computing power in the early 1980s to massive desk top and lap top power in the late 1980s.

From a focus on export potential to a realisation that we are entering the marketing driven age of the global market. From derision and fright about Far Eastern products and services to manufacture of them on 'home soil', as they infiltrate western economies. All of these environmental, economic, competitive, technological, psychological and consumer based changes have fuelled a management revolution.

This revolution has been channelled in the west by a desire to be as good as the Japanese and has been led by the gurus talked about elsewhere in this book, not least of them Peters and Crosby.

It must be noted, before going further into the 1990s, that the 1980s were still not the era of the external 'individual customer'. The focus on individuals each making up the target markets, rather than mass marketing techniques, was only just being realised. It was preached in popular terms with the advent of *In Search Of Excellence*. This, of course, was not revolutionary in itself but was based on observation of the too few organisations practising it.

1990 – The internal and external customer economy (this is no longer based on Le Marketing Interne*)*

The focus has now firmly shifted to the very specific needs of the individual external customer. 'Change' has become the norm. The speed of change has become the issue facing people in and out of the work place. The forces of change, such as technology, politics, global concerns, family and community isolation, poverty, social concerns, wars, have all become the elements creating the tensions and stresses. Communication has created a well informed society.

> ***Yet with all this marketing, or is it because of it, comes recession. People and countries have lived beyond their means. The price is now having to be paid.***

This means that greed must turn to need. However, consumer power, people's upbringing in the consumer age and an awareness that each individual has rights over the producer of products and services, mean that the customer is more demanding than ever before, even though they have less in their pockets. Indeed with less in their pockets they are looking for better and better value at lower and lower prices, yet at higher and higher 'quality'.

We therefore have a culture based on very high expectations when economies are faltering. This has produced shock waves within organisations. The need for ever more improvements in production to cut cost and increase efficiency; the need for lower prices, whilst having to invest more to keep up and the demands of the organisation on the individuals requires levels of motivation on them unheard of before. Just look at the dedication of the Japanese worker and their children at school and University.

How is this motivation to be maintained?

MEETING THE NEEDS OF THE EXTERNAL CUSTOMER

The word 'meeting', as already discussed in the phrase 'meeting the needs of the external customer', has been chosen very carefully. It has been used to describe the primary function of external marketing. Essentially the external customer really is 'king'. They have ultimate power not only over their own buying decisions but also of others. How many others was only slowly realised with the advent of consumerist power. This was manifested in all sorts of ways (from TV consumer programmes to loud complaints in shops).

The function of marketing, however pro-active, is therefore a subservient one to meet the needs of the external customers. The external marketeer in a free society cannot force the customer to do anything. The customer can, and does, make choices based on all kinds of criteria, many, if not most of them, being anything but rational or logical.

The needs of the customer must therefore be identified. They must be specified in terms of the exact type of products and services that are required. A complete and ongoing process of getting those products and services to the market place must be established.

This process has been defined and, in all but the most backward of organisations, has been accepted under the banner of marketing. It is not the intention of this book to add to the wealth of material on this subject. All that is necessary is to place marketing in the context of the instigator, creator, generator, communicator, persuader and executioner of the process that uses its skills and techniques to bring in a profit. Using a well-heeled epithet it does this by 'meeting the needs of the customer with the right products and services at the right time in the right place at the right price'.

The question is: Why have so few people realised that marketing internally can have the same power as externally?
The answer is: No one has recognised that they have had to.

The new focus is one of the most exciting and difficult challenges to face organisations yet. With the massive amounts of change affecting the organisation and its people, the process of communication and the art and science of turning that into marketed messages will be vital. No organisation will be immune to the needs of its customers, both internal and external. But how are the internal customers seen? Are they really seen as customers?

MANAGING YOUR INTERNAL CUSTOMER

Total Quality Management has created a revolution. So has the concept of Excellence. Massive changes have occurred to areas of people's life in work and the methods and practices that surround them. Very few would have predicted the rate, amount and effect would be so powerful. The amazing side effect is that, when everyone is a customer, they see themselves as having rights like they never had before.

Thus, for example, within a very short time span, organisations have changed from autocratic culture, where the hierarchy and pecking order produced an elite who were (and in some places still are) called 'Sir'; to an open egalitarian society where everyone is on first name terms.

Some of the practices, like named spaces in the car park, being replaced by a 'first come first served' rule may take a little longer, (even in the most forward companies), but it won't take long for the upward pressure and disgust at unnecessary privilege to result in further changes!

This does not mean the organisation goes soft and panders to the whims of the internal customer: the opposite is becoming the norm.

Organisations are toughening up and demanding more. The key is, is this acceptable to the individual if the organisation gives more. This does not mean money. It means the things that the individual perceives as important to them, in order to fulfil their function and be recognised in the role that they play.

Quality has not been a quiet revolution. Its strengths must not be underestimated. The effects can be increasingly seen in every aspect of organisational life. The image makers and builders of advertising and design are beginning to regard quality as a product that needs to be marketed carefully to attract the customer to buy. The same is true of the internal customer.

Excellence has produced the phenomenon of MBWA and Empowerment. Internal customers have demanded good leadership, rather than leaders suddenly deciding, or being told to, focus internally as well as externally.

Empowerment is producing increasing demands for more involvement in the jobs being done. In the past the pride people felt in the things they did may have been stifled by management's lack of concern over quality, as they strove for more and more profit. Now they know they must produce Quality.

The Quality revolution is forcing a rethink in the attitudes and practices of the leaders, managers and individuals in organisations. The customer-supplier chain has placed the emphasis on local people, providing local solutions to local customers, be they internal or external.

With this devolution of power running alongside the revolution, comes the need for everyone to be much better at managing their own customers, internally and externally. The way that they can begin to do this comes back to providing them with a model against which to work. But what are we going to put in this model dedicated to meeting customers' needs? As this book is all about marketing, surely it must include the 4 Ps.

The 4 Ps

Marketing people like branding everything. The 4 Ps are the 'brand' name given to the cornerstone of all external marketing strategies. It's what young marketing people cut their teeth on; learning about the interaction between Product, Price, Place, Promotion.

Product – What you sell
Price – How much it is
Place – Where it is sold
Promotion – How it is 'pushed'

The new 4 Ps

An integrated approach to marketing internally as well as externally should retain marketing's flair for memorable concepts. So here are the new 4 Ps that are the cornerstone to marketing internally:

Policy – The directives about the way things will be done
Procedures – The structures and systems to get things done
Plans – The future mapped out
Practices – The things that are said and done to get you to where you want to go

The next chapter covers managing the external customer and the external 4 Ps. It shows, however, that today things are no longer as simple as looking at product, price, place and promotion – the customer demands more.

After that comes managing the internal customer and the internal 4 Ps. This details the tools and techniques needed to ensure that each of these is produced in the right way to the right customer, at the right time, in the right place.

But who are these internal customers for these policies, procedures, practices, and plans? They need to be segmented as well as the external customers. There is no point in having a product with no one to buy it.

To keep the model simple we have kept the segmentation simple. See Figure 9.1 Now the segments of all the customers, external and internal can be added to the spinning top.

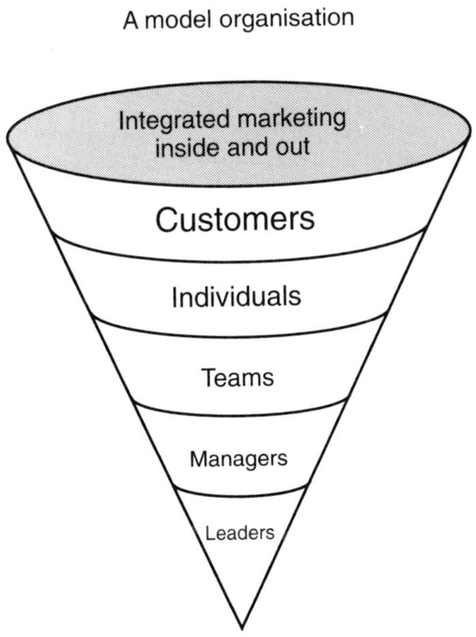

Figure 9.1 Segmenting customers – inside and out

SUMMARY

- **Excellence, Quality and Marketing together have created a focus on customers both inside and outside the organisation.**

- **Now they need to be put together for managing your internal customers successfully.**

- **Marketing to external customers is about the 4 Ps – Product, Price, Place, Promotion.**

- **Marketing to internal customers is about the New 4 Ps – Policy, Procedures, Plans, Practices**

10 THE CUSTOMER CHAIN SEGMENTED

HOW DO YOU KNOW WHAT YOUR INTERNAL AND EXTERNAL CUSTOMERS WANT FROM THE ORGANISATION?

Whilst this book is essentially about managing internal customers, not external customers, it is vital first to a good idea to let your internal customers know what your external customers want. The first part of this chapter covers the external customers segment of the model, followed by the needs of the internal customer segments.

It shows how times have changed. Things are not as simple as they used to be. This has an impact on everyone in the customer-supplier chain. You will not achieve an integrated approach without first recognising and meeting these needs.

THE EXTERNAL CUSTOMERS SEGMENT

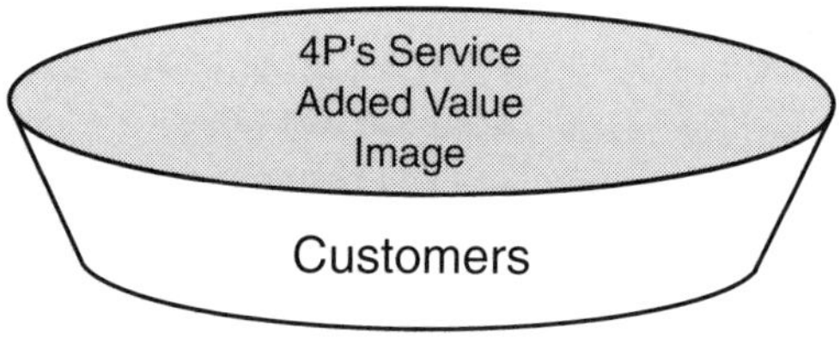

Figure 10.1 The key needs of your external customers

The 4 Ps used to be the answer – not any more!

In marketing it used to be easy. All you had to do was concentrate on the 4 Ps, and pray that your customers came flocking to buy your product.

Step 1: Get the Product right – so it was better than the competition's.

Step 2: Get the Price right – so it was cheaper or better value than the competition's.
Step 3: Get the Place right – so that the distribution and outlets maximised the sales opportunities.
Step 4: Get the Promotions right – so that people knew about the product and were encouraged to buy it.

Product

But even here, something was going wrong. The Japanese proved the Western world didn't have the product right. Quality had to become the watch word of every organisation if they were to compete. The customer didn't want a warranty any more, they wanted a product that just didn't go wrong. By the end of the 1980s they were getting it. For example, television sets that last 10 years without a hitch, not a few years. Cars that have lifetime guarantees, like Volvo now has and Vauxhall don't have – yet.

Whilst this was happening, it was creating an effect that marketing people were having to come to terms with. The quality of the product was no longer the main issue. Because customers expect the product to be 'right', the quality of the product began to turn into a 'hygiene factor' for the customer, ie only if it is *below* standard do they notice it.

> ***Whatever the customer now purchases, they expect it to meet their requirements.***

They don't expect it to go wrong. They expect that one product will be of the same 'Quality' as a similar product, because their expectations have been raised beyond measure in the last decade or so.

Price

So, what about the price of the product? Once again, Quality has done a tremendous job. The massive savings to be had through getting it right first time, had not only passed through to the bottom line in terms of profit, it had also benefited the customer in a top line reduction in prices. Once again the customer expects the price to be the keenest.

Whether it be the rates of return on an insurance policy, a bank interest rate, a car, or a packet of sweets, people believe that the price will be competitive and relatively good value from whoever provides it.

Place

Place is clearly important, but with improved logistics and distribution outlets on a local, regional, national and international scale, every producer has been able to gain the same benefits. Customers now have almost instant access to products from all around the globe in *every* High St. Place is no longer a major marketing issue.

Promotion

Promotion is vital, isn't it? Will the creativity of the advertising, branding and sales promotion ensure the success, or otherwise, of a product? It may, but it is questionable if it as critical as it used to be. Everyone's promotion is as good as the skills of their marketing people and these skills are much higher than they used to be. Creativity is not as crucial an issue as it was. In addition, most organisations now recognise the importance of marketing and marketing budgets are also kept in line with competitors. The advantage to be gained from creativity is not as strong.

In the early days of marketing, with the profession just getting started, a skilled marketeer could generate high brand awareness and loyalty on a relatively small budget. With fewer brands to compete against and easier entry into the market place, the promotion of a product could make a big difference. Additionally, it is true to say that customers were more susceptible to hype. They are much more sophisticated now and know what they want from the product.

So if it isn't product, price, place and promotion that the customer decides on, what is it?

Customers demand excellent Service

The 1980s saw a massive increase in the customers' expectation and demand for better service. This started off with a simple form of customer service and moved on to demands for more and better levels of professional service in all their dealings with an organisation. The customer service revolution hit every department that had any contact with customers. Customer service programmes, customer service videos and customer service being focused on by management became the norm.

However, with everyone concentrating on the same thing, the point of differentiation with competitors through customer service, i.e. happy, smiling and helpful staff, soon became lost. The demand for service moved from simple 'smiles' to the need for the organisation to provide a long term relationship with them as customers. The ultimate of this is 'lifetime care', be it for a car, financial service or a television set.

All of this can now be summed up with the term 'Relationship Marketing' (see Figure 10.2).

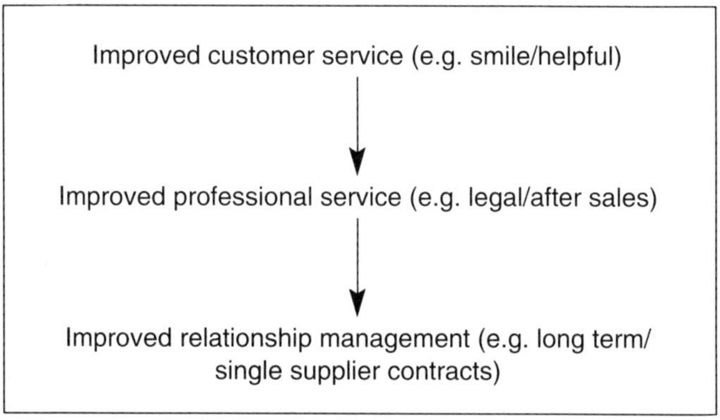

Figure 10.2 The move to improved service

So, the marketeer who has recognised this move from product focus to a focus on service has changed tack. They will be using 'service' as the key strategic plank with which to differentiate their product. Yet once again, all their competitors have recognised the same thing! On television in the early 1990s there are myriad adverts all featuring service. From Lloyds Bank and National Westminster Bank to airlines like British Airways, the smiling faces on the TV screen are there to tempt customers through the promise of excellent customer service. Many organisations have already moved from trying to differentiate their products to offering a friendly, caring, long term level of service that looks after the customer's needs.

Hold on, if everyone is now trying to differentiate by saying the same thing, then they are no longer being differentiated, so how does the customer choose? Having invested millions in customer service programmes, in all sorts of organisations from manufacturing to retail, the reality is that, whilst not perfect, the levels of service are now pretty comparable.

Service is not quite yet the 'hygiene factor' that product is; customers can still be surprised by good service. But it is no longer a key deciding factor.

A 'hygiene factor' is such that when something is 'bad' it puts people off. Big improvements in the levels of service are still possible in many areas but bad service is now more likely to turn people away rather than good service exciting them to want to stay.

In simple terms, if everyone is concentrating on service as the USP (unique selling point), then it is no longer a USP. So what's next?

Added value

'It's not what you do, it's the way that you do it'. This could have summed up the way organisations were supposed to focus in the 1980s, i.e. on the way they treated their customers. But 'the way that you do it' is no longer enough. People are looking for more. More, in the way of extras that are offered, that the competitor doesn't offer. This is 'added value', as far as the customer is concerned.

An excellent example of the move from a focus on product to service to added value is demonstrated by the pharmaceuticals company Eli Lilley. One of the divisions produces the coloured plastic capsules for pills, designed to make them easy to swallow. To get their product right they invested in a Quality programme. It worked and kept them in the forefront of their industry. To keep ahead and focus on customer service, they invested time with all their customers, researching their needs on a regular basis. This relationship management programme ensured that they knew exactly what they should be doing to keep their customers happy. But they didn't stop there.

They next concentrated, not on keeping just one step ahead, but on keeping well ahead. They did this by focusing on added value. They invested in a major programme of collecting and storing data from across the world on pharmaceutical legislation and general information on their industry.

They are now able to give their customers, the drug companies, an unrivalled fund of data which helps them in marketing their product across the world. For example, should a customer want to market a drug in a certain country, they will not only tell them if the legislation allows it, or is likely to allow it, they will also be able to tell them the colour combinations for the capsules of new drugs that are available for use in that country.

Added value not added features

It is not just extra features that people want from products any more. A classic example is all the features on a phone system or a computer system that people cannot understand or never use. It is true added value that people want – like the ability to draw cash out of the supermarket when paying for groceries by credit card, or being able to ensure that future new products can fit into an existing appliance, be it computer, TV, audio etc. Or even like the Australian supermarket chain which allows people to join a club. As a member of this club you get tremendous added value. For example, a computer builds a list of what you buy and when you buy it, creating a pattern of your shopping habits. If you forget something either at the end of a week or month the screen at the till will remind you! Not only that, if you want that product you press a touch sensitive screen. The product is added to your bill and someone brings it for you. If you haven't visited the store for some time, someone rings you up to do some research and ask you if they can help in any way. This is added value.

The main point about added value is that it is something that one supplier offers that others don't – even though they are charging the same price, i.e. it is 'added' to the value of the product or service.

You can charge more for added value but as soon as this happens this simply becomes part of the product offering and is not seen as 'special'.

Clearly, if everyone else is marketing their higher levels of quality of products and of service, the organisation which targets their customers on added value is likely to gain the marketing advantage.

Image

Product quality, Service, Added Value, what next? What is next is all of these and more, that add up to what I call 'Image'. (Some call it reputation).

A positive 'Image' of an organisation is one that makes people want to buy from that organisation. It also makes them want to stay, ideally for life.

As well as its products, its services and the extras it offers, there are a number of other factors which people will take into account when they are considering whether the 'Image' of an organisation is right for them as customers. The list below is indicative of the *positive* images that can be portrayed. It highlights some examples of organisations that are able to trade on the power of the 'Image' portrayed.'

POSITIVE IMAGES	
Environmental image	– Body shop
Historical image	– Parker pens
Staff care	– Marks & Spencer
Innovative image	– Sony
Creative image	– Saatchi & Saatchi
Personality image	– Forte
City image	– Lloyds Bank
Traditional image	– Fortnum & Mason
Shareholder image	– P&O
Entrepreneurial image	– Virgin

Added to this is the *marketing* image portrayed through the use of advertising, design, packaging, corporate logos, PR etc.

MARKETING IMAGES	
Corporate image	– ICI
Brand image	– Mars Bar
Advertising image	– Fairy Liquid
Promotional image	– Tesco
Fun image	– Ladybird Clothes
Serious image	– Bradford & Bingley
Young image	– Our Price Records

Unfortunately for some organisations there are some very strong negative images as well. If the customer is given confidence from the positive images portrayed by an organisation and will develop a relationship for life then a poor image will create lack of confidence and will lead them to stop purchasing from them. Worse than this, as everyone knows, people are far more likely to talk to others when complaining.

So, no matter how good the product quality, the levels of service or even added value, if the customer can get the same or something very similar elsewhere then image will become the deciding factor. A good image is therefore not just a nice to have, it's vital. A negative image will drive customers away and those people will in turn frighten off other customers.

NEGATIVE IMAGES

Self image	–	Ratners ('crap' products)
Advertising image	–	Benetton (AIDS advert)
Dishonesty image	–	Maxwell Corp. (pension funds)
City image	–	Guinness (Ernest Saunders)
Environmental image	–	British Nuclear Fuels (Greenpeace)
Health image	–	All cigarette companies
Political image	–	South African products
Brand image	–	Lada/Skoda/Yugo cars

The image of a product, service or organisation is not built overnight but it can be destroyed overnight. With such tremendous competition, Quality of products, high levels of service and more and more added value for the customer, image may well be the deciding factor.

It is therefore critical for the marketeer to concentrate on image – external and internal.

Having now looked at the requirements of the external customer, the next place to turn attention to is the internal customer.

FROM EMPLOYEE TO INTERNAL CUSTOMER

The term 'employee' has a wealth of meaning that creates the following types of perceptions in organisations. Some of these have been heard too often to be coincidental, and have been taken from a survey of over 2,000 managers and staff in a retail organisation facing problems in recruiting new employees:

1. Employees are 'paid' people, therefore they can be told what to do.
   Wrong – *They now leave and cost a fortune to replace, or worse still quit and stay.*
2. Employees are underlings, I am the manager, they will automatically have to respect the authority vested in me.

***Wrong** – They are too independent minded to take any nonsense from anybody these days. (I remember one research group in which a very insecure manager said that he thought that to move away from the formal title of Mr was a 'bad move'. He felt that it might reduce the respect that his employees had for him!)*

3 Employees are a homogeneous group of people who work for the organisation.
***Wrong** – Just like the outside world, you would be hard pushed, in any collection of people numbering more than a few, to come across a more disparate, fundamentally different group of individuals. The problem that the untrained person has is that they all tend to look 'pretty much the same'. It is therefore very easy to assume that the common term 'employee' can be applied.*

4 Employees work in departments, the factory, the office etc.
***Wrong** – Individuals work in these places. It is like a marketeer saying, for example, that 'Yorkshire is a target market'. Yorkshire is a county, an arbitrary area that has individuals who happen to live there. These individuals can be subdivided into target markets but any marketeer who tries to target a geographic area without further defining exactly who he is aiming at, will soon be out of a job. Not to put too fine a point on it, it is like assuming that America, to take a big example, is a target market. Yet one bank manager told me that his 'machine room' was a target market! This fundamentally ignores the fact that it is people that buy products and services.*
It would be extremely dangerous to target a 'machine room', in which there were two pregnant women, with a message aimed at convincing people about the wonders and joys of information technology, when they had just read an article about the dangers of IT output to unborn babies. This in fact did happen!
This perception only arises because the word 'employee' is seen to reduce everyone to the same status – unless of course you are a 'manager' or a 'Board Director' and then you are different, often seen as having a much greater status.

5 Employees are mainly looking for good pay and conditions.
***Wrong** – The internal products and services that they are now looking for from the organisation are not just money and perks.*

6 Employees are people with few characterstics like honesty and integrity. These qualities are difficult to find when recruiting – especially when

recruiting hourly paid staff.
Wrong – *There are very few cut-throats and thieves in society!*

7 Employees with strong characteristics like, for example, the desire to be involved in their jobs, are not needed to fill what the manager perceives as boring jobs.
Wrong – *The definition of a 'boring job' is not decided by the manager, it is decided by the individual. The feature of both internal and external marketing is that 'beauty is in the eye of the beholder'. The manager who leaps to conclusions and undersells what may be, for example, the most exciting opportunity that an individual has ever had, will be doing themselves a large injustice, and wasting a lot of money. All too frequently, this is the perception of managers when advertising positions. Indeed, in the excitement stakes, the term 'job' is on a par with the term 'employee' when it comes to expressive terminology! You only have to look at the rows of dull, factual and often off-putting job advertisements to realise that most of the people marketing these positions perceive the readers to be dull people looking for boring jobs.*

So, we have a derogatory and dull term used to describe all the amazingly complex and varied internal target markets. The term creates a perception something akin to the term 'peasant'. Unfortunately, perception is all. If this is to change with the quality revolution, where everyone is a *customer*, then the easiest way to do it is for the term to change. The word 'employee' must disappear and be replaced by 'customer' and 'supplier'. This creates different perceptions, placing the importance on the individual. It also reflects the need to apply marketing techniques, when attempting to market or sell products and services in the chain.

It is only when the word customer is mentioned that people in organisations really do begin to listen. And it is not to complain about how 'awkward' they are, as used to happen. Their significance has finally got through.

The focus that marketing has put into organisations is definitely on the external customer, with the Quality focus being on the internal customer. The concept of internal customers is understood, but unlike in marketing no one quite knows how to put in the practice of reaching them. That is where marketing comes in. So, to the biggest mental hurdle yet in changing the perceptions within an organisation. If you have accepted that the term 'employee' is no longer acceptable, then the next step must be to replace it with something that is!

To a marketeer there can only be one term used to describe people who buy products and services – customers. The same is true internally. In groups customers are called 'target markets'. The same terminology can be used internally or externally.

When talking about individuals the term is customers; put a number of them together and the term should be 'target market'.

A target market has a number of characteristics. These have similarities allowing them all to be put into one group which can be targeted with the same type and style of marketing message.

Clearly, within an organisation the number of times that an attempt will be made to target them all will be very limited. Even with a 'sheep dip' type campaign, i.e. one with the broadest of messages such as customer care, it must be recognised that the very breadth of the target market makes it inappropriate to call it a target market.

The consequent watering down of the message to cater for all tastes, means that in the truest sense of the word, all the employees in an organisation cannot be classed as a single target market. Life would be too easy if that were the case.

On top of this, because external marketing has moved such a long way since its true emergence in the 1960s, the internal marketeer is going to have to cope with a much more sophisticated set of people. These people are now used to the quality and quantity of marketing messages that they are hit with every day. This is not just true of the common perception of what marketing is all about – advertising – it is true of all the other disciplines in marketing: the design, the packaging, the branding, the promotion, the PR etc. These have yet to be truly practised in the internal market but they are already so well established in the external market place, that there is a lot of catching up to do! It also means that the impact of well produced internal campaigns is likely to be a lot less strong than might have been the case a decade or two ago. This is made worse by a symptom of internal marketing which creates more demand for better quality and quantity of the internal marketing itself and also the products that the individual demands. This is called the 'Oliver Syndrome' – but 'more' of that later (pun intended!).

Some organisations are still in the stone age when it comes to the techniques that are being used to target and reach their internal target markets. It has been said 'The memo is to internal marketing what the sandwich board is to advertising'.

The rest of the world has moved along. In fact, whilst the view is that external marketing is now light years ahead of the internal marketing of most organisations, times are definitely changing internally as well.

The comparisons that now exist are that some 'employees' are being told what to do via messages as subtle as a stone age club, while in other organisations individual target markets are being hit with messages transmitted by the latest in technology (like interactive video) sent by internal marketing and communication departments. The message becomes very clear to someone looking for a new job or looking for a move!

The 'people' in an organisation are therefore not a mass market, they are a many and varied collection of individual customers in niche target markets. The realisation and recognition of this will in itself create the biggest change in attitude, as managers begin to see that they can no longer hide behind traditional methods of 'managing'. Having begun to strongly suspect these methods are not working, managers will not start to recognise that internal target markets need as much caution in approach as external markets.

Managers are realising that the internal world is changing and that the role they traditionally played in filtering, siphoning, stopping and distorting information is one which they can no longer afford to play.

The methods of transferring information these days allow the internal target markets to be reached by working around the blockages if necessary.

If managers are to survive and grow with an organisation then they will have to adapt to the new demands being placed on them. The biggest of these will be to use all the tools and techniques of marketing to create people who are ready, willing and able to carry out the enormous demands that are being placed on them.

This pressure is part and parcel of the trade-off in organisations. This trade-off says that whilst we, the organisation, are placing demands on you as an individual, we will do our utmost to provide you with the products and services that you need from us.

In order that this can happen there needs to be a clearly defined methodology in defining the internal target markets – the next stage of the internal marketing process. There is still a long way to go, in terms of the level of sophistication, but a start has to be made somewhere!

Without the benefit of having all the marketing and research data on external customers that was mentioned earlier, such as ACORN analysis, etc. the problem is, **where to start?** ***I believe that the KISS PRINCIPLE is best (see page 21)***

The internal customer segments: individuals

Quality has helped organisations accept that people can no longer be seen as

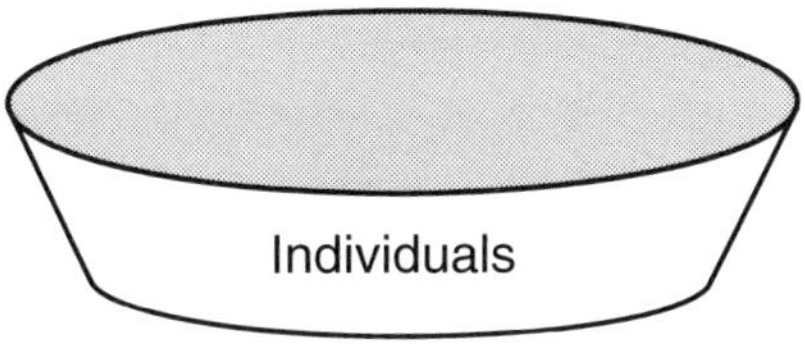

Figure 10.3 The segmented individuals

'employees' and that the next move is simply to see them as individual internal customers. Everyone in the organisation would then be seen as having a unique set of characteristics that need to be taken into account whenever they are on the receiving end of marketing tools and techniques. The picture can be built up from there as necessary.

Once the organisation buys into the new language and philosophy that internal customers actually are different to employees, and that they cannot be told what to do, the questions will be asked 'What skills do I need to be able to deal with my customers inside the organisation? How can I, as a supplier, and they, as customers with their own needs and desires, get what we both want?'

The answer to the first question, about skills, is that it is necessary to define the needs and desires of the individual customer. In other words, before a marketeer decides, for example, what the advertising campaign might look like, he needs to find out what people want and therefore what they might buy. So, it is a good idea to do your homework before attempting to answer the questions set. In this case, the homework is *research*. The answer to the second question about both organisation and individual getting what they want is revealed below.

Before going any further, it may be wise to point out that many an ill informed manager believes (too often for comfort) that they always know what their 'employees' want. The list would probably look something like this:

1 Good pay
2 Good conditions
3 Good holidays
4 Free lunches
5 Good pension
6 Good hours
7 Nice colleagues

8 Good prospects
9 Perks
10 Good annual review

The permutations may be slightly different but essentially all of these are the classic ingredients of the standard job advert. The amazing thing is, that there is nothing there that is remotely connected to the quality of the work, the quality of the leadership, or the input that the organisation will give to the individual to become effective in what they can, or might be able to do.

What do individuals want from your organisation

OK so you might have included good training! Well here's the challenge. Place the requirements in Figure 10.4 in order of importance – create the Top Ten Internal Practices for your organisation. This exercise is included

Put in order of importance 1–10

Information	(e.g. Information/Newsletters etc)	______
Pay/reward	(i.e. Financial Inducements)	______
Involvement	(With Quality and Innovation)	______
Future/security	(Length of stay/Wanting to stay)	______
Career	(Prospects)	______
Development	(Multi-Skilling)	______
Training	(Job/People/Management skills)	______
Leadership/ management	(Local and National)	______
Induction	(Joining a new/Another job)	______
Recruitment/ promotion	(Being selected)	______

Fig. 10.4 The top ten internal practices

here to make you think about what your internal customers really want from your organisation.

Is pay top of your list?

Where did you place pay? Top of the list? But pay is a given, its a hygiene factor. The only time that people can influence it is at salary review time, usually only once a year. Even then it is left up to the Unions to deal with it in most organisations.

Our experience is that pay is often raised as an issue when other things are wrong. It marks the real issue of dissatisfaction and this is usually bad leadership/management.

Of course pay can be an issue to people. If they are well trained, led, involved and more than fully contributing, then they will say that they need to be compensated, and why not?

What about job satisfaction?

Job satisfaction comes from all of these issues. Actually doing the job with no leadership, involvement, training etc. will provide little or no satisfaction. This list breaks down the job satisfaction into its key components.

So, what is the right order?

There isn't one! Just like a Top Ten, people want to hear different 'tunes' played at different times. All you have to do to find out which tune, is to ask them. The simple trick of matching the needs of the organisation with the needs of the individual, is to 'play' the tune they want to hear most. When you have done that, then you can ask or demand their involvement to meet the organisation's needs.

To take a concrete example. Say you want to get people involved in a Quality programme. If, however, they feel badly inducted, badly led, badly trained, little security and that they have no future, how can you possibly expect them to want to get it right at all. Never mind right first time! No wonder they ignore the suggestions schemes. Why should they bother? Having run a workshop with a team of Quality managers and consultants, this blinding flash of the obvious led to one person saying 'I've been running Total Quality programmes for 10 years now, no wonder people don't want to get involved and so many failed, I never once thought about meeting their needs as a customer.'

The Top Ten changes all the time

One organisation we dealt with highlights the changing needs of the internal customer. Initially, research on the Top Ten internal practices showed that the two key issues were leadership and training. Simply, the managers did not get involved with the staff, and the training was very poor at staff level.

Within months, huge overseas losses, a possible acquisition and redundancies of many thousands, put future/security at the top of the list. There is no point internally marketing training courses when people's jobs are on the line. Sadly, many organisations actually ignore the key needs of people in situations like this, often because they don't know what to do, or they think it's best to lie low. The grapevine then takes over. In my experience a policy of 'open and honest' works every time.

The top ten pattern

Having said that the Top Ten changes, it is clear from our research that it does follow a pattern. This pattern is one that you would expect would happen as a person progresses through their role. The order is in reverse to the challenge on the previous page.

1 **Recruitment/promotion**
If you haven't got the job, then this is obviously your number one issue!
Many organisations focus on this area believing this is the main plank of their internal marketing. Glossy brochures, milk rounds, local and national PR to attract people. These are all done to make people feel good about the organisation before they join. Then what happens? And how often is the marketing done only for external recruitment? Internal promotion is just as critical to people trying to move up the ladder.

2 **Induction**
How many organisations can honestly say, that they 'package' their induction programmes so that every new recruit or newly promoted person is well inducted. Do they get an induction pack, a career file to take with them during their stay, a scheduled training programme etc. Or do they get 'thrown in at the deep end'?
Research in one organisation showed that properly inducted people in one department stayed three times longer than people in a similar department. So, if induction is a key customer need, it needs marketing.

3 **Leadership**
Once recruited and inducted into a new role, the most important need following this is that of the 'local leader' or boss.

There is no ideal leader. However, how he or she is seen, behaves and interacts with the internal customers is a key issue. Some say the leadership they need is very 'hands on' and 'directive'. This would especially be so for a box type internal customer. A 'squiggle' would prefer to be left alone and his ideal boss may be one he doesn't see for weeks. So, is there a magical formula?

In essence, no. What is needed is for the leader's role to be communicated and for the individual's needs to be taken into account and met. If a 'Top Ten' is carried out on a whole team, and leadership dominates the individuals and team list, this suggests some strong messages to the manager concerned. Interestingly, there is a strong correlation point between 'poor' leadership, a leadership featuring highly on people's Top Ten and 'pay and reward'. When people's leadership need is met, pay too, is not a major influencer.

4 Training

High on the list of internal customers' needs must be how they are trained to do their job. If this is an important need, then why is training marketed so badly? The actual courses may be fine, but the promotion and packaging are often totally ignored. A typical approach is 'there is a course on XYZ – I want to go on it next week'. Where is the research, design, testing, targeting etc?

If people feel their needs are being well looked after by the organisation, they will give more and stay happier and longer.

5 Development

Training allows you to do the job, development prepares you for promotion or multi-skilling. With flatter structures, multi-skilling becomes the only outlet for people's needs to grow their skills and talents. And not just in work. Development outside work is as vital to some people to retain motivation. Ford run the Employee Development Assistance Programme (EDAP), which provides a cash allowance to learn new skills outside the workplace e.g. languages, yoga etc. Imagine the increased commitment to the organisation if it truly looks after its internal customers.

Midland Bank run LEAP, a free to use library and training materials service. Kellogg's do the same. Rover run a scheme similar to Ford.

If 'Development' is marketed well it is one step nearer to gaining involvement in Quality programmes.

6 Future/security

In the 1980s this was not very high on internal customer's lists in a lot of organisations. Indeed for some, keeping people was an almost impossible task. Spiralling wages chased low levels of people on the job market. The economic climate has changed and this is now number one on people's list.

But how are their needs to be met? Does the organisation have a strategic and tactical approach to the bad news. External PR organisations see bad news as a core issue to an organisation's external marketing strategy. Does the same apply to internally? How often do the leaders communicate what is happening? Is it as open and honest as it is with shareholders and the City? This doesn't mean revealing sensitive data. It does mean communicating often and responding to feedback. Otherwise demotivation, rumour and strife are likely to occur. The answer may not be the company magazine! If this is already perceived propaganda, as is so often the case, then other internal marketing media and methods are required.

7 **Career**

Flat structures make promotion more difficult, but not impossible! How are your organisation's career prospects marketed? Do they live up to the promise made during recruitment? Are there photocopied notices on the notice boards? Are successful people marketed?

If a career is number one on people's list and prospects look bleaker than they really are, they will look elsewhere – once recession is over.

8 **Involvement – in Quality and innovation**

And here is the crunch. It is only now that they are well recruited, well inducted, well led, well trained and developed, feel secure and confident about the organisation and their role now and in the future, that people want to be involved in improving, innovating and being involved in the organisation. Indeed, it will be their 'Number One'. They will *want* to be involved. They will welcome Quality programmes. Q.E.D. Quality won't fail because no one will want it to fail.

There are two sorts of involvement. The first is in Quality issues, i.e. constant improvement on what *exists*. The second is in innovation, i.e. coming up with *new* ideas and selling them through introduction.

Too often organisations concentrate on good ideas, i.e. new ways of doing things. This is innovation, often described as what you *should* do. Constant improvement via Best Practice focuses on what you *are* doing. The two are totally different. Best Practice is covered in depth later.

9 **Pay and reward**

This is *financial* or other physical reward, e.g. incentives. It is my fundamental belief that pay is not a key ongoing issue. Once a level of pay is accepted it is not a motivator. It is only a demotivator if it is below a person's perceived self worth and all the other motivators are not enough to counteract 'low' pay.

People will work in the most appalling conditions with very low levels of pay if the leadership is good.

This suggests that an investment in management skills should be a fundamental part of dealing with pay issues, i.e. too much is paid to compensate for poor leadership.

When it comes to incentives, these are only generally needed once people really are providing *extra* worth. This occurs when they are involved in Quality and Innovation. It happens when they really are over-delivering against expectation. Incentives are not necessary to motivate average performers, a 'thank you' and good leadership should do that. Too often incentive schemes are introduced to replace poor management motivation. They don't. They then lead to major problems from those who don't gain the incentives. On top of this, the levels of expectation rise higher and higher. As Oliver Twist said, 'more'!

10 Communication

This is perceived as a key requirement in most organisations. Attitude survey after attitude survey says, for example, 86 per cent of people think our communication is poor'. What do they mean?

They mean no-one is telling them about the things they think are important. Well, we have just covered them. Improve the marketing of the other nine areas and 'communication' is not a problem. What is left is what I call 'Information'. This covers the rest of the news and data that are not covered in the rest of the Top Ten.

It is no wonder that people feel badly communicated with, when there is a lack of any cohesive policy on the issues that affect them. Training does its own thing. Head Office news covers another area. Team Briefing cascades something else. Very little is labelled, branded, packaged, marketed, sold, or sustained. Very little is pulled together.

Yet without realising it most organisations are doing a lot in all of these areas. Once they pull it together, then real communication starts to occur. This is what individual internal customers want, to feel that their needs are met. Once they have that, they will usually give their all. This is when they cease to become just individuals and start to act as part of a team.

The internal customer segments: teams

Enough has been written by training experts and psychologists on the subject of teams in terms of their composition, their dynamics and the 'how

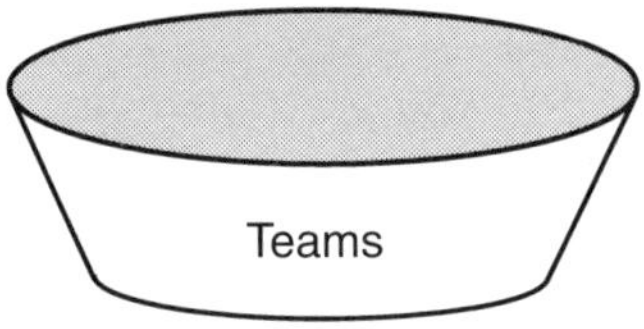

Figure 10.5 The segmented teams

to', when it comes to being part of them. What is unique to the marketeer is that they do not usually have to target their message to more than one, or at most two people. Even in a family situation there is one key decision maker.

The dynamics of team based environments are such that even the decision maker is likely to be heavily influenced, on a permanent basis, by the team. The politics, jockeying for position, the posturing, the emotions, the styles, the back stabbing, will all play a part. In short, the Attitudes, Awareness, and Abilities of the individuals will impact on each other.

The requirements of the team to produce, so that all the inputs of the individuals will influence the outcome, often mean they are effectively performing as one unit.

The problem is – how to market a group of disparate individuals with one consistent message that will be targeted to them all!

In addition to this, the problem is intensified by the changing nature of business. The flatter structures, the looser hierarchies, and the fast responses required today are all producing more and more teams. By their nature they are less formal, they come together very quickly and disband again, they are issue orientated, and rely on very effective communication processes. These processes also need to be effective with the rest of the organisation. A classic example of this would be the Service circle/Quality circle. Their importance has now been recognised in the UK.

The key to ensuring that the Quality message does spread, is in the way the information is gathered and shared. One excellent example, or should I say hundreds of examples, of Quality circles, is in the Royal Mail. The Quality concept has taken such a hold in the organisation that Quality circles provide a tremendous amount of drive and innovation throughout the Royal Mail, and its various divisions such as Streamline and Quadrant.

To market the ideas generated by the Quality circles and teams, an annual Quality event is held in Milton Keynes. Teams from all over the country in each of the divisions exhibit their ideas. In addition to this, there is a data bank of Best Practices held on a computer that anyone can access. This contains information from moving an office to operational systems. The problem is making sure that enough people are aware of the Best Practice data bank and want to access it.

The marketing of Best Practice is crucial to stop a major malaise that occurs in all organisations, that of 'reinventing the wheel'. The wheel continues to be reinvented despite the introduction of Quality. In fact there may be even more people and teams inventing and reinventing the same policies, procedures and practices throughout organisations. This costs organisations dearly and subverts the process of Quality spreading throughout the customer-supplier chain.

A key need of teams to be well communicated with

Now that many organisations rely on team-based structures, communication to teams is critical. These may be permanent teams, or as is increasingly the case, they may be ad hoc teams that have been put together for a specific purpose, for example a project or problem solving. The nature of a team-based environment is that there is no real formal structure or reporting lines. But communication is exceedingly difficult without the formal structures in place.

It is worth pointing out here that one solution that a considerable number of organisations tried to adopt was that of 'Team Briefing'. As a process this has a number of flaws which are highlighted in the 'egg timer' effect. How do you overcome these? In short, instead of attempting to go around the people, like managers or team leaders who provide the bottleneck, the process called 'Team Listening' allows these people simply to act as facilitators. They check the knowledge, and motivate their team members who have been *previously* targeted with the information.

So how does the team listening approach work?

The individuals receive a targeted piece of information in the form of a magazine or partwork from their manager *prior* to the meeting. This contains both policy/strategic information and local tactical news, and team members will be able to read, understand and digest the contents before attending the meeting.

The benefits to the manager are such that he or she becomes a facilitator or coach, checking understanding and agreeing goals as opposed to presenting or talking at his people.

The benefits to the organisation are that the meetings are shorter, the core message is understood and a move towards an involvement and

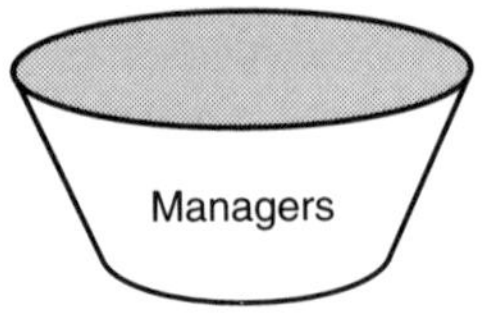

Figure 10.6 The managers segmented

listening culture is achieved. (Team Listening is covered in greater depth later.)

The internal customer segments: managers

If plenty has been written about teams, then even more has been written about managers. In the context of the customer-supplier chain, managers make an interesting internal target market. The only reason that they can justify being an internal target market is their position, which creates a set of characteristics, sufficient to allow the overriding position of these people to produce a target group.

This is a similar classification to the one of 'Leader', in that the position is itself the deciding factor of their targeting. There is one big difference however, as you will see.

Saying the word 'manager' is like saying that the position of say 'father' or 'mother' provides a target market. Of course there are products and services that these people will have to buy that are pertinent to their position, but to suggest that it is the position itself and not the people who occupy them will lead to producing some generalisations which could lead up a blind alley. Thus, for example, a father or mother living in a high rise flat with 10 children and no income, will be a totally different proposition to a father or mother whose children have left home and who are enjoying the benefits of no mortgage and high incomes.

The differences within the classification 'manager' may seem obvious, but having suggested that 'managers' can be seen as internal target markets, to leave it at that would be to consent that the classification is valid.

> ***In the absence of effective research, and a great deal more work on the classification of people in management positions, the use of 'manager' as a term for target markets will have to suffice for the present.***

Why is this classification important? It is only necessary to think of the myriad pieces of information and 'communication' that flow at this internal target market to realise that the classification already exists in people's minds. What does not exist is the realisation that the recipients of this deluge are not just 'managers'; it is only their title! They are people who effectively need to be put into defined segments. These would then have to become target markets, by having similar needs, desires and likes and dislikes in terms of the design and style of messages. They would also need to be marketed to with a piece of communication targeted at them.

Not only are managers a target market, they are also the source of a great deal of communication, information, motivation and integration.

Managers need to be able to practise marketing on their own internal customers. Of course the same holds true of everyone in the organisation who has customers. It is however, especially true of the manager who, being in a position of authority, has more customers and more responsibility for these customers.

The concept of the 'marketing' manager should be no more alien than the concept of the customer-supplier chain. Yet how many organisations train their managers, other than those in marketing, in marketing techniques? Even where they do, the marketing techniques are for dealing with the external customer.

British Rail have got there!

One organisation that has made a start in training their managers in an integrated approach to marketing is British Rail. Their management centre at The Grove, in Hertfordshire, now has courses to teach managers to use marketing skills in their everyday jobs, looking after internal as well as external customers.

Figure 10.7 is the first three pages of a pre-course, magazine style communication and the last page shows the workshop outline. This explains how to turn an inward facing manager into a customer facing 'marketing' manager.

The internal customer segments: leaders

Are your leaders providing the organisation with direction?

Does the process of segmenting apply to leaders as it applies to managers? Are leaders as identifiable as managers who have titles and obvious areas of responsibility?

Practical Marketing from within

ADVANCED BUSINESS SKILLS

Pre-Workshop Workbook

WHAT'S THIS WORKSHOP ALL ABOUT?

This workshop will not only take the mystery out of marketing for you, but also give you a chance to learn and use the secrets of the magic behind this key business discipline.

Marketing has really only one key objective:-

"To satisfy customer needs in order to generate profit"

With this in mind this workshop will cover:-

- A SWOT research analysis - Strengths, Weaknesses, Opportunities and Threats.
- The use of targeting, using hooks and benefits.
- The tools and techniques of marketing.
- How to apply the principles of marketing in your everyday work experience.

THE TOOLS TO USE

"It's all very well knowing that you have to do some marketing but how do you do it?" It's like knowing you need to fix the car but you don't even have the spanner. We'll give you enough in the toolbox for you to do a routine service. For example, you'll be able to carry out a 'SWOT' check on all your customers.

WHAT ARE OUR OBJECTIVES IN RUNNING THE WORKSHOP?

We want you to:-

- Broaden your perspective - to see the business through the eyes of Marketers.
- Develop your knowledge - We believe you will gain a tremendous advantage from learning about the discipline of marketing.
- Enjoy learning how to apply the skills internally and externally in the organisation.

WHAT'S IN IT FOR YOU?

Below, we've outlined some of the 'hooks' or benefits for you to attend this workshop:-

These break down into 4 main learning areas. We call these the 4 'A's - after all, this is a marketing course!

Attitude - You'll feel and be confident about using marketing skills in your everyday environment.

Awareness - You'll understand and be able to use the methods of reacting to and targeting your customers with the right messages.

Ability - You'll develop some real tools and techniques, such as copy writing skills, useful for every type of communication.

Actual - You'll have at your finger tips the data on your internal and external customers to market effectively to them.

Figure 10.7 Pre-workshop workbook – practical marketing from within

The Buzz Words!

...Marketing made simple

THE 'SWOT' CHECK

This is another one of those acronyms! It simply means Strengths, Weaknesses, Opportunities, Threats.

Marketing people use these simple headings to generate the analysis that is needed when making long term and short-term decisions. The 'SWOT' analysis can be used on just about any topic e.g. Products, Services, People, Structure, Competitors etc.

We'll show you how to take this a few stages further, on page 4.

TARGETING

In the early days of marketing, advertising people used to target their customers in a buckshot type approach! Lots of money was wasted on expensive campaigns, Companies advertised in magazines, or on television, to people, the majority of whom would never buy, just to catch the few who would. Today, direct mail into your home targets you with the precision of a laser rifle. So how can you target your messages with the same precision? The Thomson Whitwell Customer Style Indicator on page 6 will help you do just that!

THE HOOKS

This is a form used to identify what makes people want to buy. It's the "What's in it for them" factor. Why do so many products and services fail to attract customers? Why is it that so many internal campaigns e.g. Quality, Customer Service, fail to get people motivated?

Our research of the Top 10 of people's needs goes a long way to explaining this! You'll find out more about the Hooks on page 7.

Figure 10.7 continued

Getting Your Customers Interested

Targeting

Once you've researched your customers and found out what they think and what they want from you, how do you now get them to 'buy' from you? Why should they be interested in what you have to say, after all, they are bombarded with thousands of messages and images every day?

Opposite is a technique, based on the use of colour, design and language to help you target your message more effectively. It's called The Customer Style Indicator - photocopy this and you and your customers can have a go at filling it in.

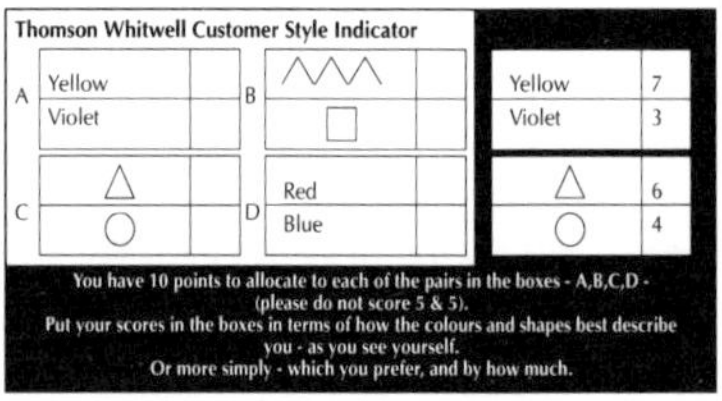

Thomson Whitwell Customer Style Indicator
A
Yellow
Violet
B
C
D
Red
Blue
Yellow 7
Violet 3
6
4
You have 10 points to allocate to each of the pairs in the boxes - A,B,C,D - (please do not score 5 & 5).
Put your scores in the boxes in terms of how the colours and shapes best describe you - as you see yourself.
Or more simply - which you prefer, and by how much.

COLOUR

Marketing people use colour in just about everything. It is used to differentiate and to create appeal. Here are some obvious examples where colour makes a big difference.

PRODUCTS	-	CARS, CLOTHES
PACKAGING	-	SOAP POWDER, SWEETS
PRINT	-	MAGAZINES, MAIL SHOTS
PROMOTIONS	-	COUPONS, COUNTER DISPLAYS

What's not so obvious is why people are attracted to certain colours and what the colours can mean.

Exercise

What do the following colour schemes convey in one or two words.

BP	-	Green & Yellow
McDonalds	-	Red & Yellow
ICI	-	Blue

We'll discuss the implications on the workshop.

LANGUAGE

The first way you express yourself to customers is in the language you use. The following is a simple test showing some extremes.

Simply tick which in the following pairs of words appeal to you

A	New	☐	Safe	☐
B	Exciting	☐	Tried and Tested	☐
C	Ideas	☐	Facts	☐
D	Uncertain	☐	Certain	☐

So what will turn on your target audience when you talk to them, make presentations, write a memo, or even design posters and magazines?

DESIGN

Just like colour, the design of something, from a product like a car to the layout of an advert on a page, is vital to attracting people.

Exercise - Pull out any advert from a magazine you like and bring it along. What attracts you to the advert, the way the advert is designed, or the way products are designed?

Figure 10.7 continued

Practical Marketing
ADVANCED BUSINESS SKILLS

i

WORKSHOP OUTLINE

Stage 1 Introductions - Ice breakers

Researching the backgrounds of course delegates.

Stage 2 Course Objectives - The 'WHY' concept

What's the module about?
Hooks - What's in it for you?
Your aim when marketing.

Stage 3 Buzz Words - Introducing Key Marketing Concepts

'SWOT' - A marketing analysis
'Hooks' - Benefits
'Targeting' - Right messages

Stage 4 Customer Profile - Understanding customers

Typical data from course delegates.
Group analysis

Stage 5 'SWOT' The Marketing Audit

Group feedback pre-course work
One to one exercise.
Case study

Stage 6 Targeting -Customer Style Indicator

Individual styles
Group styles
Colour and case study (Midland Bank)
Design and case study (Esso)
Language and case study (Royal Mail)

Stage 7 Hooks - Top Ten Customer Needs

External customer needs
Internal business needs
Internal customer needs.

Stage 8 A Marketing Model - Marketing Meets Quality

External customers
Products and services
Marketing and sales
Internal customers
Customer Supplier Chain

Figure 10.7 continued

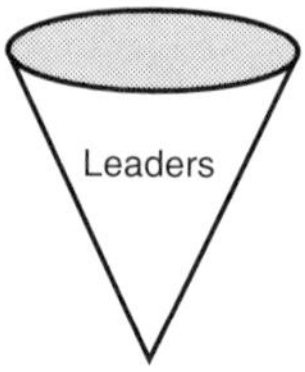

Figure 10.8 The segmented leaders

Yes, but the one important difference is that the 'leaders' of an organisation do not have to be in formal positions of authority. They can be anywhere in the organisation, holding any position. They will tend to be leaders as a result of their personality, charisma and strength of character. It is therefore more likely that there will be more similarities between them, in comparison to the much wider group of 'managers'. Once again, however, the classification is really only one of immediate convenience until more accurate targeting can be done.

The one thing that can be said of most leaders in any organisation wherever they may be in that organisation, is that they like to be at the top! A leader will inevitably choose the triangle shape on the Customer Style Indicator where the pinnacle is at the top. This represents their position, be it as chief executive, departmental manager, team leader or supervisor. The pinnacle they perceive represents themselves. It may be their position now or where they would like to be in the future.

The model of a spinning top does not allow for this quirk of human nature. The leader is placed firmly at the bottom which would appear to undermine their authority. Is this the case?

No. Not if the leader sees their position as being crucial to the future success and direction of the organisation. They are at the point of this spinning top. They control its direction.

> ***Will the leader take the organisation in a straight line? Will they go all over the place, or will they even go backwards! How quickly will they get there? How smooth or bumpy will the journey be?***

The leader's role is a supportive one. They cannot do it all by themselves. However, in this model they must bear the weight of the rest of the organisation as they take it forward. Their role is in determining how, when and where it goes – whether they are local, national or international. The rest of the customers in the chain will be carried with them. The leader supports their actions and provides clarity of thought and purpose. Their role is to create the right policies.

Because the personality of the leader is important, as well as the policies that they create, it is vital that both of these are marketed to the customer-supplier chain.

It is the leaders role to market themselves and their policies. They do this by adopting the practices of marketing, e.g. MBMA. They also need to ensure that everyone else in the organisation is capable of meeting customer needs. So everyone needs MBMA. This is often a huge culture shift.

Surprisingly, with the massive changes going on in the public sector many leaders are recognising this culture shift much more.

Examples of leaders deciding to turn their organisation upside down and create a marketing-driven environment are: Richard Prescott in ITSA Procurement Services mentioned earlier, and John Morgan and Richard Bullard in British Rail Business Systems. Their policy is to ensure all their people are capable of delivering a quality service to their customers, be they internal or external. This includes giving them the skills to do this, e.g. marketing sales, consultancy, customer care. This is what leadership is all about, providing the direction then letting people create and sustain their own momentum.

The four internal target markets – a summary

It is interesting that this set of internal target markets, individual internal customers, teams, managers and leaders is reminiscent of the socio-economic groupings ABC1.

However, it is not necessary at this stage of the development of marketing in the customer-supplier chain to invent new groupings, classifications or titles. The conceptual leap of recognising that internal customers are, in reality, internal target markets, is sufficient. This will create the realisation that if 'communication' is to get better, the only way to do it is for the 'communicator' to recognise that they must become internal marketeers.

People need to be comfortable with having to deal with only four internal target markets. These need to correspond to their present conception of an organisation structure. Experience using the classifications to date indicates that people are very comfortable with the four internal target markets. If from here, the level of sophistication can grow, as has happened in external marketing, then so be it.

BUT WHAT DO YOU MARKET?

The apparent complexity of organisations is enough to create confusion in the best of corporate planners. So what chance does the average individual stand when it comes to knowing what the organisation can give to them and expect from them? What chance does the supplier in the customer-supplier chain have of knowing what their customers want, be they internal or external.

Each day people turn up for work and things just happen to be there. Someone somewhere, is always responsible for having produced or organised things, and in general terms it is pretty obvious why they are there – or is it? The next chapter describes *what* to market.

SUMMARY

- Customers expect more than the 4 Ps. They want service, added value and a positive organisational image.
- Constantly research what individuals want from your organisation. Their needs are not static.
- Teams are important parts of the organisation. They need to be well communicated with – and be able to communicate themselves.
- The classification 'manager' may contain many different types of people, but they all need to know how to 'market'.
- Leaders need to market themselves and their policies. Their role is critical at the point of the spinning top.

11 WHAT TO MARKET TO YOUR INTERNAL CUSTOMERS – THE NEW 4 Ps

WHAT ARE THE PRODUCTS AND SERVICES THAT THE ORGANISATION NEEDS TO MARKET TO ITS INTERNAL CUSTOMERS?

The last chapter dealt with the internal target markets in order to establish the existence of internal customer segments in the organisation. This chapter looks at doing the same for what the organisation produces for its internal customers. This is the starting point to put everything that the organisation does into context. Now, there are only two more steps to go in the process of marketing throughout the customer-supplier chain.

Step 1: If you accept that the people in the organisation are internal target markets, then the next step is to recognise that these markets buy internal 'products' and 'services'.

Step 2: Internal 'products' (like a training manual) and 'services' (like a Mission) must be viewed as the outputs the organisation provides its internal customers. These outputs allow the internal customers to fulfil their function. To keep it simple, we have called these the New 4 Ps – Policy, Procedures, Plans, Practices.

> ***Suddenly a whole new light is cast on the way that the organisational issues are put across to the people. Marketing to the internal customer-supplier chain becomes a reality.***

In external marketing terms the concepts are plain. If someone says or does something to assist you to achieve a desired result, it is called a 'service'. If someone provides you with a physical article that is designed to meet specific needs, then it is a 'product'.

In marketing to the internal customer, the service is generally of a consultancy nature (Policy, Products, Plans). It is what most managers and leaders spend a lot of their time doing. They provide consultancy, on behalf of the organisation, in order to facilitate the processes necessary for producing the product. The output of this consultancy, be it a method, solution etc., is the service.

The internal products provided can be anything physical which the individuals can utilise to help them achieve the goals they are set. Thus, a training manual is a 'product', as is a staff room, notice board, meals at work, a pension, etc. (Practices).

Having gone to all the trouble to produce these internal 'products' and 'services' the methodology of marketing ensures that their use is maximised. All this adds up to a policy of MBMA by the leaders.

These tools and techniques are all documented throughout this book and include research, creative, development of products and services, testing them, launch, measurement, systemising, sustaining, promoting and improving.

Once everyone is trained in marketing it doesn't matter who or where their customers are. They will recognise the importance of being closer to the customer. This is the vital cultural change needed in all organisations, so that everyone benefits.

Each of the new 4 Ps is particularly important for one of the four segments of the internal customer-supplier chain. In the previous chapter we built the customer chain segments 'top down' from the most important person, the external customer. In order to build up the model with regard to the internal products and services, it is more logical to do it 'bottom up'.

THE FIRST OF THE NEW 4 Ps – POLICY

The whole essence of this model is to put the leaders at the base of the organisation. If the leaders are at the point of the spinning top then the key service that they provide is the direction of the organisation. It is on this issue that all else sits.

Direction is fundamental to the organisation. It provides the goals that people strive for. The way that leaders market the direction that they are taking the organisation, is through the first of the internal 4 Ps – Policy.

It is not the purpose of this book to discuss the actual internal products and services themselves in any great depth. The role of marketing is to take those products and services and ensure that they meet the requirements of the organisation and the individuals so that they can be successfully integrated.

The way in which Policy is internally marketed is interesting because it is probably among the worst examples of this form of marketing that can be

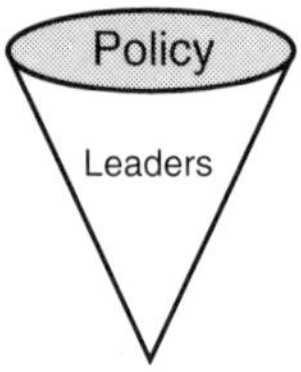

Figure 11.1 What 'direction' will be marketed?

found! It isn't for the want of trying. I believe that most CEOs and the Boards of virtually all organisations would be upset to think that their key output is not being, at the very least, transmitted, and at best, bought into. For example, how many 'mission statements' produced on pieces of laminated card are forgotten or discarded?

The key problem is recognising the difference between 'absorption' and 'impact' of the message. The key decision makers in organisations spend many hours in debate to produce the future direction. The problem is, they have had the benefit of this debate, and in the process of the debate, have had plenty of time to absorb the changes. The rest of the organisation is left to change their thinking, or otherwise, from, at worst, a paragraph or two on the wall and, at best, a conference supported by a front page spread on the company newspaper.

By mistaking impact for absorption, many organisations believed that they were able to change cultures in one fell swoop and then forget about it.

Marketing does not stop

When CEOs recognise that the discipline of marketing must also be used internally, then the organisation will start to move – in the direction that they want!

When CEOs also start to recognise that what is good for them, is also good for the rest of the organisation, then the rest of the organisation may become as committed and as capable as they are in their own sphere of 'excellence' – why should the individuals not have the benefit of constructive debate, well thought out presentations, sound logic and reasoning behind all the proposals being put forward etc.

Unfortunately, even if the people responsible for putting the policies across believe in the messages, if they have not been trained in how to effectively market and sell them internally, then the process breaks down. If this is true of apparently simple things like mission statements, (which, when boiled down, can be one or two sentences long) then what chance more complicated issues?

Add to this the problem of leaders themselves only showing temporary commitment to the internal service they provide, and is it no wonder that there is a great deal of cynicism about it. It is like a salesman selling something which neither he, nor you, really believe does the job required. Alternatively, the product may have taken lots of preparation and launching, but if it is then forgotten for something new, or left to others less qualified to champion, once again it will fail.

The other side of the coin is that, if marketed correctly, the policies will provide an almost unstoppable momentum for the future direction. The spinning top will go where the leaders want it to go. But what are the policies? There are four key policies critical to all organisations. These are the Vision, Mission, Values and Quality policy.

The key policies – some marketing based definitions

As a marketeer it is extremely difficult not to try to simplify things. In everything undertaken, from pack design to advertisements, the customer must be able to comprehend what is being said. To make things more complicated for the marketeer, the average attention span of the customer has been reduced by the very process itself. Whereas a 90 second TV commercial was considered acceptable to get over the concepts of even simple products, this is now too long for the attention span of many consumers. The way around this has been to turn these slots into mini soap operas. Indeed, some of these have become classics in themselves. We are living in a very fast paced society which is used to everything in 'bite sized chunks' – or 'sound bites' as they are called.

It makes sense to give the terms 'Vision, Mission, Values and Quality' a simple and short set of marketing based definitions before we precede to the marketing of these concepts as they apply to the organisation. It may be interesting to research the words themselves within the organisation, as I suspect to the average person, their elitist terminology would be somewhat esoteric sounding – in short off-putting!

Vision – how I, the leader, 'see' the future

Whoever is perceived to be able to see into the future, will almost always find followers. It almost doesn't matter whether it is good or bad! The often quoted examples at two ends of the spectrum are Jesus Christ and Adolf Hitler.

Within organisations people expect the Leader to be able to see into the future and to be able to chart a way forward for the rest of the organisation, be it international, national, or local. The leader of a local branch or team can and must provide Vision as much as the national leaders. Our research shows it is what almost every local internal customer wants: local leadership.

The problem with the word Vision is that its mystical overtones may, or may not, help get the simple message across, e.g.:

> ***'This is what I believe the economy/market/local branch will look like in two years' time.' The Vision must be strongly marketed as a personal view of the leaders – whoever they may be.***

Unlike the Mission which is team-based, when it comes to the vision, the leader responsible must be marketed, as well as their vision. Think of a political party. It is not just *what* is said, it is *who* said it. Imagine Mickey Mouse delivering a Churchill speech!

Mission – the goal and sense of purpose of the people

Is your mission to be biggest, best, most respected, most caring, most innovative etc? These may be sub-sets of a goal, but according to Eli Goldrat in *The Goal*, the goal is to make money. According to the Chartered Institute of Marketing it's more simple than that – to make a profit. The size of that profit will in turn be affected by the 'values' held by the organisation, and how much is invested in upholding those values.

The problem with a goal like making money is that the individual looks to having a bigger share than they can either have, or justify. Individuals also need something more than just money as a focus.

> ***A mission statement creates an almost quasi religious sense of purpose. It enables the organisation to work to achieving its place in the future (i.e. it is held within the vision of the leader).***

This sense of purpose is as vital to the followers of the leader with the vision as the vision itself. The way it is internally marketed and kept fresh in the eyes of the organisation is of the utmost importance. A recent survey shows that, as far as internal customers are concerned, there is only one word that motivates everyone to want to perform. The word is *best*. That is why this was included in the Mission of integrated marketing in Chapter 1:

In simple terms, for every supplier to be able to say to every customer in the chain, 'We are the best'.

Values – things held dear to our hearts

Many organisations have numerous Values. A Value is easy to describe, all you have to be able to do is to say 'We value . . .'. So, for example, your organisation could say 'We value hard work'. We value teamwork/integrity/honesty/loyalty/our suppliers/our reputation etc.'

The critical part of this is the use of the pronoun *we*. There is no point in just some of the people in the organisation working towards a new morality (for that is what it is) if there are those who do not subscribe to it.

However, those organisations that have tried to market these types of Values to their internal customers have hit a major stumbling block – no one can remember them all.

Out of a list of items like these, how many would you remember, especially when you have more important things to think about that are actually job related? Our research indicates that at best it is two Values that are remembered, at worst it is one. This can even happen after an extensive campaign including video, poster and plastic cards showing the Vision. So let's take the worst possible case. Rather than fret about people's bad memories, why not turn this into a marketing opportunity? If people can only remember one thing at a time then focus on this one thing.

Advertising to the external customer recognises that it is critical to only focus on one thing, e.g. 'We're with the Woolwich', 'A Mars a day', 'Coke is it'. There is usually one key attribute in most organisations, just as there is one key attribute to the product or service that is being marketed externally. This attribute should form the one core Value to be marketed to the organisation. From this core Value, repeated again and again in every form of communication, flows the other intrinsic values. To take a concrete example from our own organisation:

OUR CORE VALUE

We are dedicated to DELIGHTING our customers – internally and externally.

To ensure this happens we therefore intrinsically Value:

Our Clients	Our People
Our Products	Our Creativity
Our Services	Our Track Record

And so a list like this can go on without people having to remember it. The key is that the core Value can be repeatedly marketed and thus repeatedly reinforced.

A quality policy

Throughout this book we have attempted to show that the word Quality should be synonymous with marketing; both are striving to achieve the same thing. The definition of marketing is that it meets the needs of the customer now and in the future whilst achieving the goal of the organisation (e.g. making a profit).

> ***A Quality policy will put customers first. Just like marketing, it will strive to maximise the resources of the organisation.***

It does this by creating a belief in meeting the needs of every customer throughout the customer-supplier chain. As previously stated, this may be achieved through the Total Quality concepts such as, 'Right First Time', 'PDCA', 'KAIZEN'. In addition to this, to achieve BS5750/ISO9000 registration a Quality policy is fundamental.

An illustration of this is taken from the Marketing and Communication Agency (MCA) Quality Manual. This is entitled *Partners In Quality* (see p. 157).

THE SECOND OF THE NEW 4 Ps – PROCEDURES

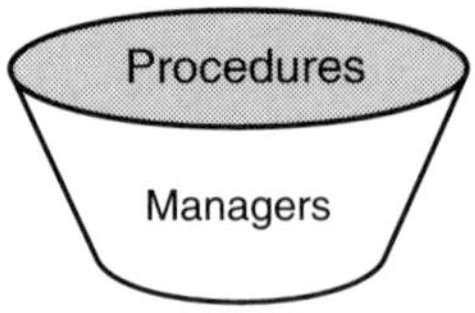

Figure 11.2 To BS5750 or not to BS5750

Attention: This is a section not to be missed!

Attention grabbing is a vital necessity when it comes to procedures. Many of you reading this book may well be marketing professionals who see the title,

QUALITY POLICY STATEMENT

Partners In Quality

The Marketing and Communication Agency Ltd has, since its inception, been committed to the achievement of quality at every level, throughout all our activities.

Quality to us, is a process of continuous improvement through:

- identifying what's good, by listening to our customers – internally and externally.
- continually seeking to make it better, by gathering the best of what we and others do.
- sharing the best practices throughout our organisation for the benefit of all our customers.
- creating new ideas and innovating new products and services to keep ahead.

Quality is about partnerships between:

- our organisation and our customers.
- our organisation and our people.
- our people with each other.
- our organisation with our partners in joint projects.
- our organisation and our suppliers.
- our organisation and the community.
- our organisation and the environment.

Through these partnerships, and by following our Quality Management System, we strive to be right first time, every time. We do this by ensuring that everyone within our organisation understands our policy. We want everyone to be committed to being 'Partners in Quality'.

All our people are fully aware of, understand, and are committed to our Quality Policy. We undertake all our activities in accordance with the procedures stated in the Procedures Manual.

Kathy Whitwell
Partner

'Procedures' and decide to skip the section. That is because they are often seen as dull and a boring necessity. Things are changing however. The move towards TQM and BS5750 has put procedures into the limelight and there will be very few readers who can afford to miss this opportunity.

To go back to basics, what is a procedure? *Collin's Dictionary* defines it as:

> '**Procedure**: A way of acting or progressing in a course of action, especially an established method.'

So why should we be afraid?

All of us, every day of our lives, progress on courses of action based on what we know will be successful. The difference is that procedures are written down in most companies and have to be followed. The person who devised them originally, probably had good reason to do so, but those reasons are seldom known and understood by the person pushing the paper around; the reasons why are never 'sold' or marketed.

Many references have been made to target markets and, when it comes to procedures, there are distinct target markets. One way of defining them is by their reaction to procedures themselves.

'It's more than my job's worth!'

Nearly everyone at some time in their professional or domestic lives has come across a 'job's worth' attitude. To some, procedures are a haven of security. They are something to hide behind and a good way of keeping the customer at a safe distance. This can often be to the extent that the mindless adherence to procedure surpasses all common sense.

'I've got more important things to worry about!'

At the other end of the scale, many people see procedures as an unnecessary evil that gets in the way of 'real' business. (Whatever they may mean by that.) They simply can't, or won't, follow basic procedures or guidelines and, as a result, cause headaches for the people who have to pick up the pieces.

With the advent of BS5750, I firmly believe that these people will be forced to comply or find an alternative occupation in a company that isn't registered. Increasing competition, flatter structures and fewer people to do the job, make sensible, customer-focused procedures increasingly important.

Procedures can be a framework around which to build a firm focus on the customer and see that everyone in the customer-supplier chain gets a consistently high standard of service.

For those of you who have not spotted it, the above takes for granted the fact that the procedure itself is one that is sensible and customer-focused. All of us have come across ones that are not. In fact, some seem to have been created solely with the objective of upsetting the customer, so much so, that they go elsewhere for their products and services. This is another good reason why external marketeers should examine the internal market and integrate their marketing before they spend millions of pounds on an external campaign.

Excellence in defining and putting effective and sensible procedures into practice, therefore begins to impact upon the whole area of Quality. This was recognised many years ago and much has been done to put controls in place and thus ensure effective processes and procedures. Perhaps the most well known of these recent initiatives is that of BS5750, which has grown in its profile at such a pace as to match and even overtake the previous monopoly of TQM advocates.

How to market your procedures – to BS5750 or not to BS5750?

That is the question that has or will be presented at the majority of company board meetings throughout the country. 'Whether 'tis nobler in the mind to suffer the slings and arrows of inefficiency or to take arms against the sea of unrest and implement BS5750?' Those companies faced with this question, who also have a TQM advocate in their midst could be faced with a heated discussion.

Let's examine then the two options and see if either of them have the answer to the procedural phenomenon.

As has been indicated, there is much rivalry between disciples of TQM and BS5750, the former concentrating on generating enthusiasm and commitment to Quality and the latter on having procedures defined, understood and adhered to, on the premise that this ensures Quality. This was covered in *Personnel Management* who highlighted two core studies.

Bosch, in Cardiff, who preferred to take the TQM option, state of internal customers:

> 'Our approach stresses the customer-supplier relationship; every supplier must agree what product or service is to be delivered to the customer, then deliver it 'right first time, on time and every time'. But this applies not only to the service to our external customers, the car makers, but to our internal customers too. The value of this approach is that it makes everyone aware that we all have customers.'

This is all very applaudable and, as stated earlier, there is no doubt that many companies have benefited greatly from TQM and the like. As Bosch stated 'we have found that implementing Total Quality is like a continuous organisation development initiative.'

However, it does not address the question of how to ensure that everyone within the customer-supplier chain is genuinely committed to turning its philosophies into a living and breathing reality. The only way to do this and ensure the procedures, processes and controls within the organisation are put into practice, to the benefit of all customers and suppliers, is to internally market them so they are 'bought into' and turned into reality by every leader, team and individual within the organisation.

Without the integration of marketing and quality to 'sell' the processes and procedures to the organisation, TQM can only be an initiative; it can never become the driving force behind a focus on delivering total quality to every member of the customer-supplier chain.

Dow experienced just this 'initiative' problem with Quality:

> In 1989 we had been through the first flush of enthusiasm for Quality (including all the dinners, presentations and enthusiastic debate) but nothing had seemed to last.'

Dow decided therefore, to pursue the other approach and opted for the BS5750 route.

Much has been written about BS5750 and this is not the place to present it in detail. However, there is a need perhaps for those of you who do not have knowledge of BS5750, to explain my understanding of it.

The British Standard Quality System Part 1 1987, explains the scope and field of application of BS5750/ISO9000 (for those who are already confused, BS5750 (British Standard) and ISO9000 (International Standards Organisation) are one and the same. A European version (EN 29000) also exists, but for the purposes of this chapter they will be referred to collectively as BS5750.

BS5750 defined – 'twenty questions'

> The International Standard specifies quality system requirements for use where a contract between two parties requires the demonstration of a supplier's capability to design and supply product (*or service*). The requirements specified in this International Standard are aimed primarily at preventing nonconformity at all stages from design through to servicing.'[1]

In other words, say what your policy is with regard to customers, specify what needs to be done to achieve those standards and prove you meet them.

[1]*BS5750* Part 1, page 1, Scope and Field of Application.

Should mistakes occur you should also specify a method for ensuring they don't happen again and take preventable action wherever possible.

In short, have sensible, customer-focused procedures and stick to them.

So, what does BS5750 specify as the key procedures in this process?

For those of you who want the official version, you will find it contained within your Quality Systems BS5750 Part 1. For those of you who prefer an easier, more targeted route, here it is as 'Twenty Questions'.

1. *Management responsibility*: Do you have a quality policy statement defining who is responsible for what? The assurance of everyone's commitment to putting that policy into practice.
2. *Quality system*: is there a Quality Manual that defines standards and procedures?
3. *Contract review*: Do you regularly ensure that both parties understand what is expected of them and can satisfy that expectation?
4. *Design control*: Do you define the purpose and standards for new products or services and do they meet the customer's needs?
5. *Document control*: Can you prove you have done what you said you were going to do?
6. *Purchasing*: Do you always get what you paid for?
7. *Purchaser supplied product*: Do you have adequate quality controls over things you buy on behalf of others?
8. *Product/service identification and traceability*: Is someone accountable at every stage of the process and do they know they are?
9. *Process control*: Do you have procedures written down for all your processes?
10. *Inspection and testing*: Do you make sure your products/services are of the requisite quality at every stage of the process?
11. *Pre-specified inspection, measuring and test equipment*: Do you always ensure that equipment is safe and effective?
12. *Inspection and test status*: Do you have records to prove you've complied with No. 11?
13. *Control of non-conforming product and service*: Do you have a way of picking up faults before delivery to the customer?
14. *Corrective action*: Do you always find out what went wrong and make sure it doesn't happen again?
15. *Handling, storing, packaging and delivery*: Do you have systems for the proper storage, etc. of materials, and do you always know where they are at any given time?
16. *Quality records*: Do you have a good filing system and does everyone

know where to find everything?

17 *Internal quality audits*: Do you check you're doing what you said you would and does it work?

18 *Training*: Are all your people adequately trained so they can deliver quality in everything they do?

19 *Servicing*: If you service your product, do you state what you will do and prove you've done it?

20 *Statistical techniques*: Can you prove your product does what it claims to do?

The emphasis throughout is, say what you're doing and prove you've done it.

This may seem an exhaustive list. However, BS5750 is not a panacea for all Quality ills. What it will do is ensure that relevant, efficient and effective systems and procedures are in place. It looks to ensure that these operate *intelligently*. It will not stop things going wrong. All the systems and procedures in the world cannot make people follow them. That's why the internal marketing of BS5750 to the customer-supplier chain is so vital.

The attitude shift required to achieve the greatest benefit from BS5750 can, in my experience, only be achieved through a concerted and systematic internal marketing campaign.

Unless attitudes are addressed, you can kiss BS5750 goodbye. ICI Engineering, for example, were taking their people down the quality route via BS5750. Whilst progress towards the goal was being made, it was not being done at the speed or with the commitment that was essential to achieve registration within the timescales set. The fact was that the BS5750 team had assumed, because of their own commitment and enthusiasm, that everyone was of the same mind. Talking to ICI's group of pragmatic engineers revealed a very different story. They were full of objections as to why BS5750 was not practical to their design environment, how it was no guarantee of quality and could quote endless examples of receiving poor quality from BS5750 registered suppliers, through non customer-facing procedures.

This brings us to where we started with a definition of a procedure – an established method. Some companies have gone too far with BS5750 and get buried under a pile of paperwork. One Midlands company for example, planted a tree outside their office to make up for the guilt they felt at the amount of paper generated as a result of BS5750! The more you specify, the more you have to write down what you are going to do, and the more pieces of paper you need to prove you've done it! Moreover, the more there is for the inspectors to 'trip you up' when they come round to check you out!

'So beware ye who enter here', but do not abandon hope, BS5750 is great, if seen as a tool for use in the achievement of an effective business and administrative customer focus. But manage *it*, don't let it manage *you*.

So, back to Dow and their BS5750 implementation. As with Bosch and TQM, Dow found that implementation of BS5750 required not only changes to procedure, but a culture change as well.

> 'The aim (now) is to encourage people to be pro-active in finding and fixing problems and not frighten them into hiding them or 'cooking' the data to tell management what it wants to hear.'

Agreeing policy and documenting procedures is one thing, but how do you make sure people:

1 Carry out the procedures.
2 Document them.
3 Are committed to the Quality Policy (see Twenty Questions Point 1).

The answer is to effectively internally market the changes (and there will be changes if you move towards BS5750). No matter how efficient you are, or think you are, there *will* be changes; changes to policy, to the way you do things, to where you file things, to how you write things down etc . . .

As mentioned in Chapter 2, change is a very emotive subject for the majority of people. On the one hand, everyone knows that change is a necessity; without it there can be no progress. It is inevitable that change and progress go hand in hand with progressive organisations. On the other hand, change is also people's greatest fear.

The human being has a natural tendency to avoid change (homeostasis) and stay in the safe, cosy world of the things they know. As the old saying goes 'better the devil you know . . .'

Take elections, for example. The incumbent of any post is far more likely to retain his/her position than any newcomer is to take over; especially if the newcomer represents a different party. That's why last year's US Presidential elections were such a shock. Not only was Clinton a 'newcomer', but he also represented a political party that had not been in power for 12 years!

What makes people want to change?

Why did he win and how can you?

People will only accept change if they believe it will be for the better.

(Hence, on the home front, many Americans believed 'whatever Clinton does, it just be better than the situation we're in now!'.)

The only way to get people to accept change is to make sure they believe it will be for the better. This is the reason that electioneering adverts make statements like, 'look forward to a better future with "X" party'. They try to make us believe that voting for a new person will bring a brighter future.

How does this relate to BS5750, TQM and procedures?

Implementation of all of the above brings about a huge amount of change. It has been established that, for change to be accepted, it has to be seen to be positive.

Changes to procedures or the implementation of BS5750 or TQM on the other hand, are often seen as negative. More work is created, there seems more bureaucracy, etc. The benefits of, for example BS5750, are not foreseen by the majority of people and are very seldom marketed.

Throughout this chapter, the constant emphasis has been upon the need to market the value of procedures and their context to the internal market place. External marketing departments can ill afford to ignore the procedural framework of their company, especially where it interfaces with external customers. If properly managed, TQM and BS5750 both have the *potential* to increase the efficiency, speed and quality of service within your organisation.

Wherever you lay your hat, you will undoubtedly have to convince your people to see everyone they come into contact with either internally or externally, as customers, and you must market the benefits of carrying out procedure.

> ***Without internally marketing your message to your people, you will ultimately fail, whichever option you choose.***

THE THIRD OF THE NEW 4 Ps – PLANS

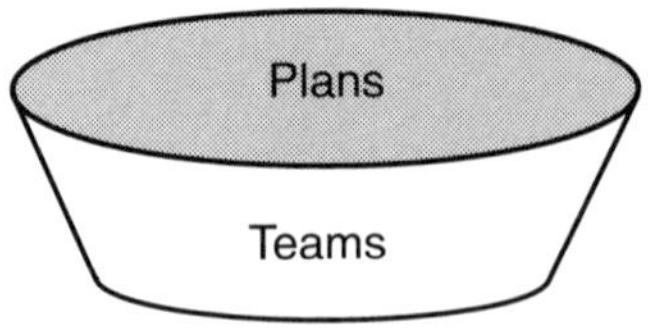

Figure 11.3 Plans – who needs them?

Personal observation suggests that the old business adage about 'people doing the urgent rather than the important', holds true, especially in the fast paced environment people live in today. It is especially applicable to the planning process. The 'day to day' crisis style of management allows the manager to do what he is best at (or at least what he thinks he is best at) and that is, solving problems. Effective planning prevents the problems occurring, but then the manager may feel he is not as important.

All of this may be happening at subliminal level, but, nevertheless it seems to point to one conclusion. That, either planning per se is not a 'service' that people are capable of undertaking, or that there is a degree of difficulty in the internal marketing of those plans. Probably, both of these are true.

Firstly, in business, there appears to be a distinct lack of training in producing plans. Very few organisations put those responsible for planning (i.e. most managers/supervisors) on training programmes to look at the 'process skills' of management. These being problem prevention, planning and, the most important of all, once you have all the problems out of the way, decision making.

Secondly, it may seem to most managers that, having spent time on the plans, there is a distinct lack of enthusiasm for carrying them out. Questions that may arise from this may be:

Is it the plan or the quality of the presentation?
Is the target market willing to take them on?
Is there on-going promotion?
Are the ideas and information good enough? or
Is some other factor affecting the acceptance of this service?

The training is not being carried out and the plans are not being accepted, but the root problem is highly likely to be the quality of the marketing of the plan to the customer in the customer-supplier chain.

Forward planning – now and forever more!

So, once again we have a 'service' provided by the internal producers and it must be internally marketed to enable the business to function. What if the plans are badly marketed? The internal customers may be able to stumble on, from day to day, they are after all resilient, aren't they? The problem is that this leads to frustration. As we come out of recession, people's feelings have built up behind a dam which is ready to burst. In simple terms, people may well leave. They will want to find an organisation which *will* provide them with the way forward in achieving a mission which is set by the leaders who then empower their people to get there.

If the mission has been effectively marketed internally, the demand for good planning at every level of the business, is going to be high. But how far forward do the plans have to be focused?

Until recently, it was quite acceptable to think in strategic terms of five years. Many a five-year marketing plan has been produced with, often detailed, projections. In today's market place, the speed of change, the constant threat from new products, new competitors and many other unpredictable circumstances, often only allow for two- to three-year strategic plans. Tactical planning is now a continuous process, whereas in the past, it could often be done on a six monthly or yearly basis. I will not comment here on whether organisations should be like the Japanese and have 20-year plans!

> ***This constant revision of plans, both strategic and tactical, means that they will require constant marketing if the people in the business are to know 'what the hell is going on'.***

The sense of bewilderment that exists in many organisations, through lack of awareness, is only made worse by the increasing demands of the individuals today to know more of what is going on. It is not good enough, therefore, to be seen to be lumbering on from crisis to crisis, or to have inadequate or conflicting plans.

> ***What has changed is that previously plans were prepared essentially for the benefit of the organisation. Today the customers in the customer-supplier chain demand a service that meets their individual needs. Increasingly, these needs are for awareness, involvement and belief in the future of the organisation.***

The belief will come when the individuals are convinced about the capability of those responsible for ensuring the organisation's survival in a tough market place. Those responsible therefore, need to be skilled, not only in the planning process, but in being able to internally market those plans.

To give an example. The planning process for ensuring a total approach to the human resource development needs of the business within Butlins Holiday Worlds involved all the key functions of marketing, operations, personnel, and training in a company-wide launch to all its management and staff. This launch of 'The Personal Development Plan' involved providing the individuals in the business with the planning information, both strategic (e.g. how to meet the challenge of the new Euro Disney) and tactical (e.g.

how the managers were going to train and develop every single person no matter how long they were with the organisation. In some cases this amounts to only a matter of weeks).

Plans, what plans? Business, Finance, HR, Marketing, Operational, IT

No department is safe! Everyone must work to a plan, therefore everyone in the organisation should have the benefit of knowing what they are working to, and why. All these plans add up to an overall business plan.

The people who should be best at internally marketing their plans should be the marketing department. Too often however, the perception within marketing is that their function is an external one. If they get involved internally, it is likely to be, for example, with new product launches in order to ensure that 'sales' people make their products successful – a somewhat selfish reason. Is this unfair? Having 'been there' I have to admit to this from a personal point of view. If any external marketeers have wandered down the corridor recently to chat to the human resource development specialists about the needs of the internal market place, I suspect they are few and far between.

If the external marketing people are not well versed in internally marketing the strategic and tactical plans of the business, what chance is there for accountants, works people and even the strategic planners themselves?

THE FOURTH OF THE NEW 4 Ps – PRACTICES

The practices of the organisation are the actions that the individuals take in carrying out the functions they perform. Every one of those practices needs to be conveyed to the individuals in a way that tackles their attitude,

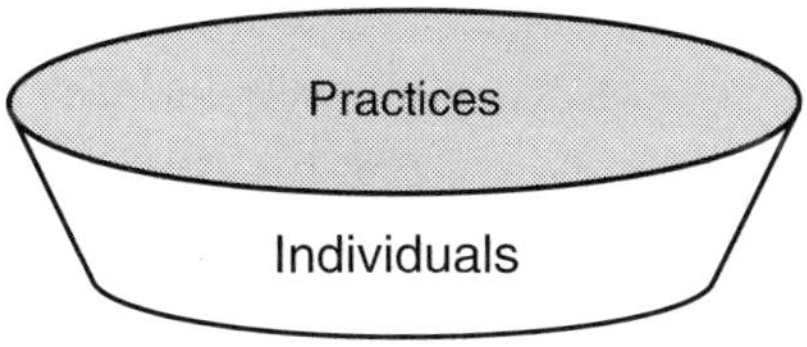

Figure 11.4 Do you practise what you preach?

awareness and ability. Every one of these practices has to be conveyed in a way that allows the methods to be transferable to a number of individuals. The way to do this is to view them as products, which then have to be marketed, or sold to the internal target markets.

In the past, employees have often seen the organisation's practices as imposed from above, by a management that does not understand what the workforce actually does. The practices of the organisation have usually been referred to as 'standards' or 'systems' or 'working methods'. The way of getting them across has been to write them down in heavy tomes, called manuals. The people responsible for the production of these tomes have often not been the people responsible for the work itself. It was usually reserved for the 'experts' at writing manuals, e.g. administrative or training people.

Whether or not these manuals on the 'standards of practice' were good – the problem is that no-one wanted to buy the product. The targeting, the creativity, the packaging, the incentives and rewards were all either ignored or at best handled by untrained people.

It all leads us back to where we started, with the people issues: The people who were supposed to read manuals were seen as 'employees' who were paid to do as they were told and acting according to the book was one of the things that they were told to do!

When the current period of massive change came along, the book was constantly being rewritten. The amount of information that people are supposed to read, the number of functions and responsibilities that they are supposed to perform, means that there is always a good reason why people are not paying the attention to certain things that they should. Following recommended practices is the first thing to go.

Then Jan Carlzon, Philip Crosby and Tom Peters all appeared and told everyone that what is now important is rewriting the book every day!

Finally the Japanese proved that the constant attention to making things better, i.e. creating new standards which everyone should be performing against, can hit people at the rate of millions per annum. In some major Japanese organisations, the reported rate of suggestions in the 'suggestion scheme' varies from 4,000,000 to 6,000,000 per annum. In one UK organisation, with approximately 50,000 employees, the number of reported suggestions in the 'suggestion scheme' numbered approximately 5,000!

Yet two suggestions per week on how to improve the business, or new ideas that might be tried, from each individual, is not a lot to ask. Indeed, if you were to listen carefully, people are probably making at least two suggestions per week, and they may be making a lot more. With 50,000 employees, two suggestion per week is equivalent to five million per annum.

The point is, that if the business is going to be improved from 'above' (note that the direction has now changed to match the inverted top structure!) the transferal of the information to enable everyone to benefit, is vital.

Gathering the best practices from the people

The methodology being adopted by many organisations to gather and transfer this information for the benefit of all, is called 'Best Practice', gathering and sharing the wisdom of the people. Many of the organisations we are currently working with, see this as a major opportunity.

The organisation finds out the people and functions which are doing well, or better than others. It then examines what is said and done within this practice that makes it better. The next stage is to replicate this in other areas. Unlike a 'good idea', this is now a tried and tested practice that can be adopted by all. Unlike a 'standard', this does not come from 'top down' as an instruction but from peer groups. As such, experience shows it is more easily and quickly adopted by other internal target groups, enabling cultural change towards 'excellence' to happen at a greater speed and with less resistance.

The benefits to the organisation are obvious. There is far less reinventing the wheel, as Best Practice is shared, thus reducing costs. In one organisations, after five days research, they realised the cost of not adopting Best Practice in one area of the business in the region of £2 million, mainly in duplication of effort.

By gathering Best Practice in a structured way as a result of the research methodologies used by marketing, the organisation stands to benefit from the might of the collective brain power of its people. If the principles and practices can then be disseminated in a way that encourages 'ownership' then the organisation stands to benefit. Everyone will be less precious about taking up new and improved internal products or services.

It is when these Best Practices lie around with no-one to pick them up that the individuals who know their worth get very demotivated. It is when they are picked up and others will not use them because of poor internal marketing, that they can also get even more demotivated. By the same token if the people who are using existing methodologies are not sold the new ideas and Best Practices in an effective way, they will fail to 'take them on board'. They will also become demotivated if they know they are using practices which are recognised as inferior.

The marketing task is three-fold when it comes to 'tactics from below'.

These can be summed up by a wonderful phrase which I heard from Robert Crawford, Service Circle Co-ordinator of the Royal Bank Of Scotland. His role in essence was to collect the Best Practices and to disseminate these throughout the Bank. They come from the work and ideas of each branch and departmental team charged with collecting and generating ideas locally. He calls it:

The Gathering and Sharing of the wisdom of the people

To this simply needs to be added:

after listening to the voice of the customer

Many organisations have gone down the route of having teams of people who get together to improve the methods and practices. Once the ideas are generated the main issue for the organisation is in ensuring that their use is maximised. In order that this can happen the ideas have to be gathered. This is not only true of teams of people coming up with new ideas, it is true of individuals as well.

Even more fundamental than dreaming up new ideas is identifying whether the internal or external customer has a need for them. If no one wants a better mouse trap then a lot of time can be wasted inventing and launching it! In ordinary language this is called 'listening', in marketing it is called research!

It may be either qualitative or quantitative research. The skills can be taught. They often only require a simple process of using structured, 'open' or 'closed' questions. But why should managers in an organisation believe this is important? The following example illustrates why.

Back in the mid 1980s we were faced with a major challenge: how to get 2,500 managers in one organisation closer to their customers. These managers were no ordinary managers, working in a close knit corporate environment. They were part of the contract catering giant Gardner Merchant.

Each of these managers worked in a client company, such as Ford, Midland Bank and Commercial Union, as well as smaller organisations. These organisations commissioned Gardner Merchant to run their catering. Each manager worked in an environment which they believed was totally different to all other outlets. They often related more to the client company than to Gardner Merchant, as their only real contact was an area manager visiting once or twice a month. The client could visit once a day.

Yet one thing doesn't change: customers have needs that must be discovered before producing products and marketing them. Interestingly catering people all too often produce what they like to produce, or what they think the customer wants, rather than what the customer actually wants. This approach had to change.

So, we trained its managers in sales, merchandising and research techniques. They were given a guide which included a series of customer questionnaires. This encouraged the managers to go and find out the customer requirements, before they attempted to introduce Best Practices, or any new ideas. More of this later. Suffice to say that the overall results added £½ million p.a. to Gardner Merchant's profit.

A further benefit of listening to customers first is that it can then be said that the introduction of ideas was as a 'response' to a customer need, not an imposition from 'on high'.

The strengths of using the recognised techniques of research enhance the transference of Best Practices. Everyone knows that the research process has validity in the external marketing of products and services. No one in their right mind launches a product today without the need being established and the likely take up being estimated. Both of these are highlighted in the research.

This process is given further credence by the assumption in Quality Programmes that everyone is part of a customer-supplier chain. So, the first thing that needs to be done is to 'establish the customers' requirements'. Yet, the connection with research has not been made. Crosby, in his book *Quality is Free*, talks of the fundamental definition of quality as 'conformance to requirements' and goes on to say that 'measurements' must then be continually taken to 'determine conformance to those requirements'. This is absolutely valid, but the system and language used bears no relation to that used and practised externally. Research does exactly the same thing. Up until now, the organisation has an internal language of 'quality' and an external language of 'marketing'. Never the twain shall meet. The aim must be to put the two together for the benefit of customers – everywhere.

The benefits to the internal target markets are great. People feel listened to and involved. They are happier to adopt other tried and tested practices rather than Head Office suggestions or changes that 'won't work out here in the real world'.

The benefits to the customers are that excellence in the form of sales and service etc, is increased, as more become like 'that nice Miss Smith who looks after me so well – thus building on long-term relationships. This can only benefit everyone.

This critical area for organisational improvement is covered in more detail in Chapter 12.

SUMMARY

- **Policy, Procedures, Plans and Practices need internal marketing if they are to be bought into by the internal customers.**
- **Targeting the New 4 Ps is not about issuing 'statements' on pieces of card or posters on walls.**
- **Policy is 'Bottom Up' direction from Leaders, it needs marketing.**
- **Procedures – To BS5750 or not to BS5750, that is the question! If yes, it needs marketing.**
- **Plans – Planning for the future isn't enough, they need marketing.**
- **Practices – Whether six million or six in number, the best practices of an organisation need marketing.**

12 PUTTING THE THEORY INTO PRACTICE

HOW DO I PULL IT ALL TOGETHER?

This chapter pulls together all the theory and provides a real life example of how to successfully implement integrated marketing. In the example, Best Practice is the 'product' to be marketed, using a three staged approach.

Stage One: listening to customers
Stage Two: gathering the Best Practices
Stage Three: sharing the wisdom of the people

STAGE ONE – LISTENING TO CUSTOMERS

There can be no better way of finding out about your organisation than by listening to customers. What will they tell you?

How well are you doing?
Could anything be better?
Does anything else need changing?
Who is likely to oust you?

Marketing people do this all the time with research. The methods of qualitative and quantitative research have been discussed in Chapter 5. However, whilst customer research is clearly vital, it often ends up only being used by marketing in limited areas. The typical areas for marketing to research are product development, corporate and brand image, and product testing.

Very little of this type of research, apart from attitude surveys, is conducted throughout the customer-supplier chain. So, with so few people owning, or being involved in the data collection, or its analysis, research has tended to remain a mysterious area practised only by the initiated.

Why research throughout the customer-supplier chain?

While people might think that research is a good idea, they may not see how it applies to their own work. As we have said, *everyone* has customers, and *everyone* needs to understand the techniques of marketing, in order to market to their customers.

With the word marketing must come research. No marketeer worth his salt would make any decisions without having the research data to back up the decisions he or she would make on the future direction of the organisation.

These decisions may be of a strategic nature such as the product areas or ranges to invest in. Alternatively they may be of a tactical nature, such as the design, style, nature of the product, branding, packaging, advertising etc.

Yet here we are with organisations having spent millions on introducing the Quality concept of the customer-supplier chain, but there has been no real attempt to back up this concept with the practical and pragmatic approach that the marketeer takes when looking to meet the needs and requirements of the customer through research.

How to research throughout the customer-supplier chain

Is it as simple as that? Can the tools and techniques of research simply be lifted out of the standard research manual and applied to the concept of the customer-supplier chain? Yes, with some major modifications to the format. No, not using the existing method of paying someone else to do the work.

It would be unbelievably expensive to call in any research organisation to interview every type of customer throughout the customer-supplier chain.

Certainly, limited samples could be undertaken but, as we have discussed, the requirements of internal customers are becoming so specific that the generic type of data that is produced in, for example, attitude surveys, is now recognised to be of little or no use at local level.

Unlike the type of research done by the local manager, as in the case in Trusthouse Forte (see below), there are other major limitations to both forms of external research (qualitative and quantitative) where applied to the customer-supplier chain. These are:

1 They are usually commissioned by marketing, and have no real ownership within the rest of the organisation.
2 The data, being collected by a third party, is second hand.
3 No one quite knows what to do when the mass of data hits them.

The net result, without labouring the point, is that external market research, whilst providing valuable data for marketing, is not as useful, powerful or practical for everyone else. So, if not standard market research, what can be used?

Two examples of internal research

In *The Employee Revolution* I talked about a brand new concept that could be used within organisations. This was developed during my time with the catering part of Trusthouse Forte in the early 1980s. It was done to get everyone at the local level closer to the customer.

Each of the sites on the large multi-operational motorway service areas was given its own version of a local marketing manager. Chosen from one of the management team, their responsibility was to focus the merchandising on the sites to the needs of the customer. They were responsible for examining all customer comments on a specially introduced customer comments scheme. They were responsible for the introduction of customer service and sales skills.

As well as having personal marketing responsibility, they also trained staff to question customers about their needs and to discuss ways to meet these needs. In simple terms they were given basic sales and marketing skills and given the opportunity to apply these at a local level.

> ***The effects on the organisation were not just extremely positive, they were electric.***

With the introduction of local merchandising and sales, and a major rebranding of the sites taking the name of the parent company – not hiding behind a brand no-one recognised – the new name, brand image and a national TV campaign were launched. The advertising campaign was able to show motivated staff, who previously were researched as being highly demotivated. The advertising on TV and in the press also featured staff interacting with customers, when previously they were often surly or even rude.

> ***The concept of local people responsible for their own sales, marketing, research, innovation and even product development and launch is not just a good idea, it is essential in meeting local customer needs.***

With this experience, the concept of local marketing was applied later in the mid-1980s for Gardner Merchant, the industrial catering company, also a part of Trusthouse Forte (as it was then). Their need was also to get close to customers, to find their needs, and then get local management and staff to go the same route as those in the retail catering division.

With over one million customers served per day, and over 2,500 outlets spread all over the UK it would have been a very expensive first step in this process to get a research organisation to visit every one, and interview customers. Yet it was felt vital to get the managers to get close to their customers and find out what they wanted. The simplest ideas are often the best, so, following the initial basic sales and merchandising training, the recommendation was to then get the managers of each site to do the research on their site themselves.

Colour photographs of this process, taken from the training guide, *The Good Ideas Book*, were included in *The Employee Revolution*.

This concept, part of the wider one of managers being responsible for their own sales and marketing on each site, consisted of training the managers to:

1 Talk to customers, or better, listen to them.
2 Collect data on what was successful – gather Best Practice.
3 Communicate to others what worked – share Best Practice

The process was formalised in the launch of a guide to best practice called *The Good Ideas Book*. Subsequent research into every one of the concepts and ideas to satisfy customers and increase revenue proved that bar one, they all worked. These Best Practices then changed from simply being ideas to becoming standards of practice.

These standards were built into the fabric of the organisation, such as in training sessions, design of new outlets and in joint promotions with suppliers such as Coca Cola. And no wonder they became operational standards.

The computer analysis of the 'Best Practices' showed that an average of approximately 10 per cent increase in sales revenue was possible. In some outlets the figures achieved were 20 to 30 per cent increase in sales.

These figures came firstly from introducing new customers. This happened by researching the needs of the non-user. Secondly, they achieved an increase in the average spend from the existing customers. They did this by offering them extra items not previously offered, or even totally new ranges of goods such as sweets and medicines.

This massive increase in turnover, representing additional revenue translated to over £½ million extra profit.

Provide measurable data

So, the process of listening to customers at a local level works:

- It gives the local people the data that they need.
- It gets local people close to customers, providing a fast response to the rapid changes in requirements and demands, be it for products, service, added value or in image.
- It is sustained through a structured, well accepted marketing process that the customers can relate to and approve of i.e. research.
- Listening also ensures the one thing that is needed to drive any Quality improvements – measurement.

Is measurement important? The question almost answers itself. Peter Hazzard, Food services Director has a saying which goes:

People work against three main criteria:

1 what they like doing
2 what they are good at
3 what they are measured on.

The short version of this which most people are familiar with is,

WHAT GETS MEASURED GETS DONE!

Imagine then, like Gardner Merchant managers, being able to measure any and every form of customer requirement through the customer-supplier chain. Powerful stuff! Measurable data about what is good, what can be better, and who does it best can be assessed at local level to improve local customer retention. It can then be collected, i.e. gathered at area, regional and head office level, to assess whether the Best Practice is applicable across the whole customer-supplier chain.

All that remains is then 'sharing' this data and Best Practice information in such a way that everybody wants to buy into the ideas. Did I say all that remains? With team briefing and just about every other form of internal communication getting bad press, the sharing of this information on Best Practice is not as easy as saying 'all that remains'. But more of this in the section about 'Sharing'.

Best Practice – who decides?

Quality has not only developed the concept of the customer-supplier chain, it has also given us the concept of continuous improvement. This is all about doing 'things right'. This is why people are encouraged to sit in quality circles, put forward suggestions, and generally enter into the innovative spirit of organisations that are looking to get better and better. There is, in my opinion, one major flaw with the idea of doing 'things right'. From a marketing point of view is it what you, the supplier believe is right, or is it what your customer is saying is right?

If you ask your customers what they believe you should be doing you are no longer doing 'things right', you are now doing the 'right things'. This is the crux of the concept of putting marketing and Quality together.

> ***By putting marketing and quality together you make sure you are doing the right things right!***

How this happens at the moment, when Quality and marketing have not got together, can best be illustrated by an example of an internationally known manufacturing organisation who have adopted Quality as a watchword. In their UK factory they have over 250 quality circles working on their programme of continuous improvement. Virtually all of these circles are working on issues which have been decided on by the quality teams themselves. Customer feedback is, of course, taken into account, but they have no formal process for benchmarking the requirements of their customers. They are all concentrating on doing 'things right' but are not necessarily doing the 'right things'. What a waste of time, money and valuable resource.

Quality ensures that everyone in the customer-supplier chain is responsible for setting down their requirements. What happens from there, however, is left to chance. Only by adding marketing to the process will the customers' requirements be included in the process.

But shouldn't a quality assurance system ensure that nothing is left to chance, like gaining feedback from customers? If you have set up and are running to BS5750 doesn't this mean that you have all the checks in place to make sure you are meeting customer requirements?

Yes, there is a requirement in BS5750 that there is a review of the contract with your customers to ensure that you are meeting their needs. However, it doesn't say how you should do this, and it doesn't say that this requirement must be met throughout the entire customer-supplier chain. So a formal meeting would be enough to meet BS5750 requirements where there are customers involved in a long term relationship.

BS5750 was originally designed for a manufacturing situation where the bond between the customer and the supplier is such that the review process entails feedback meetings. But what about a retail or a service situation, which often only has one off customers. And what about the manufacturing situation where it is not just the formal contract which provides the customer with the motivation to want to deal with the organisation?

Every marketeer will tell you that the decision-making process 'to buy or not to buy' is a complex one.

In other words BS5750 is a quality assurance check on an organisation's *systems*. It is not a check on its customer requirements. From a marketing point of view it has severe limitations.

The BS5750 quality assurance system

BS5750 may not provide the best means for researching your customers' requirements, but it has some tremendously powerful attributes that can be used to assist in marketing to customers.

The first is a check-list of your quality system requirements. This check-list is there to ensure that an organisation gains and keeps its registration, and it forms the criteria for gaining certification. The check-list provides an established set of criteria that enable a supplier to go and ask the customer whether or not the organisation is meeting their requirements. The only problem with the check-list is that it is system orientated.

Recent research shows that only 2 per cent of all BS5750 registered companies go into liquidation. So Quality assurance works, but is necessary to put the marketing and Quality assurance together. A SWOT analysis of the topics covered by BS5750 does just that.

The quality assurance check-list of BS5750 provides the ideal guide to establish exactly what it is that you want to be asking your customer. Clearly this is only a check-list, as no customer will be faced with having to deal with all of the topics impacting them at the same time.

Once the key topics are decided for each particular piece of research they can then be used again as a benchmark for later research, or changed if it is obvious that they don't provide a problem or opportunity for the customer. Before that, however, it is necessary to put one final piece of the marketing process into place.

The SWOT analysis

If you are going to measure what the customer thinks of you, what type of measurement are you going to use? It may be a bar chart, %, pie chart, or simple 1 to 4, 1 to 5, 7, or 10. Whatever you choose, the statistical measurement will give a figure-based reading. This is usually all that is required in quantitative research, but it is not enough to drive marketing improvements. From this quantitative base it is necessary to get 'under the skin' of the customer to find the *reasons* for the customers' perception. The simplest way to do that is to apply a qualitative methodology; simply ask 'why?'. Remember, this data provides the 'Best Practices' from a strengths and weaknesses analysis. It is a strategic as well as tactical research tool. As recommended by Malcolm McDonald, and quoted at the beginning of the book:

> '. . . a summary of reasons for good or bad performance should be included. It should be a concise interesting analysis which appears in the eventual marketing plan.'

By asking why they have given a certain rating, the reasons for success, or otherwise, will be given.

So it is not the rating which is the only important thing, it is the *reasons* for it which provide the solid information that a manager can act on. This can be on any specific topic. But the tools and techniques of marketing aren't just found in research organisations.

In addition to producing figures on specific topic areas the marketeer also uses the SWOT analysis. You used a SWOT analysis in Chapter 1, to assess where you are now. It is often a quick and easy analysis, and may be produced by the marketeer working individually, or with others in a team meeting, on a flip chart. Its strength is that everyone can understand the process, and it provides simple and contrasting information for making decisions on future issues. These may be on a new product introduction, the state of the organisation compared to others, or the state of one part of the organisation, such as the sales function.

> ***SWOT is an acronym for Strengths, Weaknesses, Opportunities and Threats. Being a classic marketing technique, it has one major advantage: marketing people understand it. So do a lot of other people in many organisations, as it has become an accepted method for analysis.***

The SWOT analysis is the first step to getting your customers to give you the marketing information that you as a supplier will need to keep them satisfied. The good thing about the process is that the steps are very positive ones that encourage a customer to provide constructive feedback rather than complaints or whinges! By its very nature SWOT takes you down a route which looks for Best Practice, and if you aren't doing that Best Practice it will allow each supplier of goods or services in the customer-supplier chain to find out who is. So what are the steps to take when using the SWOT process?

Step 1: Strengths

The customer will be asked to analyse your 'strengths' by providing you with details of what they like about you, your products, services, organisation etc. The question you need simply ask is:

'When looking at our strengths, what would you say we are good at?

The customer will then be providing you with either the best of what you produce, or what you do. These will point you to the 'Best Practices' in your organisation.

Step 2: Weaknesses

This could be looked at negatively, but if you ask the right question your customer will not be looking to criticise but to assist you. The question to ask is:

'When looking at our weaknesses, what could we be better at?'

This will ensure that the customer is looking to assist you in your quest for constant improvement. By looking at this in a positive light it will also ensure that the person doing the research doesn't get demotivated. You are not saying, what are we bad at, hit me over the head with a stick! You are asking for all those improvements which the Quality process has said are vital to look for if you are to keep your customer.

The nice thing is that the customer is giving you the data about which areas of improvement you the supplier should look at. If your customer is a regular one, imagine the power of getting them involved in your business.

Step 3: Opportunities

Where do most opportunities come from? They come from filling the gaps that others have not yet filled. They come from spotting a need that others have not yet spotted. They come from being one step ahead of the competition. How do you do all of this? You could try sitting in a darkened room with a dim light and a crystal ball, or you could simply go out and talk to your customers. They may not come up with totally new concepts like the Sony Walkman but they will usually be able to give you hints, tips and guidance about their present and future needs. They will be able to say 'It would be nice if you could just do . . .' To get them to do that, ask them:

> *'When it comes to possible opportunities, what new ideas would you like us to try?'*

Unless you ask them, then they will not be able to tell you. This will not only give you totally new ideas, it will also provide you with benchmark data about other organisations. For example they may say, 'XYZ have a very good idea which they use all the time which would definitely enhance your offering.'

Customer-driven new product development throughout the customer-supplier chain is a powerful addition to any organisation. Relying on in-house research and development is both short sighted and introverted.

Step 4: Threats

This does not have to come across that you are afraid, just that you are not complacent. Too many organisations have failed by resting on their laurels. Take the classic case of IBM, where two of its greatest competitors came out of people who left IBM to develop products which the company decided not to invest in – Apple and Compaq. IBM are now looking to effectively merge with Apple recognising that they have superior technology in the area of desk top publishing. The people who developed the Apple and Compaq products knew what was threatening IBM; in the case of Apple the complexity of working a computer. The windows and mouse concept has done more to attract the average user than any number of extra features on a system that is already perceived as complicated.

The fate of those organisations that are too arrogant to look over their shoulder is legion in the brands of yesteryear. One wonders if organisations had taken the trouble to say to their customers:

> *'When it comes to possible threats to our relationship, who or what would make you go elsewhere?'*

Once again by asking the question it will give you the information that you need to act. If in addition you ask your customer to rank the threat from weak to strong you will see how vulnerable you are. The same applies to all of the SWOT criteria. Now you have the data to move to the next stage.

STAGE 2 – GATHERING THE BEST PRACTICES

Before talking about the process of gathering Best Practice it may be worth looking at how important it is to an organisation. Our experience of many organisations suggests that Pareto strikes again. Whether it be individuals, managers, teams, departments, outlets or even whole companies 80 per cent of the best ideas come from 20 per cent of the people.

When it comes to Best Practice many organisations, of whatever size, are egg shaped. The 'hat' of the egg produces most of the best ideas, product, service, innovation etc. (see Figure 12.1). The obvious conclusion is that if this is the best part, then it needs to be opened there first.

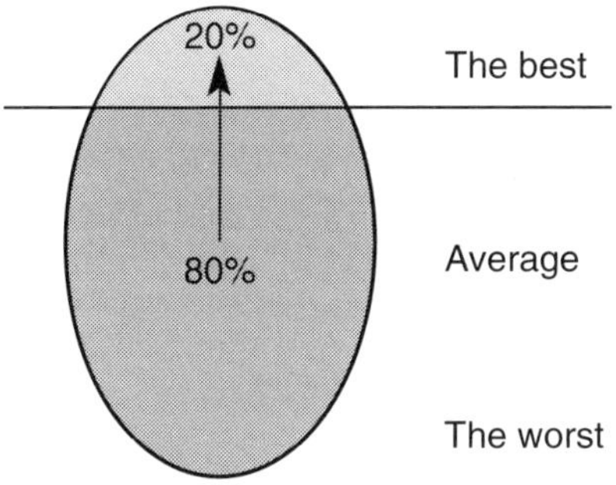

Figure 12.1 The 20/80 rule – the best are the least

The Best Practices discovered in the 20 per cent then need to be shared so they can be adopted by the rest of the organisation. The object of the exercise is to change the shape of the organisation so that it looks more like an egg on its side, with 80 per cent of the top being above the line. It is this part that delights the customer! Imagine having the hat contain the yoke too! It looks more like Figure 12.2.

There are other benefits of adopting Best Practice from within the organisation. These can be contrasted with the other alternatives for improving

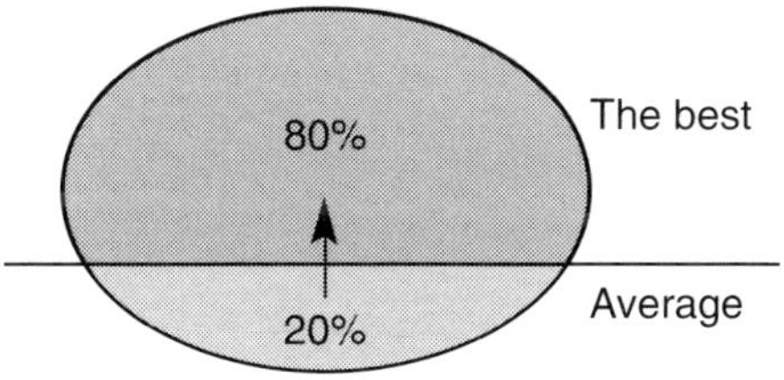

Figure 12.2 The 80/20 rule – the best are the most

things. The first of these is to call in outside help. This may be in the form of consultants, management 'gurus', training experts, academics etc. The second is to go out and 'benchmark' against similar organisations and learn from them.

Outside help moves in – but does it stay in?

The main problem with this can best be described by continuing the analogy of the egg. Imagine now this egg is soft boiled. The top is off. Introducing change from outside the organisation is like taking a soldier of toast and thrusting it firmly in the middle. The taste doesn't change but the yoke pours out. Imagine this as people's motivation. They are being told forcibly and without regard for everything they have done, that it isn't enough. Someone on high is shoving something in to change the taste!

And what happens when the toast is taken out? This is the point at which the consultants or gurus disappear. Without constant dipping in by outside intervention the egg remains below the level of being the best. A lot (of motivation) is missing. Finally, the toast hits the part that is hard boiled – which may have been all of it, and fails to make any impression at all!

Best Practice adopted from within by rolling the egg onto its side so that it is all above the line prevents the outside interference that has been the bane of many organisations. Best Practice from within works.

As has already been pointed out in the examples like Gardner Merchant, the effect of everyone practising Best Practice can be considerable. Changes in all of the following areas can be expected:

1 Customer satisfaction up – inside and out!
2 Sales up
3 Costs down
4 Reinventing the wheel reduced
5 Profitability up

All of this is happening in the top slice of every single organisation in the world. How different is your organisation? Are 80 per cent of your ideas coming from 20 per cent of your people? Transferring Best Practice not only makes sense, it makes money too.

Gathering Best Practice – an example

There is nothing like a good case study to prove a point. Midland Bank, mentioned previously, was almost on its knees at the end of the 1980s. It is a classic example of the results obtainable from Best Practice. One of its problems lay in the way it was motivating its people. It was being done by a Head Office based scheme run with an incentives company. The scheme called, 'Building on Success', was remote from the branches and deliberately circumvented the branch manager.

So, instead of getting an incentives company to motivate people to improve sales and customer service, with a points mean prizes scheme, Best Practice was used. It saved the organisation over £4,000,000 per annum. It also pulled managers and staff together in a way that had never been achieved before.

Before the introduction of Best Practice, research into staff requirements from the bank showed that they did not want a prize like a set of glasses or even a microwave at the end of the year. (They 'won' this by having collected 'points' for selling products to customers who didn't always want them.) The scheme actually turned as many off as on! It also spent millions simply to say 'thank you'. Research showed that what the staff actually wanted was for the manager to be **involved**.

Staff wanted the manager to be involved in setting them goals, helping them achieve the goals, then involved in rewarding them with a thank you. They also liked a small token from the manager as well, not for its own sake but to ensure that they were recognised when they had done well. How did they know they wanted this? Because they had all experienced either the excellent manager or the manager doing some of the excellent things. The problem goes back to Pareto, only 20 per cent of the managers were above the line of Best Practice.

The solution was to:

1 Stop the national 'points mean prizes' scheme.
2 Gather the 'Best People Practices' of the excellent managers.
3 Share those'Best People Practices' with all the managers.
4 Give the local manager a small branch budget to support them in providing the recognition that people needed.

At first some of the managers did not know what to do with the money. The budgets in some branches were left untouched. Slowly but surely, however, the culture started to change. 'Building on Success', the national scheme, had been retitled 'Building on Success Goes Local'. The concept started to take hold and the process is continuing now. This is further helped by a change of corporate direction as the new owners, Hong Kong and Shanghai Bank, believe that local autonomy and responsibility is the key to success.

Graham Couldwell, responsible for marketing at the time of the move to

'Building on Success goes Local', and now Project Director, responsible for integration of the Hong Kong and Shanghai policy, draws an analogy about the need for local motivation which demonstrates the power of the fundamental concepts involved in motivating people as described in the guide *Best People Practice*. This analogy is also worth telling as it graphically describes the need for constant marketing to all customers.

The vitamin C analogy

The body needs vitamin C to keep it alive, well and vital. The body is unable to retain vitamin C and must get it from outside itself. Regular doses are critical to keep the levels up. The same is true of motivation. Motivation in the work place must come regularly from others.

Managers are able to provide this, providing they in turn know what to do and will make the effort to do it. (This does beg the question who is providing their dose?) The doses must be received regularly or motivation dies. The same is true of any customer feeling motivated to buy a product or service. Marketing to customers must be constant.

This is why in the next section on sharing Best Practice we will be recommending a classic marketing approach. Rather than asking people to buy the whole of an *Encyclopædia Britannica* in one hit, Best Practice is best produced in an ongoing regular 'partwork' style approach. Just like the sort of monthly magazine that builds up into volumes.

This is exactly what was done with the Midland's guides to Best Practice. It was done for the managers on how to motivate people. It was done for the staff on how to improve the operations. It was done for the sales people on how to provide excellent service.

In this way the gathering of Best Practice need not all be done at the one time. It can also be taken in small doses, just like Vitamin C!

How is Best Practice gathered?

There are only two things that need to be analysed to gather Best Practice. These are 'what is said' and 'what is done'. You might, therefore, assume that gathering Best Practice would appear to be relatively easy. After all, an individual Best Practice is only made up of these two basic components – what people do and what people say.

In reality, gathering Best Practice needs a systematic approach that calls into play a full spectrum of skills.

Psychology and behavioural analysis
Questioning techniques
Listening techniques
Objection handling
Monitoring and evaluating techniques
Measurement criteria

In fact, gathering Best Practice will need precisely the same skills you would expect any professional market researcher to possess.

Identifying where to look for Best Practice

Techniques like the SWOT analysis are a superb tool for identifying precisely where in the organisation you need to look for current Best Practice. Knowing exactly where your 'best' performers are in the organisation is an essential first step in the gathering process.

Analysis of the initial data received from SWOT, will provide you with a range of performance for each topic. Once you have the customer-driven data, the starting point is easy.

In order to gather Best Practice, talk to those who fall into the strongest performance criteria! Your aim is to find out exactly what the best performers are doing and saying that contributes to their results.

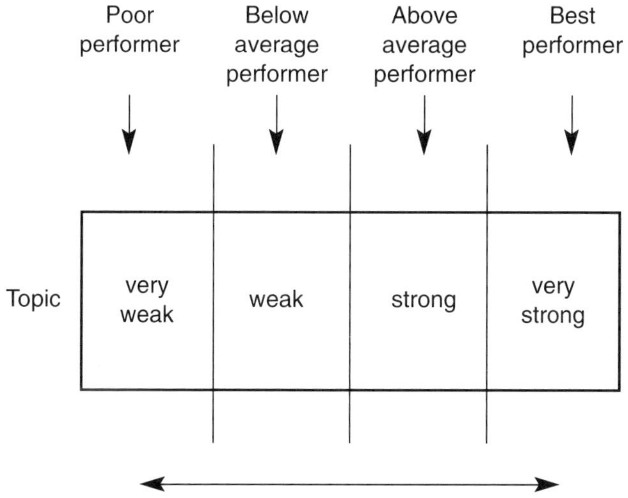

Figure 12.3 Where are you? Where do you need to be?

Overcoming the Best Practice barrier

Best Practice gathering can be compared to searching for a 'blinding flash of the bloody obvious'. It is precisely because best practitioners regard much of what they do and say in their jobs as (to quote our own research) 'common sense', 'just part of the job', or 'I just thought everyone did it this way', that the job of gathering Best Practice can be difficult.

> ***People need to be coaxed, and reassured, that the things they do and say, really are the best, and of vital interest to the rest of the organisation.***

However, be careful. Ask people for what they regard as their 'Best Practices' and they're likely to provide you with a list of 'good ideas' or 'important suggestions'. They will do this rather than putting forward their own tried and tested working methods. This natural modesty can be one of the problems of trying to gather Best Practice.

The difference between a good idea and a Best Practice is easy to discover. The key words to look for are '*should* be doing', and '*are* doing'. The first is a good idea – these run in plentiful supply, but do nothing if not put into practice. The second is a real money spinner in the best sites or people.

Methods of gathering Best Practice

There are a range of options, as with any research, for gathering Best Practice. We have made use of various types of self completion questionnaires and telephone interviewing. However, in our own experience, gathering of Best Practice is best achieved through face to face interviewing conducted by someone who has received training in how to undertake the interview, using a structured format.

Thomas Cook, for example, in its Best Practice gathering exercise, has trained a group of 'Best Practice champions'. Their task is to visit branches, identify where the branch is performing particularly well and then search for the Best Practices associated with the strong performance through structured interviews. The information they gather is fed back to a Best Practice project manager so that Best Practices can be shared throughout the country.

Other organisations have chosen to use external researchers to assist in the Best Practice gathering exercise. This can offer the advantages of being both less subjective and providing greater opportunities for spotting potential Best Practices. However, a well managed internal scheme should yield the same results, if there is sufficient attention to detail, and enough investment in time and training.

Gathering skills

Having identified where the best performers are in the organisation, you then need to identify their precise Best Practices. The key skill here is questioning techniques. People gathering Best Practices should always go armed with open ended questions. To keep it simple we refer to these as the Kiplings. These are named after his famous rhyme and cover all the open questions. They are: what, why, when, how, where and who. The rhyme goes like this:

I keep six honest serving men
They taught me all I knew
Their names are what and why and when
And how and where and who

The Kiplings form the basis for identifying the components of a particular Best Practice. By building up an interview in this way, all the key parts of a Best Practice can be gathered.

What did you do?
Why did you do it?
When do you do it?
How do you measure it?
Where does it happen best?
Who was involved?

Encourage the interviewee to think

Before you are in a position to discuss the precise elements of a Best Practice, you need to get the interviewee thinking about the job, working methods and results achieved. Key questions that could be used are:

What works well in helping you achieve results?
What have you changed in the way you do your job to improve results?
Tell me about the parts of the job you feel particularly proud of?
What do you think you did that made this particularly successful?

Using the Kiplings format, a particular Best Practice revealed during the initial conversation can be fully explored. Even if an interview does not reveal any additional Best Practice it is a useful technique to ask some 'networking' questions. Some examples of these are:

Who else do you know whose method of tackling their job has impressed you?
Who else do you know whose results have been particularly good?

It is astounding how many additional 'leads' to help in the gathering of Best Practice can be gained from asking these types of questions. Spreading the net further helps bring about the self-generation of Best Practice that tends to be the hall mark of a well run scheme. People start wanting to share their Best Practices with you rather than you having to actively search for them.

The importance of measurement

A Best Practice becomes far more meaningful if it has some form of measurement criterion by which its success can be effectively measured. The person gathering the Best Practice should always be looking out for such measurement methods. One particular topic area where such measurement is vital is customer service.

> ***There may be many actions that could be deemed as useful to achieve a Best Practice, like improved customer service. It is those that can be shown to have measurable, demonstrable success which win hands down every time.***

Successful customer service should be demonstrated by successful repeat sales.

A measurement method is vital in the subsequent sharing of Best Practice. People want *proof* that a practice has worked. They also need to be able to assess for themselves whether it will work for them.

Sustaining the gathering of Best Practice

Once a Best Practice programme is underway in an organisation it will begin to develop a momentum of its own. This happens when people begin to see the value of sharing in the success of others. Communication channels then open up and individuals want to contribute their own Best Practices.

It is for this reason that feedback loops need to be put into place. These will allow people in the organisation the opportunity to contribute their own Best Practices. They will also be able to improve on those which have already been shared. Clearly this is the philosophy of constant improvement that Quality attempts to engender. The user friendly approach of Best Practice creates a much more open attitude.

The feedback loop can take the form of a simple questionnaire that can be sent through a management chain, or alternatively sent directly to a central source. The questionnaire should also be a core element of the Team Listening process described at the end of the book. The beauty of the self perpetuating nature of Best Practice is that the process of continuous improvement becomes embedded in the culture of the organisation.

This self-sustaining process comes about more readily than in a quality driven programme which focuses on doing 'things right'. Best Practice is driven by customers giving constant feedback. Once a Best Practice is identified by a customer the gathering process swings into action. For example, in a branch network situation there will be some good sites and some bad. Even the good sites can learn from others where they have weaknesses that can be improved.

Best Practice of whatever topic is the root to marketing Quality in an organisation

Gathering Best Practice has a further benefit: it gets the people in the organisation close to those suppliers in the customer supplier chain who really do it 'best'. The final step in the process after having gathered what is good, is to 'share' this information.

STAGE 3 – SHARING THE WISDOM OF THE PEOPLE

As I have said, marketing is about the 4 Ps externally and now internally. In this last stage of the process of introducing Best Practice to the rest of the organisation I will stick to using the four internal Ps. By doing this it is intended to show the practical application of using these headings to market a live issue.

The 4 Ps – a policy of Best Practice

If the message has not got home that it must become a policy to treat all customers throughout the customer-supplier chain with the same marketing based commitment, then I have failed.

The policy must, therefore, be to apply a strategic, long term marketing approach to the marketing in the customer-supplier chain.

The move from a solely Quality-based approach, to an integrated marketing approach must be a policy decision. Without the three Cs – Commitment of the leaders, Concentrated use of the marketing tools and techniques by everyone and the Cash to launch and sustain a campaign, then any attempt to change to a culture of Best Practice is doomed to go the way of 86 per cent of Quality programmes: failure. We know, we learnt by making mistakes!

This won't be an easy policy to get adopted. It has few champions, and indeed few real practitioners. Still, marketing in its present external facing format, as a discipline, took over 20 years to be accepted. Only in the late 1980s did the Institute of Marketing become the Chartered Institute of Marketing. So there has to be a start somewhere. Since writing *The Employee Revolution* in 1989 the concept of Internal Marketing has become widely known.

However, a recent survey shows the perceived importance of communication within organisations:

> 'Only 11 per cent of all UK companies employ an internal communications specialist, of whom only a handful are board members. The implication is that the majority of UK companies have failed to recognise the value of on-going communication with their staff. Still fewer have realised the positive effects that communication can have on their bottom line'

An extract from an invitation to the launch of a film by Island World entitled *The Science of Internal Communication*.

Perhaps it is because even the practitioners have not yet made the leap from internal communication to integrated marketing. At least everyone knows that marketing is vital. My experience with senior managers in a variety of market sectors shows that most of them believe that good internal communication is just a 'nice to have'. When it is perceived that an integrated marketing policy is just as good an idea as a sound external marketing policy then the pace of change will quicken.

Best Practice is, I believe, one of the most important of the products, that needs to be introduced under the new integrated marketing policy. It is also a wise move to let everyone know that it is also a *policy* to improve the organisation from within using Best Practice. If people know that they are going to be the prime source of improvements and change rather than the external consultants or guru, then you can expect them to give far more of themselves.

The 4 Ps – the Procedures for introducing Best Practice

Deming, the Quality guru, has a fundamental belief: get the procedures right and Quality must pop out at the other end. So he devised the Deming Wheel with four very simple parts to it: **PDCA – Plan, Do, Check, Action.**

Not to be outdone I have added to this basic approach with an integrated marketing wheel. Keeping up with the Demings I have (tongue in cheek) called this the Thomson Wheel. It is shown in Figure 12.4. It is basically the same approach, but has one huge difference.

A WHEEL NEEDS A HUB IF IT IS TO MOVE.

Deming's hasn't got one! An integrated marketing process wheel can only move if it does so around what customers think.

The only way to find out what they think is research. In an external marketing process the customers' reactions are checked and tested at every stage of the process. The same procedure must apply to marketing to customers throughout the customer-supplier chain.

The hub of the integrated marketing procedure must be research. The rest of this integrated marketing process wheel is very similar to procedures in an external marketing environment. It is also a more detailed version of the simpler PDCA.

To introduce any concept from Best Practice to a training programme, all

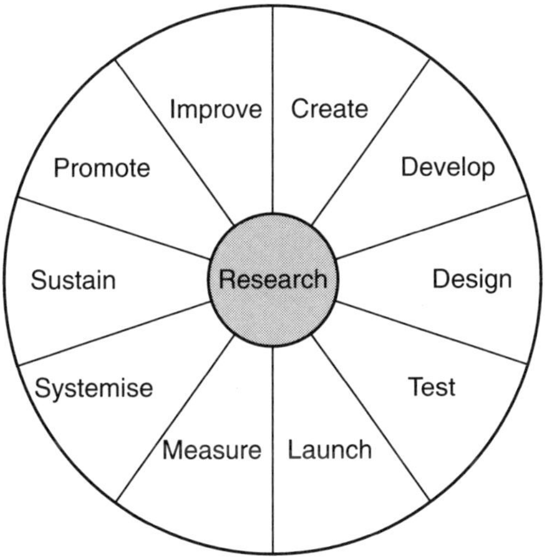

Figure 12.4 The Thomson Wheel – the integrated marketing process

that needs to be done is to move forward on the wheel. Not that it will guarantee success! Over 90 per cent of external products that are launched still fail, but then it is a tough market out there. Few companies would trust to luck and so have marketing and sales processes, even so:

> ***There are no guarantees when it comes to the customer buying what you have to offer, but what is guaranteed is that the success rate would be non-existent if there were no marketing process at all.***

The 4 Ps – a ten stage Procedure for introducing Best Practice

1 Create

If the customer wants it and you haven't got it then you may have to create it. If you have created something, then you will only sell it if the customer wants it. Either way this is the first procedure in the process, and you will need to be listening to the customer before and after, if you are to end up with a success.

In the case of Best Practice, the practice may well have been created and/or have come from a customer need. It then remains to research it with other customers. It must be checked to see if it is one that will work elsewhere.

2 Develop

Having got the core concept, it now needs to move from the idea stage to development.

In the case of Best Practice this will entail thinking through all the ramifications of introducing a change into an organisation. It will often require the development of training materials to get the idea across. It will require the development of a project plan to introduce it.

The development stage will usually, as in modern manufacturing, require the simultaneous development from a number of people involved, from designers to printers, from trainers to operators.

Once again researching the customer will pay dividends. Especially in the closed environment of an organisation, the involvement of customers not only ensures that what is developed is the 'right thing', it gains the commitment and ownership of the customers to the final products and services.

3 Design

This is not just the artistic, or technical design, but also the design of the written materials. Materials such as the communication and training package that will surround the introduction of Best Practice or any other form of change in an organisation.

Research in this phase is not just vital, it is likely to be the making or breaking of any new introduction. *The Employee Revolution* showed a wonderful example of some concept boards designed for a training package in the Royal Mail. The designers had chosen yellow as the base colour and a squiggle shape to the graphics. (This was before the Customer Style indicator which was developed from this programme!) The design, when it was researched, went down like a lead balloon. The ultimate design was in traditional Royal Mail red with a royal blue wavy line that represented a face. Postmen are people, not necessarily ideas people – obvious when you think about it.

The design for the launch of the Midland Bank's programme of Best Practice did research exceedingly well. Instead of the corporate logo looming large over everything, it was 'relegated' to one corner of design. The Griffin shape virtually disappeared. In its place one of the circles (yellow spots) surrounding the Griffin logo was coloured differently to the others and produced in red. This red spot became a spot on a local map representing a local branch on the High Street. This backed up the title 'Building on Success – Goes Local'.

What was interesting about the graphic design of the magazine and Best Practice inserts, was that initial research indicated that a colourful, energetic style was preferred. The constant feedback from each magazine issue, required that the style was toned down more and more. Subsequent research showed that the testing had been done on volunteers. Most of these were outgoing, young cashiers (yellow squiggles). The majority of the rest of the target market, of administrative people behind the scenes (violet boxes), wanted a less colourful and more structured design style.

4 Test

This is the same as the 'do' stage in Deming's wheel. It means go out and trial it before actually launching it. Tom Peters calls it 'chicken testing', after the huge failure of the Rolls Royce carbon fibre jet turbines to stand up to (dead) chickens being thrown into the engines. This was to simulate a flock of birds flying into the plane. The chicken test in this case was done, not right at the beginning, but after years of development and multi-millions of pounds being spent on the development phase.

The moral of the story is that testing (early) is vital. And so is getting the reactions of the people that are affected by the test, throughout the customer-supplier chain, not just the final customer. This means going back to the research hub before moving on.

NB: If at any stage the research shows you have to make amendments, or maybe even have got to start again, this is good news. This is going to save a lot of money. Too often people are afraid to research something in case it does come out badly. They may fear loss of face. Surely any news from research is good news? Customer feedback cannot be a bad thing.

In Thomas Cook, as I write, we are in the test stage of a programme already described, to introduce Best Practice to the Foreign Exchange part of the retail chain. The test is in two regions, one in the north of England and one in the south.

By testing the concept of all the 'glitches' can be ironed out, the programme can be more tightly controlled and the lessons can be learned. Most important of all, testing allows for the successes to be established. These then produce the case for going forward with the programme – or not!

Obviously, testing is done in all spheres of organisational life. In marketing, test marketing is often also done in controlled regions, e.g. a TV region. So there is nothing new in the concept of testing. What is new, is applying it to the launch of internal issues.

How often are things tested inside organisations? From Mission Statements to new corporate initiatives, all too often they are launched without testing. This can be to the whole organisation, for example with a video, which itself may not even have been tested!

5 Launch

Sadly this usually means 'launch into', sometimes blindly. Often nothing more happens after that. It must be said at this point that Best Practice should not be launched into. Just like any other method of introducing major change into an organisation it must be seen as a cultural change.

This must also be seen as a long term programme. If Best Practice is launched into it will fail. It will also fail if it is just launched and left. It would be unheard of in external marketing to develop a product where the marketing stopped at the launch. This is often the norm in the internal market.

Figure 12.5 is a self completion test. I believe it makes the point. External marketing does not stop at the launch stage, internal marketing all too often does. People within an organisation seem to believe that once the video has gone out, once the conference is over, once the company newspaper has been distributed, etc. then they can relax as their job is done. They somehow know that whilst the impact may be high the absorption may be low, but that doesn't seem to matter.

Tick which of the following in your organisation have had a **sustained** internal marketing-based programme around them.

Put a cross next to those that were launched and had **no real follow up**:

Mission Statement	☐	Vision	☐
Values	☐	Quality Programme	☐
Customer Service	☐	Management Skills	☐
BS5750/ISO9000	☐	New Advertising	☐
New Products	☐	Investors In People	☐
Just In Time	☐		

Now do the same with this **external** marketing list. Tick which are followed up as part of an overall sales and marketing strategy. There should be no crosses.

Product Launches	☐	Sales	☐
Brand Image	☐	Advertising	☐
Corporate Image	☐	Promotions	☐
Public Relations	☐	Direct Mail	☐

Fig. 12.5 Marketing self-completion test

It does matter to ESSO in the UK. The existing programme, entitled 'You make the difference' is being refocused on Best Practice. Currently it is based on product knowledge being transmitted to cashiers throughout the chain. This is followed up with a prize for anyone answering questions correctly about the information sent out. The programme is driven by ESSO, not the local retailer, who often ignores the scheme entirely. Why? Because there are no real 'hooks'.

The new scheme isn't just being launched and left. ESSO have commissioned a two year contract to ensure the Best Practice concept is successfully introduced. The same degree of commitment must be given to any introduction of a new concept into an organisation. But it doesn't often happen that way.

In external marketing you can watch the effect on sales when a campaign stops. In internal marketing the effects are almost impossible to judge.

Why? Because no one is measuring them. Which moves us onto the next stage of the process and starts us on the left hand side of the Thomson Wheel.

6 Measurement

Like the left side of the brain, the left side of the wheel is all about the facts and the figures. Like the right side of the brain the right side of the wheel is all about creation and innovation.

In the early days of marketing it was often the right brained people who were responsible for the function. The next result was that apart from a few simple measures like readerships, OTS (opportunities to see an advert) and of course top line sales, marketeers could concentrate on the creative side of the marketing process. Times have changed, and the people in marketing have also changed.

Nowadays measurement is vital. Every technique in the book is used to generate the data that tells you if you are succeeding. Management information systems driven by previously undreamed of computing power are now driving marketing strategy and tactics. Research is of course the main technique when it comes to customer measurement.

Quality itself has helped organisations focus on measurement. Statistical Process Control (SPC) uses all the standard statistical tools like Pareto diagrams, bar charts, pie charts, etc. to measure levels of Quality. This can be done from measuring the speed of response to calls at the switchboard, through to measuring complaints on goods after they have been sold and shipped.

How often do the people in the customer-supplier chain actually measure customers' perceptions? Not enough.

Enough has been said about research in this book. Where something is being measured which shows that someone is doing or saying something that is better than the rest, this is simply providing the organisation with a Best Practice. The good news is that the systems exist through BS5750/ISO9000 to ensure that once information is captured it should be incorporated into the documentation of the organisation. Whether it is bought into is another matter.

7 *Systemise*

Enough has also been said about BS5750 to endorse the importance of a systematic, documented approach to running an organisation. Whilst the requirements of BS5750 are mainly manufacturing driven, this does not negate the need to *systemise* the marketing procedures and practices. The same is true of Best Practice wherever it happens in an organisation, even if it falls outside the scope of BS5750. At present to extend the scope of the current requirements, work is being done by organisations like the British Standards Institute and Marketing Quality Assurance to apply the procedures to marketing.

BS5750 Part 8 produced by the British Standards Institute for the service industry does have within it a requirement to ensure internal communication is systemised. Excellent! The problem is that the requirement does not define how powerful the system needs to be, and in my opinion requires considerable clarification. It also requires a much stronger focus on marketing to customers as well as on the channels of communication, like team meetings.

EXTRACT FROM BSI QUALITY SYSTEMS BS5750 PART 8 ISO9004–2
(My comments in italics)

5.3.2.3 Communication

Service personnel, especially those directly involved with the customer, should have adequate knowledge and the necessary skills in communication.

Does this include marketing and research?

They should be capable of forming a natural work team able to interact appropriately with external organisations and representatives to provide a timely and smooth running service.

How do they become capable?

Team activities, such as quality improvement forums, can be effective for improving communication between personnel and can provide an opportunity for supportive participation and co-operation in solving problems.

But is the focus on improving the right things, and gathering the 'Best Practices' that you 'are doing', or is it looking always at what you 'should be doing'?

Regular communication within the service organisation should be a feature at all levels of management. The existence of an appropriate information system is an essential tool for communication and for service operations. The methods of communication may include the following (*but are only a suggestion*):

- management briefings;
- information exchange meetings;
- documented information;
- information technology facilities;

The fact that communication, if only in the service industries, is recognised as being important is great news. The next stages must be to work toward an even stronger recognition for a systematic approach, approved to ISO standards.

The greatest benefit of all to having a system is that it provides an organisation with the control over its business

So without stronger guidance from ISO requirements what do you do? The Thomson process wheel is itself a systematic approach to the marketing procedures in the customer-supplier chain. At the very least if these were followed then it would be a major start. Remember that Deming believes that procedures determine Quality. If this is the case then systemising is pretty important.

Simply to get past the point of just launching something into the customer-supplier chain has to be good news. You know that with a system in place after a launch, you have to see it through. You know that after the launch you have to be measuring it, systemising it, sustaining it, promoting it and improving it. These are the final stages of the system.

8 Sustain

Once you start marketing you can't stop. The customers' demands, the competitive pressures, and the economic changes all mean that something has to be happening continually to keep sales up and a presence in the market place.

Internally the same pressures are being exerted. And there are a lot more of them. The demands being made on the internal customer are enormous, on their time, resources they can use, understanding, commitment, enthusiasm, ideas, involvement, training etc. If anything, the need to market more to the internal customer is much greater than to the external customer.

In a telephone survey of companies looking to introduce change in the form of JIT (Just In Time) over 90 per cent had failed within the first six months. Why? Because they were unable to sustain it after launch, or, even more fundamentally, assumed that all they needed to do was to launch it and the idea would then sustain itself.

Best Practice is just like any other new concept. It may be made glaringly obvious that enormous savings and improvements may be achievable through the adoption of Best Practice, but this is yet another 'better mouse trap'. As the saying goes the world won't beat a path to your door to buy one! The question is how do you sustain the momentum. The lessons from external marketing are this time totally applicable.

When you want to get your message across you say it again and again **AND DON'T STOP!**

Externally, it used not to matter too much how this was achieved. Targeting was pretty crude, so campaigns would be run using a buckshot type approach. This may have included TV, press, radio, posters, PR etc. Today targeting is all. Specific, targeted messages via direct mail for example, ensure a level of precision in saying the right thing, to the right customer, at the right time, in the right way.

Yet internally, the memo, the corporate video, the corporate newspaper and the team briefing, by managers who don't like running them, are standard forms of communication. The above extract from BS5750 is confirmation that this level of communication is all that is perceived to be required.

The way to sustain a programme of Best Practice has already been hinted at. Regular updates are the key, with information going out again, and again . . .

It is worth noting here that there are two distinct forms of Best Practice. The first is the one-off practice that applies to short term issues, e.g. a one-off promotion or new product to sell. Sustaining this type of Best Practice can be achieved by a tightly targeted monthly, bi-monthly or quarterly magazine. This can give business orientated news about current issues, e.g. product promotions. Where possible these should have gone through the trial phase and any Best Practices discovered during the trial should be included.

The second form of Best Practice is the on-going type that can form a standard practice within the organisation. Once again, these should be sent out regularly. This ensures the repetition of the message that is vital to sustain the culture. Additionally no-one could ever hope to adopt a whole manual of Best Practices in one fell swoop.

This is where the marketing concept works using the idea of a build up of information with a 'partwork' format. This is the type of magazine where the first issue is often advertised with a free bidder. Issue two may be 'free'. If it works for the customer externally then it should work for the customer internally. And it does, provided that they have been properly researched, and provided that the organisation stays committed. Provided also that another marketing concept is used to keep up people's interest – promotion!

9 Promote

Promoting products and services comes naturally to people, not just to the trained marketeer. The shopkeeper in the local shops knows just what to do to get customers to notice what they are doing.

Free! Reduced! Special Offer! Two for the price of one! Buy now pay later! Prices slashed! Sale! Save Save Save! Hurry! Stock clearance! Look! And all of these are visible from my office window!

We, as customers, need to have our attention attracted. No one is ashamed to admit it. No marketing organisation is ashamed to have to do it. Things are revitalised by making them exciting, attractive, a bargain, a good deal or whatever else is needed to be done to make us want to buy. Compare this to what happens internally.

Internally we are sent another memo, reminding us about the things we 'should be doing'. The management sit in review meetings trying to decide what went wrong and how to put it right. If things get really desperate the chairman preens himself up for another video.

The stark contrast illustrates the way that internal customers are treated in a totally different way to external customers. But surely I'm not going to advocate using these brash external marketing concepts internally? Yes, why not. Why shouldn't a prize draw be used to get people to complete questionnaires, for example on product knowledge or Best Practice? It only takes a few prizes, and little administration to pull out 'the first five correct entries'. Why shouldn't the local manager have a competition to reach a certain target, or get the most out of adopting a Best Practice? The prizes can be as simple as a silver cup full of Smarties. Both of the above are Best Practices. It doesn't all have to be hype. Even something as simple as holding a meeting can be used to promote something. And, simply spending time with some extra training on the subject may help.

If it is recognised that the nature of customers is such that they will forget and need to be 'reminded', then promoting must be seen as part of the process.

As with all the other stages in the wheel, it must be remembered that any form of promotion must itself be researched, prior to a full scale introduction. There will come a time, however, when no amount of promotion will entice a customer to buy. Quite simply they need something new, or something else is more attractive to them. This is the stage when the basic product may need to be improved.

10 Improve

Constant improvement is the well spring of all Quality programmes. If this dries up the Quality concept will die. Plenty has been written about this subject, from holding quality circles to suggestion schemes. One area of constant improvement can be included here, and that's the constant improvement that comes from the customer.

Once again listening to the customer is the most powerful way of producing the right sort of change within an organisation. If you ask the customer what needs to be improved, they will not only tell you that, they will also often be able to tell you how best to do it.

So, why waste all that time in Quality meetings when a large percentage of your improvements could come from the customer themselves.

This area has been discussed whilst looking at the SWOT analysis and forms the basis for starting the process all over again. If the research shows that improvements that the customer wants are significant enough then it may be necessary to go back to the beginning and 'create' something new.

The wheel takes you where you want it to go

The 10 procedures in the Thomson Wheel that have been described, will help ensure that the communication of any concept, initiative, training programme, etc. is more likely to succeed. It can be used by any supplier in the organisation for any number of customers.

The concept of Best Practice has been used to illustrate how the Wheel operates and I am delighted to say that we have created the Wheel from Best Practices. It has come from all the work that we have done with organisations, large and small. Once you have the wheel, it is up to the organisation to decide where it goes. Having set the Policies, the Procedures in the wheel simply allow the organisation to get there, more quickly, and more smoothly. In other words, *you* keep hold of the steering, but the 10 point wheel is the fastest way to get you from A to B.

These are the 10 steps of the Best Practice process; plans are next.

The 4 Ps – Plans

Once it has been decided at policy level that marketing throughout the customer-supplier chain must take place, and that the best way for everyone to improve is through Best Practice, then these decisions need to be communicated. People need to know the Plans that are going to affect them. Even more than that, they need to buy in to them. 'Ownership' becomes a critical issue when introducing change.

In those organisations where people aren't brought 'on board' the result of introducing change is often failure. The question is how to get people involved in the plans when they haven't necessarily been involved in developing them. The answer is often to simply give them what I call 'a good listening to'. Let them air their views. Let them say what they think the organisation should be doing. Let them feel as though they can affect the final outcome, albeit if it is only in a minor way. Give them this 'good listening to', and change is much more readily accepted. The process also provides the methodology for finding out the attitudes of the customers in the customer-supplier chain. The process is similar to focus groups.

It helps if everybody is given the opportunity to go through this process, but even if only a representative sample of people are selected then it can be said that people were consulted.

The methodology that we have developed to do this is called 'Listening Groups' or 'Issues Groups'. These were first conceived when assisting Lloyds Bank with a massive cultural change programme helping them introduce information technology throughout the branch network. The problem was that the focus of the programme changed half way through its development. It was originally conceived as an opportunity to provide the 'paperless office', but increasing competition and customer demand led to the programme becoming totally customer focused. The question was, how to let a network of over 50,000 people buy into the change.

The Issues Group concept allowed every one of their managers and assistant managers to participate in a discussion about the future plans. They were provided with a pack of information that also allowed them to discuss these plans in the same way with the people in the branches.

Involvement in plans – the listening group concept

Listening Groups or Issues Groups as we call them, are structured to go through a three staged process. The analogy that best describes this process is traffic lights at red, amber and green. The first thing to do when you are coming up to a red light is stop!

When stopping at a red light the heat generated when applying the brakes can be enough to boil a kettle. The velocity and weight behind the vehicle is also enough to do serious damage to anyone who gets in the way. In many organisations the tendency when introducing any new plans is to jump in front of the oncoming vehicle and hope that it stops, picks you up and carries on having taken you on board. The reality is totally different. The vehicle will either run you over or swerve to avoid you. Either way, you aren't taken on board.

The energy needs to be dissipated in another way. The vehicle must be brought to a stop before anything new can be added. The 'red' section of Listening Groups allows people to get it off their chest, having their say, speak their mind, and feel they have had 'a good listening to'. Almost without exception this is all that is required before moving on to the amber section.

Going back to the analogy of the vehicle, it is now at the traffic lights and they have just changed to amber. Which way should the vehicle turn? Should it go straight on, turn left, turn right? Should it start off straight away or wait for the mother with a pram who is hesitating at the side of the road? In exactly the same way as this car waiting at the lights, there are many decisions that an organisation can take. If people have not been given a good listening to, then they will want to be involved in the decisions in order to provide them with a feeling of knowing where they are going. If they have been given a good listening to and got everything off their chest, then they are more likely to be ready and willing to listen to the plans that have been put together, by the people who are responsible for them.

The amber section is positioned as being the plans or the potential plans of the people responsible. If some room is left for ideas on how best to implement these plans from the participants, then this does help. If not, it does show that all the options were at least looked at.

Once these have been talked through, then and only then will people be ready to move off, when the light goes green.

In organisations today with such massive changes going on, people have enough to do to play their part in the change without worrying about getting involved in other people's area of responsibility. All they need to have felt is that they were involved in discussing the issues. So when the green light for action planning is given, and their roles and responsibilities defined, then they will be far more likely to move off in the right direction at the right time without endangering themselves or others.

The 4 Ps – Practices

A lot of what has been talked about in this book has been a totally new concept of introducing marketing skills throughout the organisation. However, it is not only the concept which is new, the marketing practices that have been involved have also had to be adapted to meet the specific needs of the customer-supplier chain.

The concept of Best Practice advocates that instead of bringing gurus or consultants into organisations to introduce change, the change should come from within. How can this be reconciled with introducing changes which are totally new?

The answer is that within most organisations there are examples of virtually everything that has been talked about. It may not be as obvious as has been described, but one way or another, there will be people who are, for example, targeting their messages. One way or another, there will be people who are researching their customer's needs. One way or another, there will be people who will be sustaining concepts like Quality by promoting them to their customers. All that needs to be done is to find these Best Practices and pull them together in such a way as to fit in to the Policies, Procedures, Plans and Practices of the organisation. All that remains is to let everyone else know about these marketing Best Practices.

Externally the practices in what is called the 'marketing mix' include advertising, promotion, PR, product launches, packaging, etc. What does the marketing mix include when looking specifically at internal marketing. As this is a 'how to' book, the next chapter illustrates the Best Practices in the internal marketing mix.

SUMMARY

- **Listening to customers must be the first stage of the process.**
- **Gathering the data on what is 'the best' they do and say is the key to reversing the 80/20 rule of Best Practice.**
- **Sharing the information gets the whole organisation as good as 'the best'.**
- **Follow the 10 point Thomson Marketing Process Wheel for a successful implementation and long term integration into your organisation.**

13 HELP AVAILABLE FOR YOU TO DRAW ON

This chapter highlights the external and internal help available and looks at the pitfalls in simply adopting external marketing practices.

THE DIFFERENCES BETWEEN INTERNAL AND EXTERNAL MARKETING

The reasoning so far about the use of marketing skills to meet the needs of internal customers has been based on the concept that it works on the external customer it must work on the internal customer. There is however, one big difference between external marketing and an integrated approach to marketing. This needs to be explored.

It has been said that the skills of external marketing are to 'meet' the needs of the customer with the products and services that are being demanded and are expected to be in demand. It is, of course, also possible to create demand that people do not even know exist, with innovative ideas.

> ***The main proviso that the external marketeer must work to is that, if the customer fundamentally does not want, or cannot afford, his products and services there is no point, in the short term at least, in trying to persuade them otherwise.***

The role of an external marketeer is clearly based on 'meeting' the needs of the customer, who may have to be persuaded that the products and services on offer are better than the competition. This is where the skills of marketing and selling come into play. The customer does, however, have the last word in the matter.

In the internal world of an organisation things are different. To take an extreme example to make the point; if 'meeting' the needs of the internal customer was the objective of the internal marketeer, then the organisation would soon be out of business! For example, to 'meet' the needs of an individual within the organisation it might be necessary to pay them a million pounds a year! Clearly, this does not 'meet' the needs of the organisation.

This relates back to the flaw that organisations found when they tried to introduce McGregor's X and Y theory. The internal customer, if treated totally as 'king', is highly likely to take advantage of the situation, to the detriment of the other stakeholders in the organisation and therefore the organisation itself. This can be summarised as follows:

1 The needs of the organisation, and the needs of the individual will inevitably be different.
2 The role of internal marketing cannot be to 'meet' the needs of one to the detriment of the other.
3 The key element in the whole process will be to 'match' the needs of both the organisation and the individuals.

Clearly, there will be times when there will be direct conflict, but in the main, the recognition of individuals in any organisation will be that they cannot allow its downfall through unreasonable demands to satisfy needs that cannot be met. It may be necessary through internal marketing to create the awareness and acceptance that their need must be 'matched', and if this is unacceptable, the inevitable result is either compromise or confrontation.

The reason for much of the confrontation in the past has been that individuals in organisations have not perceived there to have been a 'matching' of needs, far less an attempt to 'meet' their needs.

For the organisation that actually starts to market, its internal products and services in a way that creates recognition of the strength of commitment to the individual, then the payback can be tremendous. Many organisations *are* doing a wonderful job of matching the needs of the people who work in them, yet if you were to ask the individuals about the internal products and services on offer, there would be little perception of a co-ordinated policy.

How many organisations can claim that they have an internal image as strong as Marks and Spencer's. Or to take a specific example, how many individuals feel that the 'free' catering they get is really part of a package, or is it more a right? Apart from recruitment, virtually nothing is done to put together a totally co-ordinated package, targeted at the employee, once they have joined the organisation.

One excellent example of this total approach to internal marketing is that of Trusthouse Fote's Catering Division. The interesting aspect of this programme called 'Winners' is that it was run by someone who was, I believe, Britain's first internal Brand Manager. Robin Turner worked within the marketing department, yet his remit was, in current parlance, human resource development.

The ITSA Procurement Services division is another organisation that has embarked upon a major communications test programme. It is envisaged that this will save the organisation considerable sums. It builds on the success of its own people by transferring Best Practice.

The Butlins Holiday Worlds 'People Development Programme', already quoted, is another example of a total approach to matching the needs of the organisation to the individuals.

The Royal Mail also runs one of the UK's largest internal marketing programmes. One of the items at the top of the list of issues to tackle, is to enable everyone in the organisation to be able to 'communicate'. This is done by transferring the marketing skills to the key internal target market, the managers. This programme has now been taken up by Streamline, its direct mail division.

Knowingly, or unknowingly, other organisations that are now looking at this area are many of the large and respected market leaders. There are also many small organisations – size has very little to do with the need.

This highlights the growing realisation in organisations of the importance of running a range of internal products and services for all internal customers. This will soon be recognised by more and more organisations.

The first practical move that an organisation can make is to ensure that there is someone, or indeed a department, responsible for integrating marketing and Quality. Whilst everyone at local level must be responsible for their own marketing to their customers, an overview is critical. This person or department would fulfil a 'gate-keeping' role. At the same time they would be responsible for transferring the marketing skills to the individuals in the organisation.

In other words, the role is not to build up a large team of (costly) people as a power base. The internal marketeer, like his external counterpart, does not have to attempt to actually do the physical production and carrying out of internal marketing. The role is fundamentally strategic, and the internal people who fulfil it should use the internal and external experts to carry out the tasks necessary to make it happen at a tactical level.

So, just as the external marketing department plays a liaison role with the internal departments and the external agencies, the same will happen with internal marketing. For the external marketing departments these agencies include advertising, PR, sales promotion, direct mail etc. For the internal marketeer the likelihood is that the outside skills will come from a number of sources, such as these agencies, plus a number of others. They will all have at some time, assisted people internally. Not surprisingly, moves are afoot amongst of all these companies to look to exploiting this new business opportunity and to winning the potentially large accounts.

The agencies that are moving, or have moved into this area, include an array of companies. They specialise both in external marketing support, and those which have been involved in particular aspects of internal services and are listed later in this section. All will have particular strengths, but most of them will have one weakness; they do not have the combination of marketing, human resource development and Quality. There are some who do, but they are few and far between.

Beware of those who only bolt the skills that they know already onto this very complex area. I have seen large amounts of money being squandered, that need not have been. As stated, on incentive schemes, Midland Bank was spending £4 million on what they describe as a 'Beast' that they had created which needed feeding even greater amounts of money. The 'Beast' was killed by a well targeted campaign that invested money in training and developing people providing the Best Practice skill, and a small local incentive scheme run directly by their manager – not by providing a remote scheme of points mean prizes.

If the products and services that the individuals want, like training, are sufficient to motivate them, why is it deemed necessary to throw money at them as well? Alternatively, in external marketing terms, there is no point in going out with money-off promotions on a product which the market does not have confidence in. This is the same as providing an incentive scheme to motivate people when the leadership by the local manager doesn't inspire them.

And so to some of the fundamental misconceptions about internal marketing. The same type of misconceptions that existed in the days when the Chartered Institute of Marketing was having difficulty in being recognised. (It was only in 1988 that it was granted a Royal Charter.)

> ***Internal marketing is not about sexy campaigns, creative looking training manuals, multi screen conferences etc.; it is about*** **meeting** ***the needs of the external customer and*** **matching** ***the needs of the organisation and the internal customer.***

So beware internal detractors who may have a vested interest in attempting to say that the practice of internal marketing trivialises the complex nature of business. If this criticism were levelled now at external marketing, the cry would be 'Luddite'!

Beware as well the external agency that has a vested interest in pushing their own product. Too often they suggest an expensive campaign – inside and out. I remember one external marketeer who used to go into his advertising agency briefings and say of their approach, 'the answer is that you have to spend lots on television advertising, what is the question?' The strength of the response generally suggested that the cap fitted!

Having said that, there is a growing band of experienced professionals who are looking for long term relationships and who provide both the strategic direction and back up support needed for marketing internally. These include the following.

Human resource development organisations

Having worked for and with all the people on this list my personal inclination would be to find one of this type of organisation. They need to have merged marketing skills with a fundamental understanding and practice in human resource development. By accident or design many of the large scale training programmes that have been introduced into organisations do have many of the marketing skills applied to them.

Below the line agencies – sales promotion

Many of these agencies are involved in promotions and incentives and have experience of dealing with 'on the road' sales forces. Added to this skill, they have then moved into 'employee incentive schemes'.

My natural inclination is to say that 'nothing kills a bad product better than good marketing'. If the fundamental internal products and services are not right, then throwing prizes and money at people is a short term solution likely to lead to long term problems.

On top of an incentive base, many of the below the line agencies also offer video production, which has also prompted them to move into the area of training.

Video production companies

'The answer is a video based programme – what is the question?' Video is an excellent medium, for two key reasons. First, it creates lifelike simulations which create interest and generate what is really important – the debate. Secondly, it provides support to the person responsible for stimulating the debate. It is, therefore, an excellent tool. It is not, however, a solution to all the issues that need to be introduced by marketing into the customer-supplier chain.

Advertising agencies

The natural reaction of many advertising agencies, will be to look to this new area as it is one that potentially offers the largest opportunity for growth in marketing services in the world. The problem arises as a result of their believing that their specialist skills in external marketing can be directly transferred into internal marketing.

In the sphere of external marketing, whilst the advertising agency will get involved in strategy, their major role is to assist organisations to advertise. To do this, the solution will invariably be a combination of a number of media, e.g. TV, newspapers, magazines, posters. The one thing that can be guaranteed about each of these media is that what is transmitted gets to the final customer as it was intended. There is nothing in the way to alter the message. The media deliver a consistent message to every individual.

Additionally, the 'message' that they are skilled at putting across can usually be contained, within at most, 90 seconds of a TV commercial, or a double page spread. This means that the advert is not only consistent, it is short and simple.

It calls for one main skill. It is this skill that external marketeers go to advertising agencies to harness. It is why they change agencies if they do not succeed in creating demand for the product. This skill is creativity. This can reduce the 'essence' of the message into just a few words and designs. The most successful of these often win awards and have massive target market recall for their endurance and brillance, e.g.

HEINEKEN REFRESHES THE PARTS OTHER BEERS CANNOT REACH

A MARS A DAY HELPS YOU WORK REST AND PLAY

COKE IS IT!

MILD GREEN FAIRY LIQUID

All of these are brilliantly simple – but the simplicity of the product and its benefits lie behind the advertising message and form the main elements in the work of the agency.

In the world of internal marketing the message is not only more complex, but it will almost inevitably be best transmitted via a chain of people. These people (usually at management and supervisory level) will, almost without exception, either wittingly or otherwise be 'translating' it to suit their own needs.

In other words, the distribution channels in the customer-supplier chain are not static. They cannot be guaranteed to be totally relied upon to maintain a level of impartiality. To the advertiser, the distribution channels are just TV sets, or pieces of paper. The internal distribution channels are 'warm and breathing' and can be totally unreliable when it comes to even sticking to the message. Worse still, they may not be trained to deliver the message in a consistent way, even if they do not want to change it.

Additionally, the messages that need to be transmitted are highly unlikely to be able to be put across in 90 seconds or less. At the very least, one of the three 'As' (see page 95), but most often all of them, will need tackling when it comes to getting any message across to the internal market place. Whether the issue cuts across attitude, awareness, ability or all three, the complexity of the internal products and services mean that it is not enough just to sell the idea.

There is, however, one very important message that the advertising world can teach the internal market: the power of a campaign. For example, all too often it is felt that a one-off training course will change people. They are often subjected to what amounts to a one, two, or more days 'launch', then left to sustain the impetus on their own. The situation can actually be made worse by a high quality trainer. Just like good sales people they are able to create tremendous enthusiasm, lots of awareness and terrific course critiques. With nothing to support and sustain the high impact of the launch, the individual is then left, unable to fulfil the expectations built up within themselves.

The same is true, not just of training courses but of any other type of transfer of information, idea, or action required of the individual. In the external world the number of OTS (opportunities to see) a commercial is a vital factor in determining its impact on the uptake of the products and services that are being advertised. The repetition of a message is just as important internally. One-off courses, meetings etc. are often not enough.

Design houses

The amounts of money spent on corporate design by large organisations have almost become a legend. Millions of pounds have been poured into the identities and logo designs of the likes of ICI, BP and British Airways. Where the battle for the customer's cash is at its most fierce in retail, even more is spent on design, layout, signage etc. This has happened with virtually all of the high street retailers and financial institutions, like Midland Bank, Barclays, Debenhams, Woolworth, Marks and Spencer, Tesco, Sainsbury, plus of course the smaller niche retailers like Sock Shop, Tie Rack etc.

What is said by the design houses about corporate designs is yet another example of the same issues being raised by internal marketing. They are, however, coming at it via a different route. This issue is that the internal image of an organisation should be reflected in its outward presentation to the market place. If the image is, for example, to be one of caring for its customers, or of an innovative company, or one that looks to providing high levels of added value, then it must deliver what it promises. In order for that to happen, the internal target market must be aware of the goals and expectations that the customers will have.

The result is that the design company will start to explore many of the areas that have already been discussed. Through research and internal debate about the design issues, they will attempt to match the internal actions of the individuals with the external demands of the customer.

In terms of the 'Attitude' of the organisation, this approach is as valid as any other. If all the relevant disciplines are involved, then each will have their input as to how the organisation needs to be changed. This change will be brought about to meet the requirements set for the designers. Ultimately these must be agreed by the CEO, as the holder of the Vision and the Mission.

The one restriction that is created with the sole use of the design route is, that just like external marketing, the corporate branding process is only one part of a much larger whole. Designers may help to create the visual imagery of a brand or even corporate logo. To do this, it is vital that the designer does get 'under the skin' of the product or organisation. There is, however, nothing to suggest that they have the internal skills to change the perceptions of the people affected.

PR consultancies

There are many excellent PR consultancies who are beginning to move into the area of internal communications. Indeed some of them have been specialising in this area for many years. They have become expert at providing solutions that often entail PR type approaches. This includes corporate newsletters, videos with interviews with the Chief Executive and publicity campaigns. Like all of the others mentioned here, they are specialists, i.e. they tend to focus on one area of marketing alone, in this case, PR. Marketing uses all of the tools available to it.

A PR solution may be perfectly valid for many aspects of an integrated approach to communicating in the customer-supplier chain, but it isn't the only approach.

Total quality consultants

According to the DTI survey mentioned at the beginning of the book, 86 per cent of quality initiatives fail. Do TQM consultants have the marketing skills to make their programmes work given this level of failure? Quality may have taken off in your organisation with the help of consultants. You may have been forced to make it work in order to stave off the threat of foreign competition.

This is not to say that TQM consultants don't know their job, they probably do. They just haven't got together with marketing specialists.

Communication consultants

There is a small but growing band of consultancy companies who are saying that they offer 'total communication solutions'. Each have their own tools and techniques. All are having to work at the leading edge to develop the ideal solutions to communication, internal and even integrated marketing problems. There aren't enough of them, but then there isn't the demand! Not enough organisations have recognised that this is an area that requires budgets, money or internal people, let alone external help.

An integrated approach

I would be delighted to be able to say that the answer to integrating marketing strategy and tactics throughout the organisation would be to integrate the strategies and tactics of ALL of the above mentioned organisations. Sadly my experience in this area from as far back as the early 1980s is that integrating agencies is nigh on impossible.

Integrating internal departments is only just beginning. When budgets are at stake, trying to get agencies together creates a fear factor. They each fear the other is going to try to 'steal', or at least erode, the budget that has been allocated to them. One organisation I worked with did get very close to achieving an integrated approach amongst all its agencies. The person responsible for this, who headed up marketing, left. The whole thing fell apart very quickly, especially as his successor believed in 'divide and rule'. Still, who knows, one day?

So, there are a number of routes to choose from in order to be able to achieve the required level of professionalism in implementing an integrated approach to marketing.

SUMMARY

- Sexy, high impact incentive schemes often cost more than they achieve.
- Internal and integrated marketing is more complex than PR and external marketing agencies understand.
- External marketing 'meets' the needs of customers who need not buy what is on offer. Internal marketing must 'match' the needs of the organisation to the people in it who may have to buy what is on offer. This creates a new set of rules from those of external marketing.
- The skills of human resource are also needed to facilitate this matching process e.g. coaching the individual who cannot or does not want to buy into a new way of doing things.
- The skills and processes of Total Quality need merging with human resource development and marketing if campaigns are to work and cultural change is adopted into the fabric of the organisation.

14 HINTS, TIPS AND BEST PRACTICES FOR A SUCCESSFUL CAMPAIGN

Having got this far in the book, you probably will appreciate ideas coming from the trials and contributions of others, as they struggled to get their ideas and concepts into organisations. These are a few hints, tips and Best Practices that may help in managing your internal customer's ever changing needs and wants.

CREATIVITY

It is for their creativity that most advertising agencies are known, and upon which they build their reputations. Increasingly the other services which they once provided in-house, are being farmed out to freelance people, or to subcontractors. This includes everything from artwork to print and media buying. The one service that tends to stay within the agency and is guarded jealously, is the creative function. This is simply because it is the one service upon which all the others hang. The mysteries and aura built up around the creative aspects of advertising are fuelled by the often temperamental and outlandish dress or behaviour of these 'artistic types'.

Whole campaigns and millions of pounds can be based on concepts which the average person might feel incapable of dreaming up. Yet these ideas, in essence, have to be totally understandable by the target market in order to create the desire to purchase or increase the propensity to purchase. They are perceived to be clever because of the underlying awe of creativity. Whoever would have thought of selling off British Gas through a campaign featuring a character nobody ever saw, called Sid? The very simplicity of it captured the imagination of millions of people. A star was born.

But why bother with Sid, or any new idea in the first place? Why can't all campaigns be the same? Why not a whole series of simple messages produced in black and white on A4 pieces of paper. Why the colours, the designs, the humour, the sex, the fantasy, the enticements, the songs, the music, the well-known actors, the appealing children, the animals, the cartoons, the new campaigns, the revamped products and services etc.?

It is because people get very bored very quickly. They are soon 'switched off' by seeing the same thing again and again.

How does this equate to internal marketing? The comparison with the continuous and monotonous A4 pieces of white paper should not have been lost on anyone. They are called memos in business.

In comparison to the level of sophistication attained by external marketing, the memo is about as exciting as the 'Situations Vacant' in the local newspaper. They may be fine if you are desperate for a job and scour every inch, but if you have a job already then the chances of you reading them are very slim indeed! And today, most people who have jobs are very busy. The use of the memo, or similar pieces of communication, creates a second comparison with that of external advertising. Not only is the quality of the external advertising message usually very good, but the targeting of the message also ensures that the message hits home. The same cannot be said of much of the internal communication that takes place in organisations today.

Additionally, the consumer is not hit with products and services that the manufacturer feels he might like to sell. They are targeted with products and services that research says they want to buy. This means that the organisation starts off at a major disadvantage if all it does is attempt to push its needs to the individuals within it. As was seen with the top ten products and services, at least the individual's needs can now be assessed and met, alongside those of the organisation.

Finally, the creative process in external marketing usually lies with the naturally creative people. They have also been trained to apply their talents to the needs of the advertiser. How does the average individual suddenly become a creative person, as well as having all the other internal marketing skills? The answer is like every other skill, creativity can be taught.

There are many excellent books on the market, notably *The Innovation Handbook* by Vincent Nolan. The lessons to be learned on creativity are amazingly powerful. Others include *The Creative Marketeer* by Simon Majoro and *The Colours of Your Mind* by Jerry Rhodes and Sue Thane. In fact the increasing number of books and courses suggests that the importance of creativity is now being recognised. The main reason is to help ensure that more people in the organisation come up with the next best selling product, but the spin off in terms of the personal creativity needed for internal marketing is just as valuable.

The fact that one of those previously conservative institutions, banks, namely National Westminster actually train many of its employees in creative thinking using Jerry Rhodes, further suggests that there is growing recognition of its importance.

Having pointed out that creativity can be learned, it is worth mentioning one of the main obstacles to creativity. As individuals become more 'empowered', and therefore much stronger in their position vis à vis the organisation, the biggest inhibitor to creativity will begin to disappear. The inhibitor is fear. It is the fear that has already been discussed, preventing the mind from reaching outwards to new methods, coming up with odd suggestions and even contemplating bizarre ideas. These form the basis for creative thinking.

Add to the removal of this fear, the ability to stir the creative juices, and soon stimulating internal marketing messages will come pouring out. As one of our delegates on a creative and innovation workshop once said 'It is like being on another planet'. The comment itself symbolises the strength of the course, and their ability to change.

Create a positive atmosphere

The techniques of creativity include brainstorming, a well-known activity. There are a number of others such as one that we call 'no nos'. In other words the word no is barred. An even more potent technique is not just to stop the nos but to get people to piggy back on other people's ideas. This can be done simply by introducing the words 'yes . . . and . . .'. For example, 'Yes . . . that is excellent, and . . . it could be even better by doing . . .'. The opposite to this which is the norm in most organisations is 'no . . . but . . .'. For example 'no you can't do that but you can try my idea'. The difference is huge and the effect on individuals is a joy to watch.

> ***So, creativity becomes important at every level. It is useful every time that pen is put to paper. The external marketeer has only words and ideas to sell the products and services. The internal manager in the role of the internal marketeer is in the same boat.***

The imaginative use of many new ideas, in putting across the products and services that an organisation has to offer, are only just now beginning to blossom. The 1990s will see a move that will begin to put internal marketing on a par with the sophistication, excitement and creativity found in external marketing.

To do that of course, some key individual decision makers are going to have to see the benefits of internal marketing, but the moves are strong enough now to suggest that it is only a question of time.

It is a pleasure to see the reaction of people to creative internal marketing – for example games are a wonderful means of marketing training. Other creative techniques range from exciting and different internal videos, to local motivation schemes. These are in addition to the large, often very creative and well designed corporate programmes. They tend to be the ones that have the creative three word titles, often with the word 'people' in them. This focus on people is not surprising, as the biggest need that organisations have is to focus on their people, e.g.:

'Where People Matter' – the Royal Bank of Scotland
'People Like Us' – Bass
'Putting People First' – British Airways
'The Right People' – ESSO
'People Development Programme' – Butlins

However just to prove that using the word people isn't the only creative solution:

'Why Communicate' – Royal Mail and streamline
'Shades' – Top Shop
'A Leap in Sales' – Gardner Merchant

In summary, creativity will, and must become, a skill used by everybody.

MOCK UPS, SCAMPS, VISUALS

Tom Peters talks of quick testing of new ideas, the 'chicken test'. These must happen before large investments are committed, and time is wasted in getting products and services to the external market place that nobody wants. The advertising world had been practising this well before Peters. With so much at stake in terms of the production costs of advertising, the distribution costs through the TV networks, and the reputation of the products and services, quick tests of creative work are essential.

The methodology is very simple. Rough designs are produced for research. These can be of the brand identity, a copy line, an advert, a poster, etc. These are the 'visuals', or in very basic form 'scamps'. In addition to the visuals, (rough) examples of the packaging, and sometimes the unproduced product can also be produced; these are the mock ups. Finally, the TV advert can be visualised in a sequence of cartoons, called a story board.

These can then be filmed and a demo track, called an animatic (an animated u-matic) produced to see what the effect will be. These processes described can be initially for internal use, then they are used for testing on customers.

The same creative work and ideas for internal marketing can be visualised and tested internally. There must be constant research of scamps, visuals and story boards for videos. Mock ups can also be produced, for example, of the internal support material for a large training programme like workbooks, trainer's guides etc.

INNOVATION

Some people believe that there is a surfeit of good ideas and not enough of them get to the market place. This is the process of innovation. The interesting thing is that the only thing stopping innovation happening is people. It is the jealousies, the fear, the 'not invented here', the misconceptions, etc. which stop ideas becoming reality.

Once again as with creativity, problem solving, decision making, planning, and all other business disciplines, the process is trainable. The culture which allows it to happen also needs to be right. This may take longer to engender, but many organisations both in the east and the west have proved that continuous innovation both for the internal as well as the external market can be sustained.

It is the job of the marketeer to ensure that new products and services are steered through the internal and external maze of human and other obstacles. This is also true of the internal or external products and services. The innovation process is critical.

Edward De Bono, in his book *The Six Thinking Hats*, highlights the main problem with innovation. He points out that at any one time, the individuals who are involved in the process, will all almost invariably be thinking totally different things about the ideas before them. His recommendation is to orchestrate the process so that everyone exposes their core attitude, or mode of thinking to others. This ensures that attitudinal barriers are not raised through lack of understanding. Thus, he created six coloured thinking hats. The easiest one to explain is the black hat. If you are wearing this and tell others that they will know that you are going to oppose the idea, or a part of it. It is exactly the same as saying that you are going to play Devil's advocate.

If everyone at least knows where you stand, they are less likely to get upset about what you say – which is exactly why people do warn you that they are going to play Devil's advocate! This highlights one part of a process – exposed for all to see.

It is therefore critical to the innovation process that it is put through a process or structure. This helps steer it through the tortuous maze of people's reactions.

It is not a fanciful notion on De Bono's part. Innovation will be crucial to both the activity in the internal, and external market place. Personal experience of being involved in the development of a training product that produced a process for innovation, is that if it is ignored or circumvented, the idea will almost invariably fail. No matter how brilliant the idea, how creative the concept, in the internal market place, there are even more enormous hurdles to overcome in getting products to the external market place.

BRANDING

The 'three word titles' of the large internal marketing campaign have already been mentioned. If these are given a specific logo, or even an effective type face, they can often form the basis of the brand identity of the products and services on offer. Just as Mars, Coca-Cola, Persil, etc. form the brand names of the external products, so too can internal products and services be branded.

> ***The branding process occurs when the device used to signify it is constantly used to reinforce the identity of the product***

This can be on the covers of the training manuals, on the note paper used to send out any information, on the posters to put on the staff room walls. And so the brand is built. Once established, the range of products on offer under the brand identity can grow. This further reinforces the strength of the brand and lets the internal target market know that the organisation is serious about the products and services that it is delivering.

For example, under the brand of the 'People Development Programme' at Butlins Holiday Worlds, every aspect of the internal Top Ten products and services was addressed and put into the programme. The beauty of a campaign of this nature is that there is every reason to tell the external market place about it. If customer service is a part of the brand, then it is worth capitalising on this. The Royal Bank of Scotland used the internal brand as a strap line on all their external advertising – 'Where People

Matter'. This of course further builds the internal perception about the importance of the campaign.

It also creates a level of customer expectation which drives the people in the organisation to try to deliver. Texas, the DIY chain, have been running an 'Ask for Tom' campaign for some time. Customers will mention this, sometimes so much the staff get tired of it. Good! It has served its purpose.

The strength of an organisation, indeed its financial value is now recognised to be in its brands. Take-overs and mergers happen to create opportunities for the brands to be further exploited. However, very little attention is paid by the acquiring organisations to the strength of the human resources, and even less attention is paid to the strength of feeling internal people have towards the internal brands, and the products and services they comprise. This is a massive oversight. If the people are only one third of the equation, where customers, the organisation and people are important then they are still a very large percentage. It is these internal people who are internal customers.

Internal customers don't just buy products and services, they buy brands.

The next move after creating a brand for a programme of change, e.g. Quality people development or customer service, is to create brands for the ranges of internal products and services. These can then be linked by a corporate style. The individual products and services can reflect this style whilst having their own unique identity. This is entirely consistent with external marketing.

Referring back to the model, it can be seen that there is a very clear cut segmentation of the overall products and services that are on offer, e.g. products, service, vision, quality, plans, practices. This segmentation provides its own brands.

Take, for example, ESSO. Used in their external marketing campaign, the branding signifies the overall intent of the organisation. Very simply this is done through the words 'Quality Service Value'. The title is then used extensively in the internal campaigns, and helps to built an overall identity to the external campaign.

In the example of Renault Truck Industries, an organisation faced, at the end of the 1980s with massive change, or losing its British manufacturing base, the overall brand used, was under the banner 'The Business Development Programme'. This had a further strap line, 'Investing In Our Future'. This was even though the UK manufacturing base was going through massive staff reductions.

Sadly, few organisations pay much attention to branding their procedures. Renault have had to highlight this area out of necessity. 'The Organisational Development Plan . . . Investing in us', formed the basis for structural changes, and ties in with the overall title.

Internal brand names will often come best from those who provide the product and services. However, they should always be put through the internal marketing wheel. This will ensure that they have at least been tested on the final user, the customer.

The days in external marketing are long gone, when the MD's wife decided if the latest commercial dreamed up by the agency was accepted.
The days in internal marketing should also be over when the training manager produces every bit of the latest major campaign without reference to the internal customer – no, not just his boss!

The process of branding internal products and services in the same way as externally needs to happen automatically. Every action to build the internal brands within an organisation must be seen as adding financial value to it. As soon as that can be proved, then the case for investment becomes financial not intuitive. The position of internal marketing takes on the same strength as external marketing.

PACKAGING

I use the term packaging loosely here, to describe the methodology for putting across the organisation's products and services. In internal marketing, the product is invariably words, e.g. mission statements, strategic plans, training information. These words need to be packaged in such a way as to ensure that the customer is tempted to buy the product. The packaging may be as simple as a memo, or it may be a totally co-ordinated range of material from a video to a trainer's guide.

The nature and extent of the packaging will be dependent on a number of criteria, e.g. target audience, number, distribution costs. A few examples will illustrate the packaging produced to meet these criteria. My favourite piece of internal marketing which went through all the stages of the internal marketing mix in an exhaustive development programme, is the Royal Mail Communication Skills Package. Called 'WHY Communicate', it had four sections: WHY Talk, WHY Write, WHY Listen and WHY Meet. The title

WHY represents in mnemonic the three key elements of any communication – the most important being 'hooks'.

It was extremely successful, with over 3,000 managers attending. However, the vagaries of time, and different target audiences mean that packaging is one of the elements of the marketing mix which must be constantly reviewed and changed. So, one version was created for the letters division in the late 1980s. In 1992 the direct mail business Streamline, a separate part of the Royal Mail, had their own version produced.

The creative and innovative processes were at work during the whole development period. In addition to it being unlike any other 'training' package that they had produced before, it was the first time anything like it had been introduced into the organisation. It not only had Geometric Psychology, it also had a game played by the managers. It was considered not only an exciting and novel way of putting across a very important message, but the initial tests also showed that the learning and retention levels were higher than with most conventional training. In addition, whilst the number of messages to get across was considerable, the time taken to absorb them was much less than would have been taken in any normal method of training.

The packaging of the concept was crucial. If the internal target market felt in any way that they were being talked down to, or that the message was somehow being trivialised, then the substantial investment could have been wasted. The people involved in the project would have a difficult time also, because their credibility would obviously be affected.

The 'WHY' game was based on the brand name. The concept was researched as strong, memorable and clear in what it was supposed to achieve. The packaging of the solution was also user friendly. Everyone knows how to play games. The alternative was to have people sitting in long training sessions. The thorough testing of the game produced a product which worked well. This was vital; people will often look for any excuse to put down things which fundamentally challenge their existing *modus operandi* and their beliefs and behaviours.

In addition, when talking about research, the advance warning of things which are going to be introduced provides its own PR. The 'buzz' went around the organisation that the new training was going to be a game that was fun! All of this was part of the process.

The packaging comprised the box, with a colourful design that was thoroughly researched (in fact everything was researched and tested). This came with a separate pad to act as a reminder on the desk. Inside the box were coloured cards to show the different workstyles and situations involved in communication (later to become the Thomson Whitwell Customer Style Indicator). The object of the game is to find the 'hooks' of the internal customer before trying to get across what the manager wants. In other words communication requires marketing skills!

The often incredibly complex world of business need not always be boring

Another example of packaging a complex product is the ESSO, 'The Right People Programme' which was targeted at the independent dealers. The issues to be tackled split into three critical areas for the business. These were, and will continue to be: recruitment, induction and retention. The solution was to provide a user friendly guide, which was heralded by a pre-release mail shot.

The creative element once again was strong, using a series of cut out people all joining hands with their arms held high, as if jumping for joy. This symbolised the power of having people that are motivated.

The guide was unlike anything that ESSO had ever produced. It featured lots of graphics in full colour, line illustrations, photographs, and large type all with bullet points rather than wordy paragraphs. Once again, the style was researched and adapted to the internal target markets. The guide was designed to be readable either in short sharp bursts, or from cover to cover.

Later research showed that the experienced manager dipped into it, and the newer manager tended to use it as a complete learning package.

Research from external marketing shows that the attention span of people is reducing all the time. This meant that the guide had to have a succession of bite sized messages. Each of them had a hook that, for example, made things easier or simpler for the busy manager.

The sections were kept extremely short, and examples of any administrative procedures were always shown as hand written forms as if another manager had filled them in. This prevented the feeling of the procedures being imposed from above.

As an added learning aid, and an advert for those who wanted to know what the guide was all about before committing themselves to read it, a cassette was issued. This could be played in the car. It contained an interview featuring an unbiased third party experiencing the same problems of recruitment, induction and retention. It was Paul Chisnall, the Personnel Director of Trusthouse Forte Airports.

He commented on the fact that the biggest difference in the customer's mind between organisations, all competing for the same revenue, is the level and quality of customer service. This needs to be given by well trained and motivated staff.

Rather than send everything at once, another guide in the series was issued some six months later. This allowed time to fully research the impact of the first and to incorporate the findings. Both guides then formed the basis of a workshop, allowing the managers to discuss the most successful methods they had adopted and to hone their skills in some of the new techniques. These workshops were also put into test, and marketed to the managers.

Both of these examples serve to illustrate the creativity that can be applied to packaging internal products and services.

INTERNAL MARKETING AND THE SMALL ORGANISATION

Often at seminars people ask 'What about the smaller organisation which neither has the need for large scale productions nor the budget?' Whilst the budgets may not be as large, the need for a similar approach to internal marketing is vital. The person in the smaller organisation is no different. The external marketing influences are just as strong, and their needs and wants are much the same. It may also be that the person in the smaller organisation, will have had large organisation experience. They may be used to a degree of sophistication which makes them difficult to satisfy. The small organisation cannot afford to ignore internal marketing.

The answer to what seems like a problem lies in the advent of desk top publishing (DTP). By using simple practices like printed headed paper to give a greater degree of perceived branding, and with the relatively low cost of laser printing and high speed photocopying, the smaller organisation has no excuse for boring internal marketing. The investment will certainly be greater than before, e.g, the simple and usually boring typewritten piece of A4, stuck in the same ring binder as all the other pieces of paper. But is it the investment which is the issue, or the return on that investment?

DTP is beginning to open new worlds to every internal marketeer. Everyone can have the capability at their fingertips to be able to put information across in a way that will not only be readable but will be enjoyable. Coupled with improved skills in marketing there will be no reason why every individual in an organisation should not be treated to a high degree of targeting.

The fact that all the other elements of packaging are not available, not just the sexy manuals, but also the videos, games, cassettes, etc. make it even more important to try and use the technology that is affordable.

If you are still in doubt about the relative effectiveness of some of the pieces of communication your organisation processes, you only have to look at all the work and time wasted on some of those training manuals that are now propping open the doors. How often are they read? How much is put into practice? How often do people ask for more? Additionally, how much do people complain about 'poor communications' even when you have been pumping out memos, manuals, etc. at a very rapid rate? You try to keep up with the pace of change and the increasing demands of customers on quality, service and value, yet the level of communication is still not good?

The introduction of the internal marketing practices into small organisations does work. The difficulty with quoting small scale examples is that no one has heard of them, and the co-ordinated approach happens slowly.

If, however, it is going to take British Airways 12 years to get where it wants to go, then it is obvious that large organisations are faced with difficulties as well. It isn't just large budgets that make internal marketing work, it is the Attitude, Awareness and Ability of the individuals in the organisation!

TEST MARKETING

The external marketeer will have a variety of methods for test marketing at his disposal. There will include one to one interviews, small groups in people's houses, large tests of people pulled into halls, through to actually launching the product on the market in a test area. This is normally a TV area, or more recently, testing a whole country prior to an international launch.

The same methods of testing different numbers of people are also available to the internal marketeer. The differences that they encounter when researching target markets are twofold. The first comes from a major flattening of external cultural differences. These differences which exist between individuals externally are flattened internally, through the superimposition of the corporate culture. The wide variety of styles and approaches that need to be adopted by external marketing is therefore reduced.

Secondly, the internal target markets are used to a relatively unsophisticated level of internal marketing. This allows greater leeway in what is acceptable to the internal market place, e.g. corporate videos do not have to match the quality of TV adverts. Nevertheless, it won't take much of an improvement in internal marketing for the 'Oliver Syndrome' to start happening. The cry will not however just be 'More!' it will also be 'Better!'.

It is vital to test the creative inputs. This often applies to the later stages in the process as well, such as final artwork, and on into the actual usage of the product. As has already been mentioned, there is another benefit to internal testing of the various stages. The closed loop of communication that exists within an organisation soon allows the grapevine to work. The internal marketing methods create instant awareness of the fact that something good (or of course bad) is going to happen.

By putting concepts into test, the badly conceived elements will quickly be spotted. This should prevent mistakes.

The final benefit gained from test marketing is a sense of ownership from those being tested. The internal marketeer can also claim a high level of internal involvement, especially to those who are not tested. So what is done to test the concepts, designs, packaging and ultimately of course the product itself – be they new training methods, to the mission statement?

Basically, testing is either done on a one to one basis, or in group discussions. I am not going to discuss the techniques that are used in detail. Suffice it to say, that many of the skills are those used by most marketing specialists. Depending on the complexity of the information that is required this can either be handled internally, or by the outside organisation responsible for the research.

LAUNCHING NEW INTERNAL PRODUCTS

If handled correctly, the intitial PR about something new to hit the organisation can be done at the testing stage. Letting everyone know that something is being tested makes its introduction much easier in the later stages. This early warning can be done, for example, at briefing groups. However, anyone considering this route should watch out for the 'Chinese whispers' that occur. There are often massive distortions and additions that are used to provide personal and political benefit. In short, verbal communication such as cascading through briefing groups is dangerous. See 'Team Listening' later. Other existing channels that can also be used are internal newsletters or newspapers.

WARNING: It is worth remembering that these traditional channels do have a reputation for often being just propaganda.

If the products and services to be launched warrant special attention, then it is usually best to plan each based on its own merits.

The methods that can be used to get across new products are no different to external marketing.

Teasers

These are short sharp messages, often incomprehensible, warning that something is about to happen. They are used extremely successfully in external marketing. They can be used just as effectively in the internal market place. The ESSO teaser has already been mentioned. Another example from Gardner Merchant is a poster declaring 'WATCH THIS SPACE!'

There are lots of reasons for using this technique, but it must not be overused.

As with much of the rest of this newly emerging discipline, if seen too often, it will be perceived by some to be full of hype, and a waste of money.

Conferences

These are an excellent way of highlighting a subject's perceived importance within an organisation, because of the impact that conferences can generate. Their strength is that they can start to tackle Attitude.

They are not very good, however, at creating awareness – deep understanding

Neither do they allow the involvement people need to develop new skills. In other words, they don't address Awareness, and Ability.

As more and more people recognise the need to do more than just touch the surface of the human resource development issues in the organisation, conferences may not diminish in number, but may well diminish in importance.

Events

Not quite a conference, because the audience do not just sit in rows listening to speakers. The event can have lots of participants. There is usually more involvement from the audience, rather like a TV game show. They rely very heavily on good quality presenters or even actor(s) to provide a high level of excitement.

They have their place in the internal marketing mix but again, absorption is sacrificed for impact. If impact is required then fine, but if all the excitement is created from watching and not doing, then very little will be absorbed.

This type of training event, where a lot of ground is covered in a short space of time, is often described as a Chinese meal.
At the time you enjoy it and feel quite full, but it doesn't take long to be hungry again and forget that you have just eaten.

These are usually held for 50 to 100 people, over one or two days, using a sheep dip approach. For smaller numbers, say up to 30, using a workshop style approach, with less hype and more involvement, provides a high degree of absorption as well as impact. Holding events means that larger numbers of people can be covered when it comes to getting simple messages across in a cost effective way. This may be necessary in bigger organisations, or where budgets are limited.

Workshops

This method of imparting knowledge and of changing attitudes is beginning to take hold. Once, they were seen as a very expensive way of putting things across.

The view now is that they are one of the most cost effective and powerful tools at the disposal of the organisation.

The participative nature of workshops is the one sure way of creating the right environment for individuals to teach themselves. They have the time to think things through. Interacting with others providing an excellent stimulus. With no more than 12 people, the amount of ground that can be covered in a structured environment can be enormous.

Workshops are not necessarily training per se. It may be that the products and services being launched are simply a new approach that doesn't require any new skill input. It may be that a transference of ownership of responsibility is necessary, and the implications need to be thought through.

The environment that needs to be created is one of open debate, healthy cynicism, honest feedback and a testing of the products and services to ensure they stand up to the needs of the people who will be using them.

BOTTOM UP COMMITMENT FROM THE LEADERS (Note they are now at the bottom!)

The launch of any new products and services must be seen to have one key ingredient, commitment. That is why the external marketeer will spend a substantial part of the first year's marketing budget on the launch. The PR, the launch event, and the launch advertising will create impact and demonstrate the commitment in the new products and services to the external market place. The same must be seen internally.

Whether it is the launch of a new lunch rota in the stores department, or a major initiative on Quality, the internal market place will be looking to see the level of commitment that the organisation and the individual managers and leaders place on it.

This is why bottom up commitment is vital. If it is not seen from the beginning, it is easy for the individuals to self-justify that they do not have to take it on board.

Is this preaching to the converted? Are your leaders committed? In many organisations the word *commitment* is mistaken for *enthusiasm*. Leaders can continue to be very enthusiastic that something is done, and remain enthusiastic. However, it is the amount of time they devote, and not just the amount of mental energy, that is the key to demonstrating commitment. No launch, whatever size, will be successful without the commitment of the appropriate leader.

TOP DOWN COMMITMENT FROM CUSTOMERS

If customers are the most important focus of the organisation, then any new products and services launched, must have an effect on them. There is every reason for gaining some top down commitment from customers, either physically, or in the content of the launch. For example if dealers or agents will benefit from a new level of customer service then invite them to share in the process. It is only by being closer to customers that the organisation gets it 'right first time' in delivering its products and services.

In the external marketing, the Motor Shows in every country are aimed at both dealers and customers. Opinion gathered at these events is vital in planning the follow up marketing. The same could happen in

many other instances. Researching and involving customers creates commitment.

At the moment, it may be with closer ties such as dealers, and also with suppliers, but in the future what is to stop panels of external customers from being part of the research and launch of major internal marketing campaigns? The customer-supplier chain should not be a concept, it should be a reality.

Within my organisation, we have often initiated meetings of key customers, potential customers, and suppliers, to discuss the issues that we face in meeting their needs. This provides a forum for everyone to improve, and learn from each other. When you are busy it is not easy to devote the time, but it is worth it in the long run.

Conferences/events/workshops

These were discussed under the launch of new products and services, but may be just as valid for regular updates, for motivation exercises and for improvements to existing products and services, which do not have to be new to be under discussion.

As discussed the ability of the presenters and facilitators will determine the impact on the individuals involved. The rest of the organisation can then be affected.

Training

Very often there will be a large training element attached to the distribution of internal products and services. In addition to this, individuals in organisations today are putting training (and development) very high on their list of needs. Organisations are also recognising that they must put their training needs high on the list of priorities if they are to survive. Matching the two needs may not be difficult to start with, given a low base. Tight training budgets results in individuals looking elsewhere if their training needs are not met.

In distribution terms it is becoming increasingly clear to all levels of management that training individuals in all aspects of the three As is not the responsibility of the training department.

Training is a management responsibility. This means that they are now responsible for the delivery of the internal products and services that are necessary for the survival of the organisation. This, for some, is a major attitudinal shift in itself.

Once again it is the people who will be delivering the marketing, not a specialist department. In this case, the managers.

Team briefing

My views on one way cascades are probably clear by now. They can be made interactive, and can improve the absorption of information on the products and services being delivered. See Team Listening.

Individual meetings

Individual meetings require a whole host of skills. These necessary skills form the basis of many training programmes. These are all ultimately aimed at getting individuals to understand and buy into the 'practices', or tasks necessary for the organisation to succeed. People will fail to buy into the organisational products and services without continuous input. The management and leadership skills needed include delegation, motivation, coaching, counselling, presentation skills, to name but a few.

> ***All these skills that are needed for delivering a message have to be taken into account in the internal marketing mix. It is no use delivering a sexy package of training and development if the distribution channel cannot handle it.***

People cannot operate without the input and output of people and management skills. These skills have been classified using many different titles. These include such tried and tested techniques as Situational Leadership and its populist derivative One Minute Management, and the alternative process driven approach of Performance Management.

But none of these skills or practices admits that internal people are customers! If this is now accepted, then matching their needs with products and services requires another skill used in a one to one, or small group situation – selling!

SELLING TO THE INTERNAL CUSTOMER

The interesting phenomenon that exists in the UK is that because of our reserved attitude, we cannot cope with accepting the fact that we have to sell to be successful. The image of the double glazing salesman, with his foot in the door makes us shudder. We feel uncomfortable with the notion that people have to be persuaded to accept something by influencing them. Selling might be OK for the people on the road, but it's not something that internal people would feel necessary or even desirable.

However, people do seem to be able to cope with what is, in essence the same thing disguised under a softer title, the fact that they have to 'sell themselves', or even softer still, they have to 'sell their ideas'. It is fascinating to see the different interpretations of these three titles – selling; selling yourself; selling your ideas. The net result is exactly the same, but if the internal individual finds it more acceptable, and buys into the concept, albeit as a result of ignorance and prejudice, then there is every reason why the apparently 'softer' titles should be used – it's called psychology, and that is what forms the basis of marketing and selling!

The interesting thing about being up front with the acceptance of internal selling, under any of its three titles, is that the language used to talk about the internal customer is immeasurably strengthened. Once again, both Crosby and Peters stopped short.

Just as internal marketing is the process for matching needs of organisations to individuals, so selling is the distribution channel that puts the message across on a one to one basis. Organisations put considerable resource into their external sales activity, they know that they have to. They know that customers need persuading, they know that customers need to be handled with professional expertise, they know that the skills of the good salesperson will produce a whole host of benefits including loyalty, confidence, trust, information, and of course revenue. The salesperson in turn is targeted, feels motivated to achieve, knows the power of speech, body language, persistence etc.

If the model of marketing to the customer-supplier chain is correct, then it follows that every action by every individual in verbally putting across the products and services of the organisation, in one to one or small groups must be selling.

So why is it that selling has to be disguised under totally different names? In many situations it may appear that selling skills are not required, e.g. when interviewing, appraising, coaching. But these are the very situations where selling is extremely useful! There is always something to be sold. The specific skills involved in delicate people situations would almost invariably be enhanced by the skills of selling.

This book is not the platform for discussing selling in depth. Suffice it to say that if you regard the innumerable sales books and sales training programmes, as evidence of the breadth and depth of the subject in external terms, then there is a long, long way to go internally. Much could be done to co-ordinate the many leadership, management and people skills using the more assertive banner of selling. The experience of many organisations, especially in the financial and retail sectors in training and developing their front line individuals to sell to the customer, demonstrates the benefits to be had if everyone in the organisation were skilled in selling.

In short, once internal marketing is recognised, we're almost forced to buy into internal selling, and to reaping the tremendous rewards that will follow. (Does this sound like another book is on its way? The subject certainly deserves one). If you are not convinced, here is a list of the powerful techniques that enhance the skill of using words as the vehicle for getting things done. This means every manager, leader, supervisor and many, if not most, other individuals in the organisation. They are classified under the ABC of Selling, the Approach, the Buy, the Close. You don't have to understand or appreciate the benefits of using the techniques and skills in the list. They serve to illustrate to those who do not have a sales background the extent and depth of knowledge that exists in this field in understanding and using psychology to succeed in the external market place. The same can be done internally.

A word of warning however. The methods of delivery of these techniques and skills cannot simply be transferred from external sales to internal sales. Not to put too fine a point on it, if internal people had to face some of the styles and methods adopted to motivate external sales people they would be put off selling for life! Targeting of the internal selling message is likely to be a delicate affair.

The ABC of selling – some of the techniques and skills

1 The Approach

Attitude to selling – positive approach, goal setting, accepting rejection.

Individual customer research – assessing background, needs, personality, style of approach, using SWOT one to one.

Planning the interface – use of selling time, setting meeting objectives, arranging daily priorities, the 80/20 rule of effectiveness, pre-arrival activities.

Utilising personal strength and past experience – establishing track record, projecting image, using personality, social strengths, contacts.

Rehearsing – acting the part through preparation.

Introduction – remembering names, establishing rapport, creating confidence, backing off, adapting to different customer styles.

Using the politics and positions positively – establishing relationships, levels of authority, approaching decision-makers and influencers.

Creating business and personal relationships – establishing personal details, status, allies, enemies.

Creative starts – using visuals, stories, questions, revealing information, testing knowledge.

2 *The Buy*

Meeting the customer on equal terms – meeting negatives, meeting aggression, etc.

Identifying the irrational needs of customers – using kudos, reassurance, past experience.

Body management – sex, staying in charge by being relaxed, eye contact, gestures, expressions.

Voice management – volume, pitch, variety, emphasis.

Positive signals – expecting the order, assumptive statements, writing notes.

Question techniques – 'What' questions: general, specific, controlling, bonding, open questions, closed questions, thinking time, getting yes, testing feelings, steering.

Reflexive listening – 'So' questions, playing back, building common understanding, confirming, enhancing the need, inserting alternatives.

Utilising the customer's senses – visual, touch, sound, ownership through involvement.

The hooks – 'The nice thing for you is . . .', the benefits.

The facts – 'What it does is . . .', what the products and services comprise, the features.

3 *The Close*

Handling objections – 'Taaaa': Thank, Agree, Analyse, Act, Apologise.

Transferring rejection – moving the barriers, alternative solutions.

Asking for the order – overtly and covertly.

Negotiating – a subject in its own right! Never give anything away. Win/Win not Lose/Lose.

Agreeing the investment – the acceptable language of selling yourself.

Generating leads – asking for others likely to be interested.

Relationship marketing – keeping the customer for life.

MARKETING AND SALES SUPPORT MATERIAL

Amongst managers there is often a low base of Awareness of the need to market or sell the internal products and services of the organisation to their internal customers. So support material for them is vital. This is especially true as there is usually an equally low base of the right Attitude and Ability to deal with internal marketing issues. The size and scale of many organisations means that even with a high general level of internal marketing, there will always be constraints that necessitate giving managers strong support. These constraints include, for example, the level of people's ability to present information to others, and the time and knowledge constraints which prevent the same degree of preparation than can be given by specialists.

These are exactly the same arguments that are used for the production of external sales and marketing support material. The salesperson needs a presentation kit, just as the shopkeeper needs point of purchase material to build the display. This doesn't mean that the salesperson or shopkeeper will use the material, indeed millions of pounds are wasted on unused material. What is hoped for is that it will persuade them to stock, sell and display the main product on offer. If they do use the material that is often a bonus!

The internal marketeer must do the same to support the internal people. The sales process must be enhanced. The internal salesperson will have more credibility and more confidence in delivering the message if they have support material to help them. The internal customer will be impressed by professionally produced material, and will be more confident in the person's commitment to selling the products and services.

Having run many workshops to introduce various changes in organisations, I can testify to the relief of the attendees when they realise that they don't have to deliver the often complex messages without the backing of internal marketing support material. What does this include?

Support material – trainer/facilitator guides

Traditionally, trainer guides are wordy tomes. They are often unusable and scribbled and scrawled all over the trainer or presenter. In short, as a product in their own right, they do not meet the customer requirements.

Trainer Guides require considerable effort and time to produce. The core product may in itself be excellent, but the lack of budget and internal marketing input often means they lie on shelves, only to be reinvented by someone else who is unaware of their existence. The wasted investment in training and development in this area is frightening. It is no wonder that the move within training departments is away from being producers to being buyers of material. The next move to further prevent reinventing the wheel and being able to get instant access to products and services already developed, is towards contract training. This will perform the same function as all other contract services and allow the organisation to concentrate on its core business. The same will follow with internal marketing and all the support services it needs:

support material:
- videos
- cassettes
- workbooks
- posters
- leaflets
- mailshots
- teasers
- letters
- magazines
- books
- etc.

There are many ways of supporting the internal marketing and selling process. These are very familiar in external marketing, albeit using different terms, and their use in internal marketing can be equally valid. The way they are put together for use in the internal market place may be different, but essentially the same psychological basis exists.

So, TV adverts are effectively the same as corporate videos – both are trying to sell something using a highly visual and auditory media. TV documentaries are, in essence, the same as video training programmes. Overheads and slides are like posters. Newspaper articles are the same as memos, they may have calls to action, provide information, generate enthusiasm, tell bad news. Radio provides comparisons with messages like cassettes. Just like newspapers, they provide comment, news, information, entertainment etc.

The use of magazines and books is an interesting and new development in internal marketing. In exactly the same way as these are used externally, they can be used internally. Magazines, for example, produced for individuals, with stories, offers, hints, problem pages, etc. offer the opportunity to get across corporate messages without ever once mentioning anyone in 'management', far less the Chairman, and could be one of the strongest media used for cultural change.

Using these to get across key training messages like product knowledge, negates the need for producing the unreadable and unread reference documents, so prolific in organisations today. The Royal Mail, Trusthouse Forte and Woolworth have all invested in this internal medium and they are sure to be the first of many.

The same argument for the use of magazines to supplement the distribution media in the internal marketing mix is also true of books. *The One Minute Manager* was one of the most popular of all management books; why was this? Because it was short, simple, and based on a soap opera style of story.

The same could, and should, be done for organisations with similar messages to portray. In many ways the training video already does this, so why not a different medium which will appeal to a different target customer? Books, based on stories, or even text book style, also allow much greater flexibility in reading and speed of absorption. They can be easily produced in one colour, and in many cases drastically enhance many of the messages that an organisation wants to portray, but usually ends up doing so in more indigestible reports and manuals.

In summary without the marketing and sales support the internal marketing and sales process is doomed to fail!

INTERNAL PROMOTION

No matter how successful a product is, its sales must be supported at some time with some form of promotion. In external marketing this type of activity, along with PR is termed 'below the line' advertising. The sales promotion industry has changed from being the poor relation, to one of the key elements in any marketing budget.

The type of support given through promotion can be seen on virtually every product in the land, and increasingly it is moving into the services that are provided, from dentists to solicitors.

There is nothing wrong with this type of support, the only problem is that it suffered, and still does, from the free plastic daffodil image of the 1960s, where the 'free offer' bore little relationship to the product being promoted.

Today's external customer is still looking for something 'extra', but the tendency now is to provide added value rather than price cutting. The same is true of the needs of the internal market place. They can be tempted to make additional purchases, or to buy a trial purchase through promotional offers. In the same way as externally, the quality of these promotions must be good, and relate to the product they are supporting.

But beware, people may be taken in once, sometimes twice, but never a third time. So what is it that the internal customer will be attacted to in promotional terms?

The answer can be summed up in one word – recognition. Anything which enhances the products and services of the organisation by providing recognition will create an instant hook to increase the propensity to buy, such as the following.

Certificates

Be these internal or external certificates, as long as they have to be earned, and are perceived to improve the status of the individual, then they are an excellent method for promotion.

It must be noted that the reason why they motivate people is not just pride, but an increased potential for reward and for better prospects either inside or outside the organisation. There is no sense in denying the individual the visible signs of success that increase their personal marketability. The organisation can only hope to retain their services through everything else it does. It is for this reason that accreditation is now high on the list of priorities of individuals.

Accreditation

The added value that comes from learning new skills and receiving external recognition provides an excellent promotional platform for organisations. The current UK scheme that is attracting much attention from employers and employees alike is NCVQ – the National Council for Vocational Qualifications. Under this scheme an employer can have a training programme certified by the lead body as being pertinent to others in the same sector, or sectors, with the same needs. The certificate shows a level of competence which is marketable when looking for a new job, or used as a bargaining tool for a pay rise.

The same is happening at lower levels in the organisation with managers and leaders. Even the MBA is a promotional offer of many organisations targeted at managers, allowing free time and financial assistance, e.g. course fees, and even sending them abroad to study.

Badges

The armed forces have proved the strength of this promotional incentive – a free badge or stripe with every promotion. They are worn with pride when they are well deserved. The same can be equally true internally. There are many organisations which provide badges for all sorts of achievements. In Forte, for example, there are training badges, service badges and badges for winning internal competitions such as sales. In the words of Tony Monnickendam, in his days as Director in Charge of the Motorways Division, 'Badges are excellent as long as the wearer doesn't end up looking like Idi Amin!'.

Incentives/prizes

This is a dangerous area in terms of the spend and effectiveness of these promotional offers. As long as the individual receives constant and effective verbal praise and 'small' signs of recognition, the often vast sums spent on providing incentives can be put to much better use. This is at least until the time when the actual products and services are sufficient in themselves to motivate.

Midland Bank has already been mentioned as spending millions on the type of incentive that is akin to the ones used for external sales forces. The size of the rewards, and the fact that only half the target market can actually win them results in a major problem. Failure to win the award is probably more demotivating to the losers than the positive effect on the winners. In the words of David Young, the person responsible at the Midland in the late 1980s, 'We created a beast which we kept having to feed'.

In addition to providing good products to motivate, there is another way of providing the recognition people need. This comes from the instant praise and recognition type management technique that has its roots in performance management and *One Minute Management*. This powerful tool used in many organisations suggests that not only can a great deal of promotional money be saved, but also the response of individuals can be so much greater.

We have observed in many organisations that the most successful levels of individual and team motivation do not come from the long term expectation of promotional incentives and rewards, they come from the immediate praise of the manager and instant recognition. This may include small promotional incentives such as badges, pens, gift vouchers, etc. but the key is not in the amount, it is in the immediacy of the praise. The concept of *The One Minute Manager* was the basis of the guides that were targeted at managers in Midland's 'Best People Programme'.

It is a purely personal view, but I believe that an alteration of management style, together with some small token of the recognition would either produce the desired result if no promotional incentive is being offered, or save considerable sums where it is being offered.

BUDGETS – THE CASH TO DO THE JOB

If it is now recognised that to succeed in the external market place investment in new products and services is vital, then why should the internal market place be any different? The products and services that the organisation offers today will not only appear to be 'old hat' relatively quickly, but will also be highly likely to be out of date in terms of what they are supposed to deliver. Given the ever increasing speed of change of external products and services, the internal market place must move just as rapidly. Together with the many other forces of change such as mergers, acquisitions, privatisation etc., the chances of stability in the internal market place is slim. Whether it is mission statement or training programmes, the forces of change will affect them. To create new products and service the internal marketeer will have to put the whole process of innovation into the internal marketing mix. This will include constant research, testing, repackaging, relaunching, redistributing, and repromoting. These have all been discussed already.

They need to be happening constantly with existing as well as with new products and services. The big difference between internal marketing and the world of external marketing is that quality and quantity of the input and output is vastly different. This shouldn't be the case. Indeed, the demands of the internal market place will soon be such that the quality of internal marketing will have to strive to be as good as it is externally.

The Catch 22 of internal marketing is that no matter how good you are the external marketeer has been at your target market before you.

They will invariably have bigger budgets, which means that the internal perceptions are likely to be coloured by the level of sophistication they are used to externally. No matter how hard you try, they will very quickly expect more.

The 'Oliver Syndrome' of people wanting more, more, more, will affect every organisation as it strives for excellence and Quality. Indeed, the better you get, the more they will expect. Why not? If something is good you can hardly expect people not to want more can you?

That is the bad news. It will form part of the frustration to be felt by the internal marketeer. The poor budgets in this area and the constant cutting of them when times get tough, will continue to be the norm until internal marketing's worth is recognised.

The good news is that the rewards in trying to catch up with the external marketing will produce the host of benefits discussed throughout this book. These benefits will be felt by the individuals, to the organisations, and society as a whole as sales, production, profit, efficiency, motivation, etc. increases.

There can be no doubt that the Quality revolution is taking place in a big way. It is happening in all countries throughout the world. The only doubt now is how soon and in what way organisations will match the needs of the individuals to the products and services of the organisation, in order to meet the needs of its customers.

Marketing internally is already a major topic of debate in the United States and on the Continent. In external marketing, the UK advertising industry leads the world. Can we produce the levels of Attitude, Awareness and Ability in the UK, to build a framework which meets the needs of today's and tomorrow's organisation in the global market place. Can we do it through an integrated approach to marketing – throughout the customer-supplier chain? My vision is YES! Good luck with your part in it, if you my customer have bought into it!

SUMMARY

- **Creativity**
  A process that can be learned by everybody – once the fears and inhibitions are removed. The skill will be vital to stimulate people with new messages and new internal products and services.

- **Innovation**
  Another vital process that turns good ideas into products and services.

- **Packaging**
  From memos to videos the quality of the medium tells the user the commitment behind the message.

- **Test marketing**
  Test the issues before communicating. The benefit is that this can be used to create good PR prior to launch.

- **Launches**
  Decisions to be made between impact and absorption.

- **Selling internally**
  The key skills of selling externally should be transferred internally.

- **Marketing and sales support material**
  The sales people support needs support, the marketing messages needs support, they can't do it alone.

- **Promotions/incentives**
  Promotions create interest. Incentives are often only needed locally.

- **Budgets**
  Without them nothing will happen.

CODA
Revolution or Evolution

In the Coda in *The Employee Revolution*, I foretold of the potential battle between human resource and marketing specialists for the high ground in dealing with the new internal customer. The following articles could, I believe, be just the beginning of this battle. Hopefully, however, the message of this book is that instead of further disintegration between the disciplines of human resource, marketing and Quality, there can be a new period of integration.

The first article written by Adrian Payne, was published in the *European Journal of Management*. The second article by the author entitled 'Internally Yours', was published in *Marketing Business*, The Journal of The Institute Of Marketing. Both say the same thing, targeted at different people, HR, and marketing. The nice thing is that totally independently, they back each other up.

Marketing to internal and external customers may not be a revolution, but it is certainly now on a strong evolutionary path from the fragmented approach of the 1980s.

Internal Marketing: A New Perspective for HRM

BRETT COLLINS, *Director, MBA Programme, Deakin University, Australia;* ADRIAN PAYNE, *Professor of Services Marketing, Cranfield School of Management, UK.*

The authors argue that there are trends currently present in industry and management which require human resource (HR) managers to have much higher levels of competence and skills. Concepts and techniques from marketing can provide means by which HR managers can be more effective.

It is also pointed out that Chief Executive Officers have failed to recognize the importance of HR managers in their organizations – a weakness for which HR managers must also carry some blame.

INTRODUCTION

Over the past few years the term *internal marketing* is increasingly being used to describe the application of marketing internally within the organization. There are two dimensions relevant to our discussion of internal marketing. First, there is the notion that every department and every person within an organization is both a supplier and a customer. The second aspect relates to the organization's staff and involves ensuring they work together in a manner supporting the company strategy and goals. This has been recognized as especially important in service firms where there is a close relationship between production and consumption of the service. It is thus concerned with both quality management and customer service and involves co-ordinating people and process improvement strategies.

Internal marketing relates to all functions within the organization, but it is vitally concerned with the management of human resources. However, the traditional personnel department and the more advanced human resources department, have frequently been oriented towards control and administrative activities rather than the alignment of human resources towards achieving strategic organizational purposes and goals. In this paper we explore the marketing of a particular internal service within the organization – the human resource function. Our purpose is to illustrate how internal marketing concepts and methods used by marketing managers can provide the basis of a new perspective on meeting the opportunities and challenges faced by human resource managers. A market-oriented human resource manager is more likely to make an impact on the success of a company, through being more effective in both demonstrating the relevance of human resource movement (HRM) to all management team members, and helping other managers to increase their productivity.

Our approach is to first consider the nature of the challenges and opportunities confronting human resource (HR) managers. A view of what is seen to be a central task for the HR management professional is then outlined. The congruence between marketing function activities and HR management activities is then described. Finally, we consider how the HR manager can utilize the philosophy, ideas and tools of the marketing function to make a more effective contribution toward the organization's objectives.

CHALLENGES FACING THE HR MANAGER

The managers in a company who deal with the 'people' issues are now recognized as having an increasingly strategic role in the success of many businesses. Regardless of whether the function these managers perform is called personnel, human resources, industrial relations, or training and development, it collectively now represents a business role similar in importance to the areas of finance, marketing and operations management. This trend has been driven by a more intensely competitive business environment, increased use of technology in some industries, and the shift in corporate philosophy from asset management to operations management.

A focus on operations management has forced Chief Executive Officers (CEOs) to understand the need for skilled HR executives if they are to successfully cope with change. An organization able to adapt to change is generally found to be more able to sustain competitive advantage in an environment of increasing uncertainty. The constant stress of corporate takeovers, new ventures, the restructuring of companies, rationalization of existing operations, new technology introduction and staff lay-offs, means that the success of basic strategic decisions increasingly depends on 'matching skills with jobs, keeping key personnel after a merger, and solving the human problems that arise from introducing new technology or closing a plant'.[1] The dramatic turnaround of SAS by Jan Carlzon was driven by people rather than by an expensive investment in equipment and assets.[2]

Increasing attention is being focused on the area of external customer retention and the enormous potential for improved profitability.[3] Top management should also seek to obtain improved organizational performance through effective HRM strategies aimed at improving personnel retention. The baseline benefits are cost savings on retraining in a rapid turnover job market and cutting down the equally expensive knowledge drain. Companies able to manage this issue will reap the rewards which go with a team of committed, active individuals at a time when under-training is sapping productivity among competitors.

Increased usage of technology in some industries has led to the assumption that the quality of people performance will become a less important issue as technology becomes more pervasive. However, the maintenance of reliable performance by competent employees is becoming *more* crucial. For example, we are now in an era where electronic banking means fewer face-to-face encounters between the bank and its customers. Consequently, the importance of handling these interactions, and the 'costs' of not making the most of opportunties are greater. In a relatively homogeneous industry such as banking, a key opportunity for banks to gain a competitive edge over competitors lies in the quality of its people. In an era of electronic fund transfer there is opportunity for a bank to position itself as one that has good people, not just good machines.[4] Many of the key challenges facing retail banking involve the employee: the need to sell and cross-sell, unionization, electronic banking, affirmative action, service quality management and technology management.

It has been argued that HR professionals have failed in the past to reach their full potential within the corporate framework because they devoted themselves to the creation of ever more sophisticated programmes and forgot the whole purpose of the business.[5] HR managers have had a role in organizations dealing with outside pressures such as government, unions and safety, but their active involvement and collaboration is also needed with the production, marketing and finance functions. They have been responsible for fending off interruptions, handling and reporting requirements of regulatory bodies, and dealing with social responsibility issues, but often are not involved in activities perceived by other managers to be fundamentally important to the business.

Managing a corporation is complex, and CEOs find it necessary to simplify their task by concentrating on what appear to be the most important strategic issues. Because of resource limitations, it is necessary to focus senior management's attention and time on those aspects of the business process with the highest expected payoff. This means that some areas with extremely high potential impact, but a very low perceived probability of delivering significant results, must get less attention than one might really wish. Strategic HRM requires a significant investment of organizational resources, which directly and immediately affects profits, and can thus make it unattractive to managers under pressure for short-term results. Further, any real understanding of what competent HRM could contribute to the success of a business has only been popularized fairly recently.[6] For these reasons, senior management has often failed to grasp why HRM was relevant to business strategy business performance and the cost management function.

Clearly, the central task of HRM must be to gain the support of senior management, secure the commitment of the CEO, and ensure HRM makes the most effective contribution possible to the organization's objectives.

The HRM function in a company is never likely to be valued unless it convinces management it can provide significant payoffs, and is part of the key interactions between the organization and environment. HRM will become established as an integral part of a business through helping other managers to increase their productivity. Managers do not require more sophisticated programmes. They require someone who understands their problems, can actively contribute to the more effective and efficient management of human resources, and who has a good understanding of the business. We will now consider how the roles of marketing managers and HR managers are linked.

THE MARKETING–HRM ANALOGY

The HRM function has three distinct client groups, or markets, with which it must deal effectively:

- employees within the organization;
- other managers involved with the senior management tasks including the CEO; and
- external groups such as prospective employees, government, unions and regulatory bodies.

Consideration of the challenges faced by HR managers indicates that they are similar to those challenges faced by other senior managers, and requirements for success correspond to those needed by good marketing managers. The use of marketing ideas does not need to be narrowly confined to products and markets. Marketing has been defined as 'a social process by which individuals and groups obtain what they need and want through creating and exchanging products and value with others',[7] and implies two voluntary parties with unsatisfied needs, an expectation of mutual benefit, a means of communication, and a medium to complete the exchange.

People who buy goods and services are involved in the same type of exchange process as people who seek employment that is satisfying, interesting, and more than a well-lit work space. The relationship between buyer and seller in a labour market is such that the employee must sell labour to earn an income. A company must create goods or services and exchange them in order to earn profits. Clearly, there are times when one party to an exchange has much more bargaining power than the other party. The manager who seeks mutual benefit through working closely with the HRM department is involved in a similar exchange process to that which takes place between consumers and companies everywhere.

A source of interdepartmental conflict can be the need for a marketing manager to represent the interests of a customer against the needs of other managers. We do not lack examples of conflict between the marketing and accounting functions. For example, while the Sales department is properly concerned with maintaining a good relationship and undisrupted supply to the customer, the Accounts department is concerned with administering credit control. Accounts may seek the withholding of supply, because credit guidelines have been exceeded at a time when Sales is trying to service a sudden increase in demand, resulting in open conflict.[8] Similarly, an HR manager can become involved in interdepartmental conflict through a need to represent the interests of an employee against the needs of another manager. Like marketing, HRM is a function where success requires close cooperation with other functions, but there can be significant potential for conflict. The coalitions of power and politics at the core of fundamental conflicts such as this can be used to maximize business performance, or detract from it. The task for the HR manager is made more difficult because the quality of management performance is difficult to quantify – there is no bottom line responsibility. This can leave the HR manager without the defence available to managers of profitable business units who have tangible evidence of performance in their regular financial reports; bottom line results.

Marketing performs a valuable role in that it creates utility, the capacity to satisfy needs.[9] The HR manager is similarly concerned with the creation of utilities. The marketing philosophy or concept states that, in serving marketplace needs, the entire organization should be guided by thinking that centres around the consumer. For our purposes, the concept has three key elements:

- The HR manager requires a thorough knowledge of the needs, wants and problems of the CEO, other managers and employees. Ideally, the HR manager should start with a knowledge of client needs and work backwards to develop products and services to satisfy them.
- The second element requires that the cost, design, implementation and follow-up on HR projects should be carefully planned so all features are consistent with project goals, and the process coordinated with other functions in the organization.
- Finally, in our definition of marketing we recognize that individuals or groups engaging in the marketing process have diverse goals and objectives. If the organization itself does not gain utility from an exchange then this element of the philosophy is not met. Consequently, we would expect that if an HR activity did not lead to organizational gain the activity would be discontinued.

Quantification of performance plays a crucial role in the success of the marketing function, and the performance audit guides corrective action while providing measurements essential to supporting access to resources for projects. HR managers have sometimes been characterized by a lack of willingness to work with performance measures. Marketing strongly depends on techniques developed in the behavioural sciences for quantification of the needs, wants and perceptions of consumers. These tools can be readily adapted to requirements of the HR manager. While measures employed by marketing managers are not always of high precision, they are essential to the building of credibility through measurement and performance against explicit goals. Management performance in functions other than marketing and HRM are generally more amenable to performance measurement.

An HR manager with a market orientation would have good knowledge of the needs and wants of the client groups served, and develop a coordinated approach to servicing those requirements consistent with organization goals and with the expectation of achieving organizational gain from any exchange process. In contrast, a product-oriented HR manager would place primary emphasis on the product or services the HRM department offers, and how these are provided. It is instructive to consider the differences between these two opposing views. Consider training programmes for example: the difference between a product-oriented and a market-oriented manager is shown in Figure 1. This example is stereotypical in that the model represents two extreme positions. No one person would be expected to exhibit all of the characteristics presented for a specific orientation, but an HR practitioner would be expected to possess several if they were either market- or product-oriented and the distinction between two very different management philosophies are illustrated.

Attitudes and Procedures	*Product Orientation*	*Market Orientation*
Attitudes towards clients:	They should be glad we exist. Trying to cut costs and bring out better programmes.	Client needs determine training programmes.
Programme offering:	Department provides courses that fit our skills and interests.	Schedule programmes we know the clients need.
Interest in innovation:	Focus is on technology and cost cutting.	Focus on identifying new opportunities.
Importance of costs:	A number in the budget we cannot exceed.	A critical objective.
Number of programmes scheduled for the year:	Set with the delivery requirements in mind.	Set with client needs and costs in mind.
Role of marketing research:	To determine client reaction if used at all.	To determine client needs and if they are being met.
Attendance at programmes:	Fill all available places – repeating is good revision.	Select attendees according to their needs and coordinate this with other managers.
Promotion of programmes:	Advise managers when their staff is to attend the next course.	Demonstrate need-satisfying benefits of course to clients.

Figure 1 Stereotypical differences between market-oriented and product-oriented HR managers with respect to training programmes.

We have found it a useful exercise, in workshops with senior managers, to discuss the role of conflicting philosophies and how they affect achievement of a marketing orientation. This can be addressed in the context of both external customers[10] and internal customers.[11] Although it has been accepted for many years that a market orientation is essential to the success of a business, it has not been proven in all contingent situations. Monopoly or regulated markets provide examples of non-market orientation. As the difference between a market orientation and any one of many conflicting orientations possible is accepted as the difference between unstable short-term success and stable long-term growth, it becomes of considerable importance to senior managers to push a market orientation within their company. Similarly, the importance of HRM has gradually gained credibility and importance, as managers have come to understand how it can contribute to the achievement of business success. There exists an increasing number of well known companies where superior HRM is believed to be a key factor in their success.

We have seen the similarity in roles of the marketing and HR managers. The marketing and HRM processes both involve the creation and exchange of utilities. A need to represent the interests of a client against the narrow interests of another manager may be conducive to the well-being of the company but a source of open interdepartmental conflict. This conflict is difficult to manage and can detract from the effectiveness of the function and the organization. Both functions require commitment and support from the CEO to succeed, and performance measurement is seen to be an important tool for building credibility within the company. The market orientation can be applied equally to either the marketing or HR functions when it is accepted that success is achieving organizational goals through delivering customer satisfaction. We will now consider how the HR manager can harness the ideas and tools of the marketing function to more effectively contribute toward the organization's objectives.

THE HRM–MARKETING FUNCTION

We are concerned here with internal marketing – that form of marketing where both the 'customer' and the 'supplier' are inside the organization. In this context, we consider employees as customers or clients. These classifications are quite broad and could be further divided into such groupings as the board, managers, supervisors, foremen, clerical staff, etc. The HRM–marketing function can be described in terms of seeing managers and employees as in-house customers, viewing the tasks and activities performed by the HRM function as in-house products or services, and offering in-house or services that satisfy the needs and wants of managers and employees, while addressing the objectives of the organization.[12]

The reasons for believing marketing provides a useful framework for HRM depend largely on the congruences we have demonstrated between essential activities of the two functions. In addition to these congruences, there is a strong similarity in the constraints and difficulties facing either marketing or HR managers. Concepts and tools proven to be useful to the marketing function can also be applied to the benefit of HRM.

The HRM function provides services or programmes to employees and management, which means it sells performances that directly influence business productivity. Internal marketing can help an HR manager to attract and hold the type of people a company wants and get the best of in-house customers; the HR function can upgrade the capability of a company to satisfy the needs and wants of its external customers.

Marketing management is the process of increasing the effectiveness and/or efficiency by which marketing activities are performed. Effectiveness refers to the degree to which organizational objectives are attained, while efficiency is concerned with the expenditure of resources to accomplish these objectives. This difference is eloquently expressed in the view that it is more important to do the *right things* (improve effectiveness) than to do *things right* (improve efficiency).[13] An organization that is doing the right things wrong (effective but not efficient) can outperform organizations that are doing the wrong things right. Effectiveness and efficiency is also a concern of the HR manager seeking improved performance.

MARKETING ACTIVITIES

The marketing function in any organization is concerned with a number of related activities which include:

- Understanding of the market and competitive environment.
- Definition of the firm's Mission.
- Determination of the Target Market Segments to be emphasized.
- Developing integrated Marketing Mix strategies to accomplish this Mission in the selected segments.
- Implement Marketing Mix strategies and Control marketing activity.

This well-known model of marketing function activities, which involves the above steps, is used as a basis for a discussion on intenral HRM marketing.

Market and Competitive Environment

The starting point is for HR managers to gain a good knowledge of the needs and wants of the client groups served, the significant factors influencing the HR department's operations, and identify the 'publics' which interact with the company. This process is market analysis and involves collecting information on the different client markets into a database.

Market research should be used to identify internal client needs, wants and attitudes just as it can be used to identify the needs, wants and attitudes of external consumers or industrial buyers. For example, 'climate surveys' concerning perceptions of remuneration packages, employment conditions and performance appraisal, and opinions of quality improvement programmes provide direct benefits for the redesign and improvement of key policies, processes and programmes. There is also the positive effect on morale that flows from taking an interest in the views of employees.

This channel of communication provides an early means for pinpointing organizational breakdowns and problem areas. An important requirement before undertaking data collection is to adopt a commitment to face the issues uncovered, no matter how unpalatable. It is an ongoing process requiring that issues be resolved in order to maintain credibility of the HR department at all levels within the company. To raise the expectations of client groups without delivering can generate strongly negative effects. Finally, market research can also provide a basis for monitoring the impact of programmes on employees and check whether HR programmes are achieving what they were designed to achieve.

This market research process sometimes suffers from a condition referred to as the 'no-full-disclosure disease'.[14] It manifests itself through people within the management hierarchy who fear the things threatening them may become known to others and then used to their personal detriment. The extent of this problem depends on survey design and content. People interviewed tend to speak freely when given a chance to express their thoughts and opinions on HRM issues. However, undertaking not to reveal the content of an interview under any circumstances, without prior approval from the person interviewed, is sometimes necessary in order to get at the real problems and issues. Whether use is made of questionnaires, personal interviews, informal meetings of managers or group discussions, market research provides a clear means of identifying client needs and wants. It also provides the means for tracking performance.

Mission

The second step involves the development of a mission for the HR department. The corporate mission statement for an organization is too broad to be meaningful for a specific business function, and consequently a mission statement should be specifically developed for the HRM function. It involves asking the questions 'what is our role within the organization?' and 'what should our role be within the organization?'. Figure 2 provides an example of an HR mission statement based on one developed with a leading British service organization.

To develop and promote the highest quality human resource practices and initiatives in an ethical, cost effective and timely manner to support the current and future business objectives of the organization and to enable line managers to maximize the calibre, effectiveness and development of their human resources.

This will be achieved through working with managers and staff to:

- Develop an integrated human resource policy and implement its consistent use throughout the organization.
- Enhance managers' efficient use of human resources through the provision of responsive and adaptable services.
- Be the preferred source of core strategic HR services.
- Provide high quality tailored HR consultancy.
- Introduce methods to plan for the provision of required calibre and quantity of staff.
- Ensure consistent line accountability throughout all areas within the organization.
- Assist the organization in becoming more customer aware and responsive to changing needs.
- Define and encourage implementation of an improved communications culture throughout the organization.
- Maintain an innovative and affordable profile for HRM.

Figure 2 Human resource mission statement

At the HRM level the definition of mission does not have to be complex. It should provide a framework for explaining the HR department's role and how it can help the different levels and units of an organization to coordinate their efforts to achieve the overall objectives of the organization.

Once the mission statement has been adopted, objectives need to be formalized. Because objectives are not equally important, a hierarchy of potential services, programmes and projects should be put together. If possible these objectives should be operationalized – stated in terms that are specific and which will lead to measurable end results. It is important to understand what needs to be accomplished, when the task should be completed, and how it will be decided that the task is completed. This process links very closely with the market research function which can be used to demonstrate performance against specific objectives. A function which provides a service, and deals predominantly in intangibles, requires tangible evidence of success in order to demonstrate competent performance and help build credibility.

Market Segmentation

The third step is deciding which market groups should be emphasized. Market segmentation is a process by which we divide the total, heterogeneous group of clients into smaller, more homogeneous groups with similar needs and wants that the HR function can successfully satisfy. By developing specific services we can generally improve the effectiveness of our performance in satisfying clients. It may cost more to serve smaller groups or handle problems requiring customized solutions. Because of this, there is sometimes a need to balance the level of customization required to adequately solve a problem, against the benefits which might accrue to the organization. This is very much

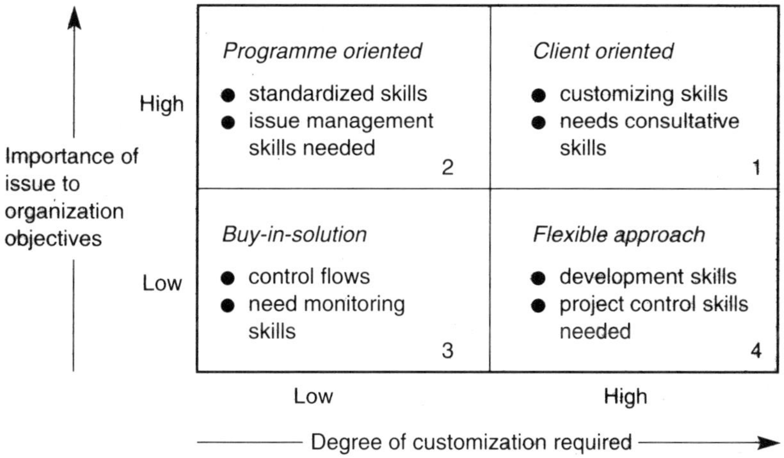

Figure 3 Characterizing HR marketing problems

a cost–benefit exercise. The characterization shown in Figure 3 can be helpful for sorting problems into classes, each of which require different capabilities.

At a high degree of customization there is increased demand for resources from the HR function. The HR cost to the organization increases with an increase in the level of customization. Programmes or projects undertaken by HR typically involve long-term benefits with short-term costs and, given limited resources, this has a direct impact on the HR department's effectiveness.

Quadrant 1 in Figure 3 represents the situation where there is need to fit a key programme to the specialized needs of a client group. A major company wishing to run an in-house strategic management seminar, enabling senior management to review and discuss current management thinking and practice, is an example. The CEO would perceive this to be of high value to the organization, while requiring this process to fit closely with the business context.

The programme-oriented task found in quadrant 2 is characterized by the opportunity for a high quality but standardized approach to be taken. For example, consider a betting agency involved in the conversion of operations from a manual to a computerized telephone betting system. There is a need to develop and implement a programme at low cost which will enable a smooth transition to the new system. Due to the large group of operators requiring new skills there is an opportunity to seek savings through standardization. The importance of this issue means effective performance by the HR department is more critical.

In quadrant 3 the degree of customization required for a task is low – for example, where factory staff are being given first-aid training. The content of a first-aid training programme will be fairly standard across a range of industries. Such a programme is not central to achievement of organization objectives, and represents a situation where service delivery can readily be obtained from outside the organization. Once the training programme was in place, knowing who had attended the course and monitoring the training process would be the key tasks.

An increase in the degree of customization required corresponds to an increase in the level of organization-specific content, as shown in quadrant 4. Consider a retail tyre organization which needs to train shop floor staff in the testing and servicing of car batteries. This more specialized course requires company-specific input, and an in-house programme is the best solution. In this quadrant the need is for course development skills, a flexible approach and the ability to manage the development process. Other examples are custom-designed employee retirement programmes, or surveys of work group satisfaction where there is a need to design and implement a project with the specific needs of a client group in mind.

Obviously most impact can be made by HRM focusing efforts in those quadrants involving problems of high importance to the organization, but not involving significant short-term investment. This type of problem area, identified because the issues involved are considered central to the achievement of business objectives, will often be more able to attract support and adequate funding. Working in areas requiring a high level of customization, which are also critical to business success, is the challenge facing HR. This is the direction in which HR requirements have moved due to the increased complexity of business, changing technology and the shift from an asset management to operations management philosophy.

Segmentation of employees on the basis of their needs and wants, as opposed to the segmentation of management clients, recognizes the need to accommodate individual differences. This is the basis for concepts such as negotiable remuneration packages, employment contracts, flexible working hours and job sharing. The techniques used for consumer segmentation by marketers can be applied directly here. It provides opportunity for companies to 'lessen the influence of unions by placing greater emphasis on direct employee communication, in addition to, or instead of, industrial relations conducted in the traditional representative way'.[15]

Developing and Implementing the Marketing Mix

Once the tasks of determining the mission of the HR department and the target market segments to be emphasized have been undertaken, a marketing-oriented HR function will focus on the 'marketing mix'. The marketing programme is developed based upon a decision on marketing mix variables over which the HR manager has some control: designing the product or service, costing it, setting up a service delivery system, promotion of the product to clients, and gaining commitment for proposals from management. Figure 4 illustrates the four elements of the marketing mix which need to be addressed. Whilst all elements need to be considered, two key variables – the design of the 'product' (i.e. courses or services) and communications are especially important. These two key variables and their relevance for the HR manager are now reviewed.

Designing the 'product'

It has been pointed out that the process of a marketing department introducing a new product, and resolution of a complex long-standing problem by the HR function are very similar. Figure 5 illustrates this, and is based on Desatnick[16] who argues that 'as the contribution of HRM is less tangible and more difficult to measure in terms of end results, it is even more important to market it effectively. This implies taking the time to reflect, to position, to package, to merchandise, and to sell'. Thus the HR manager must get the maximum impact from each situation through careful management of those elements he can control. Developing a product or service for a client group is an activity over which the HR manager has a great deal of control, and consequently provides an area where management attention can be rewarded with maximum impact.

Elements of the Marketing Mix for a Company	*Equivalent Elements for the HRM Function*
1. Products or services	1. 'Products' (services, courses, etc.)
2. Place (distribution)	2. The location and delivery means of services and courses
3. Promotion (mainly through advertising and personal selling)	3. Communications with client groups (primarily through discussion and documentation)
4. Pricing	4. Transfer pricing and expense allocation

Figure 4 The four elements of the marketing mix

Communication

Communication represents promotional activity in the form of advertising, indirect publicity and face-to-face selling which is employed by marketers to influence potential or existing customers to behave in desired ways, such as to undertake the trial purchase of a product the firm has just launched onto the market. Promotion can also be used to influence employees to reconsider attitudes, to inform managers, or alter the way in which a particular programme is perceived by the clients to whom it is directed. The use of 'publicity' through internal publications and other documentation can be used to provide feedback to employees on current issues, as well as enhance and reinforce the credibility of the research process. A well-conceived internal promotional programme can have very positive effects on employees. It can motivate, educate, or help provide a sense of belonging. The famous Avis Rent-a-Car slogan suggesting that Avis employees 'Try harder' was as effective for their employees as it was for the public image of Avis. This type of corporate advertisement primarily seeks to influence the perceptions of external publics, but management tends to forget these campaigns are also critically viewed by employees at all levels within the organization. A campaign which lacks credibility with employees is not consistent with development of a positive organizational culture. Management should develop corporate communications which are consistent with the HRM objectives of the organization. Simpler, less ambitious projects can also produce a significant impact for the HR function.

Personal interaction with other functional areas can contribute significantly to HR marketing efforts. In situations where a service or programme is either partly or fully dependent on the performance of employees for success, the communications and promotional activity should be concerned not only with encouraging clients to buy, but with encouraging employees to perform. Success in business requires the commitment of both employees and management.

The implementation and control processes represent the final step which involves the measuring of effectiveness and efficiency, taking corrective action, and iteration through the marketing planning processes. The well-established marketing planning literature[17] provides a framework to follow in undertaking this task.

Introducing the new product (1 to 3 year cycle)	Resolving a complex HR issue (1 to 3 year cycle)
DETERMINE NEED FOR NEW PRODUCT	DETERMINE NEED FOR NEW PRODUCT/PROGRAM
Who will buy it and why? How much will they spend on it? What needs will it satisfy?	What is the cost of not resolving this issue? What will be its impact on norms and values? What is cost/benefit value to internal clients?
SCREEN NEW PRODUCT IDEA	EVALUATE POSSIBLE SOLUTIONS FOR CLIENTS
What impact will it have? Will it be profitable? Is it compatible with existing products?	What impact will it have on operations? Who will manage and use the project? How does it fit with current projects/priorities?
TEST MARKET THE PRODUCT	CONDUCT A PILOT PROJECT
How do prospects view the product? What needs does it satisfy? Have we designed the right product?	Do internal clients find it useful? Will they support/pay? To what extent? Who will oppose it? Why?
EXPAND TO OTHER TEST MARKETS	ADVANCE TO OTHER POTENTIAL USERS
Are findings consistent? Are there logistic/quantity problems? Did promotions result in expected sales?	Is the project valid/reliable? Does it meet the needs of all company locations? Have the benefits been properly communicated?
ANALYSE, MEASURE, PROJECT	ASSESS OUTCOME IN ADVANCE
What impact on other functions? Detailed budget and plans. Have all implications been considered?	Which functions are affected and how? Will it cause confusion? Have times, resources and costs been detailed?
EXPAND TO A NATIONAL LAUNCH	IMPLEMENT COMPANY WIDE
Does the potential outweigh risks? Are promotions and follow-up planned? Are logistics and supply lines ready? Have we means for identifying service problems and dissatisfactions?	Does project add to HR's credibility? Who will train whom to do what, where, when? Have we an effective audit/evaluation system? Will the issue really be resolved?

Figure 5 Comparing product development to resolving a complex HR issue

CONCLUSIONS

The 1980s saw the start of a new emphasis on the HRM function. It has been pointed out that the reality is that a firm adopting 'HRM' may simply involve a retitling of the old personnel department with no obvious change in its functional role, or it may be 'strategic HRM' which represents a fundamental re-conceptualization and re-organization of personnel roles and departments.[18] The focus of strategic HRM encompasses all those decisions and actions which concern the management of employees at all levels within the organization and which are directed towards creating and sustaining competitive advantage,[19] but recent European research suggests that 'strategic HRM' is still not widespread. Findings from the Price Waterhouse/Cranfield HR research project shows that in many European organizations HR strategies follow on behind corporate strategy rather than making a positive contribution to it; and although HR representation at board level is becoming more common, this does not necessarily bring with it involvement in key decisions.[20] Some firms have been able to integrate HR and strategy but to achieve this it usually requires a concentrated and multi-dimensional effort.[21]

The scope of marketing has traditionally been limited to the exchanges that take place between organizations and their customers. More recently, this scope has been expanded to encompass the field of 'relationship marketing'[22] which suggests that marketing principles can be applied to a number of other key markets, including internal markets within the firm. We argue that there exist compelling reasons for bringing the internal marketing concept to bear on problems faced by all HR managers, but the greatest value will be obtained in those firms adopting 'strategic HRM'.

The shift in organizational philosophy from asset management to operations management, the introduction of new technologies to some industries, and the increased strategic importance of managing people resources effectively and efficiently, has meant the role performed by HR managers demands a much higher level of competence and professional skills. Marketing provides an action framework and a practical approach by which the HR manager can provide effective solutions to key corporate problems. This fresh perspective will bring market-oriented HR managers significant benefits.

In spite of the emphasis in this paper on the need for HR managers to deal effectively with the challenges they face, it must be recognized that much opportunity for the future status of HRM lies with the CEOs. Their task is to provide organizational vision, and many have still failed to recognize the value of strategic HRM in the present business environment. In spite of this, the HR manager must share the responsibility through not having convinced top management that HRM is strategically relevant to business success. Adopting a market orientation requires the HR manager to focus on the needs and wants of internal customer groups and to stimulate internal service. An investment in the marketing approach is an investment in people.

References

1. *Business Week*, 'Human Resource Managers Aren't Corporate Nobodies Anymore'. 2 December 1985, p. 58.
2. Carlzon, J., *Moments of Truth*, Ballinger Publishing Company, 1987.
3. Reincheld, F.F. and Sasser, W.E. Jr., 'Zero Defections: Quality Comes to Services', *Harvard Business Review*, September–October 1990, pp. 105–11; and Buchanan, R.W.J. and Gillies, C. S., 'Value Managed Relationships: The Key to Customer Retention and Profitability', *European Management Journal*, Vol. 8, No. 4, December 1990 pp. 523–6.
4. Berry, L.L., 'The Employee as Customer', *Journal of Retail Banking*, Vol. 3, No. 1, March 1981, pp. 33–40.
5. Baird, L. and Meshoulam, I., 'A Second Chance for HR to Make the Grade', *Personnel*, Vol. 63, No. 4, April 1986, pp. 45–8.
6. Peters, T.J. and Waterman, R.H. Jr., *In Search of Exccellence: Lessons from America's Best Run Companies*, Harper & Row, 1982.
7. Kotler, P., *Marketing Management*, 5th edition, Prentice-Hall, 1984, p. 4.
8. Collins, B.A., 'The Friction Between Marketing and Finance', *The Australian Accountant*, Vol. 55, No. 4, May 1985, pp. 45–8.
9. Murphy, P.E. and Enis, B.M., *Marketing*, Scott, Foresman & Co., 1985, p. 16.
10. Payne, A.F.T., 'Developing a Marketing Oriented Organization', *Business Horizons*, Vol. 31, No. 3, May–June 1988, pp. 46–53.
11. Vandermerwe, S. and Gilbert, D., 'Making Internal Service Market Driven', *Business Horizons*, Vol. 32, No. 6, November–December 1989, pp. 83–9.
12. Berry, *op. cit.*
13. Drucker, P.F., *Management: Tasks, Responsibilities, Practices*, Harper & Row, 1974.
14. Weinshall, T.D., 'Help for Chief Executives: The Outside Consultant', *California Management Review*, Summer 1982, Vol. 24, No. 4, pp. 47–58.
15. Cupper, L.G., 'An Employer's Viewpoint on the Use of Dialogue in Industrial and Employee Relations', *Melbourne University Business School Association Journal*, Vol. 10, No. 1, 1987.
16. Desatnick, R.L., 'Marketing HRD: The Creditability Gap That's Got To Go', *Training*, June 1983, Vol. 20, No. 6, p. 52.
17. McDonald, M., *Marketing Plans: How to Prepare Them: How to Use Them*, Heinemann, second edition, 1989.
18. See Guest, D.E., 'Human Resource Management and Industrial Relations', *Journal of Management Studies*, Vol. 24, No. 5, 1987, pp. 503–21; and Guest, D., 'Personnel and HRM: Can you Tell the Difference?', *Personnel Management*, Vol. 13, No. 1, January 1989, pp. 48–51.
19. Miller, P., 'Strategic HRM: What It Is and What It Isn't', *Personnel Management*, February 1989, pp. 46–51.
20. Brewster, C. and Smith, C., 'Corporate Strategy: A No-Go Area for Personnel?', *Personnel Management*, July 1990, pp. 36–40. For a US view also see Burack, E.H., 'Corporate Business and Human Resource Planning Practices: Strategic Issues and Concerns', *Organizational Dynamics*, Vol. 15, No. 1, Summer 1986, pp. 73–87.
21. Buller, P.F., 'Successful Partnerships: HR and Strategic Planning at Eight Top Firms', *Organizational Dynamics*, Vol 17, No. 2, Autumn 1988, pp. 27–43.
22. Christopher, M., Payne, A.F.T. and Ballantyne, D., *Relationship Marketing: Bringing Quality, Customer Service and Marketing Together*, Heinemann, 1991.

INTERNALLY YOURS

Is all your energy spent on your external customers? Are all your efforts going on external products? If the answer is 'yes' then, according to Kevin Thomson, you could be ignoring one of your most important target markets – your employees

If you walk through the office or factory each day and do little more than give a passing thought to the people around you, then you may be missing one of the greatest marketing opportunities ever to have been put in front of you. These 'employees' are not just workers, or colleagues, or staff, or 'Fred down the corridor'. They are the people who could make your marketing efforts come to nothing whenever any form of customer contact occurs. These are the people who will ensure that the product or service you are producing meets the customer requirements. These are the people who could probably tell you more about your existing products than the most expensive piece of research – they are the ones who are close to the customer, every day. They could also be the people who hold the creative answers to the next world beating product. Involvement from all, is a key maxim in any search for excellence or quest for quality.

Having studied this subject over the last 10 years it is my unshakeable belief that your position in the marketplace is as dependent on the internal customer as it is on the external one. This view is backed up by a whole host of internal research and study across the world, on subjects ranging from quality to customer service.

If total customer satisfaction is the responsibility of marketing, then it is no longer good enough for marketing people to simply look at the external customer's requirements. Quality can only come from inside the organisation, so marketing must start to turn its attention this way. It is simply not good enough for those of us in marketing to only look at the environment outside the organisation. It must be our responsibility to look at everything we can influence. By doing this we conform to the stated definition of marketing as looking at those areas that affect an organisation's bottom line through its ability to deliver the right products, in the right place, at the right time. It is the internal customer who ensures that this happens.

What is important to every marketer is that the science of marketing is expanding into areas of business that further enhance the role and influence of marketing.

Understanding this area of the 'employee' is the key to being able to produce a totally integrated business marketing strategy. The problem is, however, that the word 'employee' does not convey the need for marketing to be involved. It is when the word is replaced by the concept of 'internal customers' that marketers should recognise the need to become involved. This process of looking at the employee as an internal customer is the focus of the revolutionary new business discipline of internal marketing.

This 'revolution' is not going unnoticed. Initial research into the top 100 advertisers shows that there may not be a great understanding of what internal marketing is, or how it works, but the awareness of its importance is seeping into the minds, and the budgets of many organisations. Somewhat myopically it also shows that marketing people think internal marketing should be the responsibility of someone else in the organisation such as personnel and training or human resource development as it is now called. The view seems to be that it is they who put people on courses to train them, and they who introduce, often expensive, incentive schemes to motivate them, therefore they should pick up on internal marketing. So you may be saying, what has this inward looking subject got to do with marketing people? Increasingly, the view of 'switched-on' marketers is that marketing personnel are the only people within an organisation with a critical combination of skills:

- the overview of an organisation's strategy and organisational clout
- the core marketing understanding of external customer needs
- the marketing techniques and the tools to meet those needs
- the ability to turn those techniques toward the internal customer
- the budgets

Additionally in the UK, through internal marketing, marketers are often the only people able to redress two of Britain's most crucial problems – training and motivation. This desperate need was highlighted in a recent survey of international business confidence by the World Economic Forum. They found that managers believed that skilled labour and motivation were the top business priorities. To quote *The Sunday Times*, 'Britain fared virtually worst'.

These are also the two areas that are making organisations in other countries like Japan even more formidable. These problems may again sound as though they should belong to human resource development, but if they have failed so far, who else is left to pick up the challenge?

Internal marketing isn't just about hype, and 'selling' things, like for example a 'mission statement'. It is fundamentally about marketing anything in an organisation that needs to be bought by the internal target markets within that organisation. This includes training, and all forms of motivation, education, information, strategy, plans and many other internal products and services.

To the internal marketer the problems of skilled labout and motivation can be looked at as simply ones of 'reaching and teaching' internal markets. If this can be done with messages that make them as customers want to change their attitudes and approach, then this marketing-based methodology must be explored. This is again a marketing issue.

Add to this internal focus, the opportunity to truly co-ordinate internal marketing plans with external marketing plans, including advertising, merchandising and promotions, then internal marketing can be used to provide a total organisational marketing strategy. Cost savings and overall levels of understanding of customer needs and the subsequent motivation are driven through to the bottom line. One major high street bank saved more than

£4,000,000 through this integrated approach.

On top of this, whenever there are needs for real selling skills by internal people – at the point of sale, on the telephone or in after-sales – then those in marketing must get involved. Driving the top line is also one of the major benefits of internal marketing.

And it doesn't stop there. Why shouldn't marketing get involved when product cost, quality, delivery, service, sales, and any form of customer interface is involved? They are all part of the marketing mix. The internal customer is the one to influence all these areas, therefore they must become a target for the marketer. The impact the internal customer can have on everything in the organisation is felt when it comes to any form of maximising profit and minimising costs. The fact that increasing the top line and improving the bottom line can only be done through people suggests yet again that it is those with the skills to influence employees the most who should pick up the gauntlet.

Internal Marketing is the fusion of four key disciplines, practised as one within an organisation. These are: marketing, human resources, training and behavioural sciences. The concept of internal marketing is that it simply treats the employee as an internal customer not as someone to be patronised and ordered around. It is unique in that it 'matches' the needs and values of the workforce with the aims and objectives of the organisation. These aims, objectives and virtually everything else the organisation wants to put over to the people within it, are therefore treated in marketing terms as internal products and services.

However, the organisation must be seen as being equally important as the internal customer. This therefore requires the marketer to add the skills of human resources, training and behavioural sciences in order to be able to deal with the complex relationship that exists between the organisation and the people. There are three levels at which internal marketing operates:

- Firstly at an overall policy setting level, working with the leaders of the organisation in both creating and internally marketing what will be recognised in quality-driven organisations as 'vision, mission and values' or the future goals of the leader (the vision), the way the organisation will meet those goals, (the mission), and how it will treat its people on the way to getting there (the values).
- Secondly, strategic management works as a strategic tool at management level to fulfil the policy. It creates a demand by internally marketing and branding the processes, programmes and initiatives like quality, cost saving exercises, innovation, leadership, motivation, team building and communication. The organisation needs these to get where it is going!
- Thirdly, internal marketing works at a tactical level, as for example an advertising campaign would. It is used to assist those in an organisation who have a need to drive forward specific initiatives and working practices that are required to allow people to actually get on with the job. These would include many of the traditional areas of the internal work environment. In a lot of cases these 'internal products' as they should have been seen, have

failed; quite simply, due to a lack of effective internal marketing. This ranges from the old chestnut of customer service, to other issues that feature under training, as well as relocation, recruitment, induction and all other types of skills programmes.

Why internal marketing succeeds is because it *does* see these as internal products. It treats the internal customer in as sophisticated a way as an external customer (if not more so!). And it provides the 'Disney Dust' of creativity to counteract the traditionally boring forms of internal communication, like memos and company magazines – backed up by tried and tested techniques like research, design, development, testing and launch promotion.

If all these internal needs sound fairly complex, it is easy to see why internal customers get confused. The essence of internal marketing is to simplify things to fit the needs of the internal target markets. These overall needs can be simplified into three highly marketable concepts: best policy, best process and best practice. It is at this point that a significant benefit arises from introducing these brands which may not initially appeal to marketers but is becoming increasingly important within organisations. The added bonus for every organisation in adopting these internal concepts or products is that they fit within the overall requirements of BS5750/ISO9000 – the UK and international standards of quality assurance.

If internal marketing can provide the internal customer with the understanding, acceptance and skills to undertake quality assurance then where does quality itself fit it? The irony of all 'quality' concepts that are introduced into organisations, is that 'quality', by most of the definitions that are given to describe it, is in fact internal marketing by another name. In every definition of quality there is invariably a concept along the lines of 'meeting customer requirements, now and in the future'. Isn't this what marketing is all about? And if internal quality programmes are all about providing everyone with the awareness and ability to understand and practise the 'customer supplier chain', isn't it QED, that where you have customers, then you must have marketing? In my view, internal marketing can be seen as the logical extension of any internal quality programme. And where the quality of any product or service is involved then once again marketing must also be involved.

Whichever way you look at it, marketing, including internal marketing, has a vital role to play in the future of any organisation. It does this through matching its needs to those of its internal customers.

My vision of internal marketing as a business discipline is that just as it is the established external focus of all successful organisations, so it can also be the central driving force of successful organisations.

The science of marketing will itself be expanded if people in marketing are ready to broaden their own understanding of their subject. If you enter the 'brave new world' of the internal customer you will find it is often more exciting, challenging and rewarding – both personally as well as professionally – as external marketing. And what is more, it delivers the goods and the profits! That, surely is what marketing is all about.

The Picture is now complete

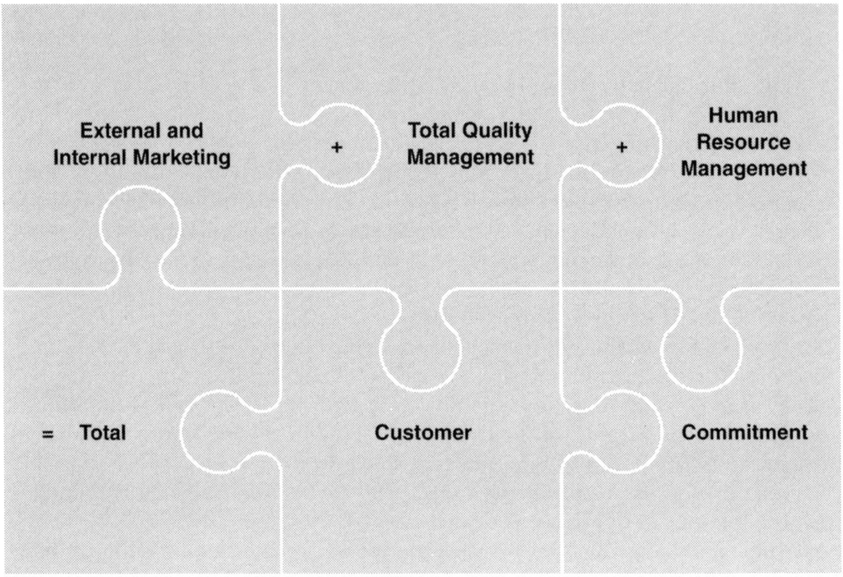

Good luck in putting together the pieces.

Enjoy colouring in the details.

Let me know the rewards it brings:

Marketing and Communication Agency Ltd. (MCA),
Century House,
19 High Street, Marlow, Bucks SL7 1AU
Tel: 0628 473217

BIBLIOGRAPHY

Adams T. *The Series Of Successful Selling* (Heinemann 1986)

Anderson P. 'Marketing, Strategic Planning, and the Theory of the Firm' *Journal of Marketing*, Vol. 46, 1982, 15–26

Argyle M. *The Psychology of Interpersonal Behaviour* (Penguin Books, 1983)

Argyris C. *Personality and Organization* (Harper & Row, 1957)

Armstrong D & Dawson C. *People in Organisations* (Elm Publications, 1985)

Arndt J. 'The Political Economy Paradigm: Foundation for Theory-marketing', *Journal of Marketing*, Vol. 47, 1983, 44–54

De Bono E. *De Bono's Thinking Course* (BBC Books, 1988)

De Bono E. *Six Thinking Hats*

Bonoma T.V. *The Marketing Edge – Making Strategies Work* (Free Press, 1985

Boulmer *Symbolic Interaction – Perspective and Method* (Prentice Hall, 1969)

Blanchard K. *Putting The One Minute Manager To Work* (Fontana, 1984)

Blanchard K. and Lorber R. *Leadership and The One Minute Manager* (Fontana, 1987)

Briggs Myers I. *Gifts Differing* (Consulting Psychologists Press, 1980)

Buzan T. *Use Your Head* (BBC Books, 1989)

Buzan T. *Memory Vision* (David & Charles, 1989)

Buzan T. *Harnessing the Para Brain* (Colt Books, 1991)

Buzzell R.D. and Gale B.T. *The Pims Principles* (Free Press, 1987)

Byham W.C. and Cox J. *Zapp! The Lightning of Empowerment* (Century, 1991)

Carnegie D. *How to Win Friends and Influence People* (Cedar Books, Revised edition, 1981)

Carzon J. *Moments of Truth* (Ballinger Publishing Co., 1987)

Cascino A.E. 'Organizational Implications of the Marketing Concept', in E.J. Kelly and W. Lazar, eds. *Managerial Marketing: Perspectives and Viewpoints* (Irwin, 1967)

Chandler A.D. *Strategy and Structure* (MIT Press, 1962)

Christopher, Martin, Payne, Adrian and Ballantyne, David. *Relationship Marketing* (Butterworth-Heinemann, 1991)

Cravens D.W. 'Strategic Forces Affecting Marketing Strategies', *Business Horizons*, Sept–Oct 1986, 77–86

Crosby P.B. *Quality is Free* (New American Library, 1979)

Cundiff M. *Kinesics: The Power of Silent Command* (Thomsons, 1989)

Daft R.L. & Weick K.E. 'Toward a Model of Organizations as Interpretation Systems', *Academy of Management Review*, 9, 1984, 284–295

Davis K. 'A method of Studying Communication Patterns in Organizations',

Personnel Psychology 6, 1953, 301–312
Dawson L.M. 'Marketing for Human Needs in a Hamane Future', *Business Horizons*, June 1980, 72–82
Dawson L.M. 'The human concept. New philosophy for business', *Business Horizons*, December 1969
Deshpande M. 'The organisational context of market research use', *Journal of Marketing*, Vol 46, No. 3. 1982
Euske & Roberts In: Jablin, F.M. et al (eds) *Handbook of Organisation Communication* (Sage, 1987)
Evans R. & Russell P. *The Creative Manager* (Unwin Hyman, 1989)
Farnham D. & Pinlott J. *Understanding Industrial Relations* (Cassell, 1979)
Feldman M.S. & March J.G. 'Information in Organizations as Signal and Symbol', *Administrative Science Quarterly*, 26, 1981, 171–186
Fisher B.A. *Perspectives on Human Communication* (Macmillan, 1978)
Fletcher W. *Creative People* (Hutchinson, 1988)
Flipo J.P. 'Service firms: Interdependence of External and Internal Marketing Strategies', *European Journal of Marketing*, Vol. 20, No. 8, 1986, 5–14
Foster R. *Innovation – The Attackers Advantage* (Pan, 1989)
Foster R. *101 Ways To Generate Great Ideas* (Kogan Page, 1991)
Fraser-Robinson J. *Total Quality Marketing* (Kogan Page, 1991)
Goldratt E. *The Goal*, (North River Press, 1984)
Goldzimer L. *Customer Driven* (Hutchinson, 1990)
Greiner L.E. 'Patterns of Organization Change', *Harvard Business Review*, 45(4) 1972, 119–130
Gronroos C. 'Internal Marketing – Theory and Practice', in Thomas M. Bloch, Gregory D. Upah and Valerie A. Zeithaml, eds. *Services Marketing in a Changing Environment* (AMA, 1985)
Gummesson E. 'Using Intenal Marketing to Develop a New Culture – The Case of Ericsson Quality', *Journal of Business and Industrial Marketing*, Vol. 2, No. 3, 1987, 23–28
Hage J., Aiken M. & Marrett C.B. 'Organization Structure and Communication', *American SOciological Review*, 36, 1971, 860–871
Handy C. *The Age Of Unreason* (Arrow, 1990)
Hopkins T. *How To Master The Art Of Selling* (Grafton, 1983)
Hopkins T. *The Official Guide To Success* (Granada, 1985)
HRD (1987) Unpublished research
Hyman R. *Industrial Relations: A Marxist Introduction* (Macmillan, 1975)
Imai M. *KAIZEN – The Key To Japan's Competitive Success* (Random House, 1986)
Jablin F.M. 'Task/Work Relationships: a Life-span Perspective', in M.L. Knapp & G.R. Miller, eds., *Handbook of Interpersonal Communication* (pp.615–654) (Sage, 1985)
Jablin F.M., Putnam L.L., Roberts K.H. & Porter L.W. (eds) *Handbook of Organisation Communication* (Sage, 1987)

Johnson S. & Wilson L. *The One Minute Sale Person* (Fontana/Collins, 1985)
Kanter R.M. *The Change Masters* (Unwin, 1983)
Karrass G. *Negotiate To Close* (Fontana, 1987)
Katz D. & Kahn R.L. *The Social Psychology of Organisations* (John Wiley, 1966)
Kotler P. *Marketing Management: Analysis, Planning and Control* (Prentice Hall, 1984)
Lawrence R.R. & Lorsch J.W. *Organization and Environment: Managing Differentiation and Integration* (Harvard University Press, 1967)
Leeds D. *Smart Questions For Successful Managers* (Piatkus, 1987)
Leeds D. *Powerspeak* (Piatkus, 1988)
Levitt T. 'Marketing Myopia', *Harvard Business Review*, July–August 1960, 45–56
Likert R. *The Human Organization* (McGraw-Hill, 1967)
Lynch D. *Strategy Of The Dolphin* (Arrow, 1990)
Luscher M. *The Luscher Colour Test* (Pan, 1987)
Maltz M. *Psycho-Cybernetics* (Wilshire Book Company, 1960)
March J.G. & Simon H.A. *Organizations* (John Wiley, 1958)
Margerison J. *If Only I Had Said* (Mercury, 1990)
Majaro S. *The Creative Marketeer* (Butterworth-Heinemann, 1991)
Majaro S. *The Creative Gap* (Longman, 1988)
Maltz M. *Psycho-Cybernetics* (Wilshire, 1960)
McDonald M. and Morris P. *The Marketing Plan* (Heinemann, 1990)
McCann D. *How To Influence Others At Work* (Heinemann, 1989)
McGregor D. *The Human Side of Enterprise* (MNcGraw-Hill, 1960)
Mead G.H. *Mind, Self Society* (Chicago University Press, 1934)
Miller R.B. and Heiman S.H. *Strategic Selling* (Kogan Page, 1988)
Minto B. *The Pyramid Principle* (BCA, 1987)
Mintzberg J. *The Nature of Managerial Work* (Harper & Row, 1973)
Monge P.R. 'Systems Theory and Research in the Study of Organizational Communication: the Correspondence Problem', *Human Communication Research*, 8, 1982, 245–261
Mudie P. 'Internal Marketring: Cause for Concern'. *Quarterly Review of Marketing*, Spring/Summer 1987, 21–24
Nolan V. *Innovation Handbook*
Peters T.J. & Austin N. *A Passion for Excellence* (Collins, 1985)
Peters T.J. *Thriving On Chaos* (Macmillan, 1988)
Peters T.J. and Waterman R.H. *In Search Of Excellence* (Harper & Row, 1982)
'Two Routes To Quality', *Personnel Management* (November 1992)
Piercy N. *Market Led Strategic Change* (Kogan Page, 1989)
Piercy N. *Market Led Strategic Change* (Thorsons, 1991)
Rein I.J., Kotler P. and Stoller M. *High Visibility* (Heinemann, 1987)
Piercy N. 'The Role and Function of the Chief Marketing Executive and the Marketing Department', *Journal of Marketing Management*, Vol. 1, No. 3, 1986, 265–290

Piercy N. 'The Marketing Budgeting Process: Marketing management implications', *Journal of Marketing*, Vol. 51, no. 4, 1987, 45–59
Piercy, N. 'The Role and Function of the Chief Marketing Executive and the Marketing Department', *Journal of Marketing Management*, Vol. 1, No. 3, 1986, 265–290
Piercy, N. 'The Role of the Marketing Department in the UK Retailing Organisations', *Internal Journal of Retailing*, 1990 (In press)
Piercy, N. & Morgan N. 'Internal Marketing: Making Marketing Happen', *Marketing Intelligence and Planning*, 199a (In press)
Piercy, N. & Morgan N. 'Internal Marketing: Strategies for Implementation and Organisational Change', *Long Range Planning*, 1990b (In press)
Piercy, N. & Peattie K. 'Matching Marketing Strategies to Corporate Culture: the parcel and the wall', *Journal of General Management*, Vol. 13, No. 4, 1988, 33–44
Putnam L.L. & Pacanowsky M.E., eds, *Communication and Organizations: An Interpretative Approach* (Sage, 1983)
Redding W.C. 'Organizational Communication Theory and Ideology: an Overview', in D. Nimmo, ed. *Communication Yearbook 3* (pp.309–341)
Rhodes J. & Thame S. *The Colours of your Mind* (Fontana/Collins, 1988)
Roberts K.H., O'Reilly C.A., Bretton G.E. & Porter L.W. 'Organizational Theory and Organizational Communication: A Communication Failure', *Human Relations*, 27, 974, 501–524
Rogers E. & Agarwala-Rogers R. *Communication in Organizations* (Free Press, 1976)
Rogers E. & Shormaker F. *Communication and Innovation* (Free Press, 1971)
Schein E. *Organizational Psychology* (Prentice Hall, 1965)
Schonberger R.J. *Building A Chain Of Customers* (Guild, 1990)
Scott Peack M. *The Road Less Travelled* (Arrow, 1990)
Singer E.J. *Effective Management Coaching* (Lonsdale, 1974)
Smith N.I. and Ainsworth M. *Managing For Innovation* (Mercury, 1989)
Tannenbaum A. *Social Psychology of the Work Organization* (Wadsworth, 1966)
Taylor F.W. *Scientific Management* (Harper, 1911)
Thomson K. *The Employee Revolution* (Pitman, 1990)
Townsend R. *Up the Organization* (Coronet Books, 1970)
Trujillo N. 'Performing Minzberg's Roles: the Nature of Managerial Communication', in L.L. Putnam & M.E. Pacanowsky, eds, *Communication and Organizations: an interpretative approach*, (pp.,73–97) (Sage, 1983)
Weber M. *The Theory of Social and Economic Organization* (Free Press, 1947)
Weick K.E. *The Social Psychology of Organising*, 2nd edn. (Addison-Wesley, 1979)

INDEX